FIELD EXPERIMENTS AND THEIR CRITICS

THE INSTITUTION FOR SOCIAL AND POLICY STUDIES AT YALE UNIVERSITY

THE YALE ISPS SERIES

FIELD EXPERIMENTS AND THEIR CRITICS

Essays on the Uses
and Abuses of
Experimentation in
the Social Sciences

Edited by
Dawn Langan Teele

Yale UNIVERSITY PRESS
New Haven & London

Yale University Press books may be purchased in quantity for educational,
business, or promotional use. For information, please e-mail sales.press@
yale.edu (U.S. office) or sales@yaleup.co.uk (U.K. office).

Set in Galliard and Copperplate 33 types by Newgen North America.
Printed in the United States of America.

Library of Congress Cataloging-in-Publication Data
Field experiments and their critics : essays on the uses and abuses of
experimentation in the social sciences / edited by Dawn Langan Teele.
     pages   cm. — (The Yale ISPS series)
   Includes bibliographical references and index.
   ISBN 978-0-300-16940-9 (alk. paper)
1. Social sciences—Research—Methodology.   I. Teele, Dawn Langan,
1983–
H62.F4195 2013
300.72—dc23   2013007487

A catalogue record for this book is available from the British Library.

This paper meets the requirements of ANSI/NISO Z39.48–1992
(Permanence of Paper).

10 9 8 7 6 5 4 3 2 1

CONTENTS

PREFACE

No graduate student in the social sciences, especially not those who spent their days tromping up Hillhouse Avenue or down Prospect Street in New Haven during the early 2000s, could have missed the fierce debates incited by our experimentalists and their compatriots across the country over empirical methodology. The clever research designs of scholars at the Institute for Social and Policy Studies (ISPS), the Economic Growth Center (EGC), and Innovations for Poverty Action (IPA) at Yale were a constant topic of discussion and disagreement. There was a hopeful feeling that economists and political scientists would finally be able to address the pressing problems of the day by using a methodology that left little room for doubt. But as more was written about experimental methods, especially those carried out in the field, more questions were raised: What factors guarantee that experiments are actually implemented according to plan? How can researchers generalize from an experimental result in one locale to a policy program in another? Can experiments answer the major questions driving most social science? Are experimental protocols ethical? What, if anything, is lost by methodological monocropping?

To explore these questions I organized a debate on field experiments at Yale in October 2009. A crowd of more than 250 assembled to hear Don Green defend the experimental "juggernaut" against strong criticisms mounted by Angus Deaton, Susan Stokes, and Ian Shapiro. Along with many in the audience, I came away from the night with a sense that the debate was far from settled. This book, which contains the original essays that inspired the debate alongside of fresh contributions, is an attempt to consider anew the arguments advocating field experiments as well as to measure and weigh criticisms of the field experimental method.

My sincerest thanks go to Ian Shapiro (of the Macmillan Center), Don Green (formerly of the ISPS), Jacob Hacker (currently at the ISPS), and Nicholas Sambanis (formerly of Yale's program in Ethics, Politics and Economics) for their support (in specie) of the original debate and for their encouragement (in spirit) for publishing this book. Thanks as well to Bill Frucht and Jaya Chatterjee at Yale University Press and to seven anonymous reviewers for their comments along the way.

Finally, I want to express gratitude to the many people who reviewed parts of this book, especially Elisabeth Wood, Susan Stokes, Frances Rosenbluth, James Robinson, Chris Udry, Matt Kocher, Casiano Hacker-Cordón, Rory Truex, Blake Emerson, and Allison Sovey Carnegie. Big thanks are due, too, to Ryan Ourada for playing with the book's theme and crafting its beautiful cover. A special shout-out is owed to my writing-group ladies, Anna Jurkeviks, Erin Pineda, and Kristin Plys, with the hope that this is only the first of many times we thank one another in actual ink. Love and gratitude to Joshua Simon for finding time to read all that I write, even when he has so much to read and write himself. In memory of my grandfather Donald H. Jones, who, despite being fully informed, never stopped volunteering for randomized trials.

INTRODUCTION

Dawn Langan Teele

A central feature of the social sciences is a keen interest in causation. Among social scientists there is widespread agreement that systematic study of the social world, of institutions, economic behavior, and social action, can lead to insights about causal relationships. This agreement is not matched, however, by consensus within or across disciplines as to which research methods are most likely to achieve that goal. Part of the disagreement stems from the inherent difficulties of studying human society: in the real world, structure, intention, and accident all interact to produce complex human behaviors whose causes can be opaque, even in hindsight. To assess the relative merits of alternative theories of human behavior we need a methodology—a means of linking evidence to statements about causation.

John Stuart Mill's early reflections on these issues remain relevant today. Distinguishing between catalysts (the "causes of effects") and outcomes ("the effects of causes"), Mill thought that the key to understanding causation lay in isolating either the causes or the effects and seeing what happens. He writes, "We must be able to meet with some of the antecedents [the causes] apart from the rest, and observe what follows from them; or some of the consequents [the effects], and observe by what they are preceded."[1] In other words, we must *vary the circumstances* of the object of study to see whether a cause always has the same effect when placed in a new context, or whether effects can be traced to the same cause in different situations.[2]

Two main approaches have been used since Mill's time to study causation. The first is *observational* inquiry. Here, in order to pinpoint causality, the researcher looks for natural differences across cases and tries to find a single input that might have caused the variation in outcomes.[3] A second technique is *experimental* inquiry. To pinpoint causality in this type of work, the researcher conducts an experiment whereby one group, the treatment group, is given a certain input that is withheld from the control group. If outcomes vary across the treatment and control groups, the researcher can argue that the difference must be due to the catalyst that she set into motion.

Mill argued that the two ways of assessing causation—experimentation and observation—were logically equivalent. But with observational inquiry he worried about the possibility that some other factor, unknown to the researcher, is actually the cause of the observed outcome. This challenges the *internal validity* of a causal inference: it is not enough to observe that *y* always follows *x* to infer that *y* was caused by *x*. As the oft-repeated phrase goes, correlation does not imply causation. In theory, random assignment in a controlled trial assures the internal validity of causal claims. In other words, if the researcher herself puts subjects into the treatment and control groups, and if she induces the catalyst whose outcome is of interest, she can say with certainty whether *x* does, or does not, cause *y*.

The insight that causal inferences must be drawn from internally valid studies was first incorporated into the natural sciences, where laboratory scientists have long analyzed treatment effects in subpopulations of bacteria and animals. In clinical medicine, randomized controlled trials are a mainstay in tracking disease progression in response to new therapies and pharmaceutical drugs.[4] These practices have been imported into the social sciences more recently, particularly in psychology, where, as the advertisements on any student union bulletin board will attest, college students are favorite subjects in behavioral research. But there are many reasons to suspect that college students are not representative of the population at large, which raises the problem of *external validity* in controlled experiments.[5] Because social scientists want to identify causal processes in society as a whole, the population that is studied and the conditions under which the study is carried out must be realistic enough to make the results applicable in nonexperimental settings. Thus even randomized experiments are not immune to criticism.

In recent decades a growing cohort of researchers in the social sciences, especially economists and political scientists, have sought to gain the advantages of internal validity under experimental controls while avoiding the difficulties of external validity by conducting *field experiments*—randomized controlled trials carried out in a real-world setting.[6] The idea is to randomly assign research participants from the real world to treatment and control groups and then intervene only in the treatment group in order to see whether the expected change actually occurs.[7] Though Mill would have been skeptical of this move—he worried that the social world is too complicated for experimental work—the modern proponents of field experiments disagree, seeing randomized controlled studies as the missing key to sound causal inference in social research.

Yet the experimental insurrection remains incomplete. If human error or cunning leads to noncompliance with experimental prescriptions—that is, if experimental subjects do not do as they are told—the internal validity of field experiments is challenged; moreover, if field experiments are carried out on groups of people that are quite unlike the rest of us, the external validity of field experiments is suspect. In addition to those who are skeptical that field experiments can overcome these problems, there are scholars who argue that field experiments only tell us about *average* effects when in fact what is needed to test a hypothesis or make a policy recommendation is more fine-grained knowledge. A still different group of critics worries about limiting what we study to questions that lend themselves to field experimental research, which may exclude many of the most pressing issues that concern social scientists. Add to these worries the ethical concerns that arise when people are assigned to treatment and control groups without their knowledge, and it becomes clear that the debate about field experiments is far from over. The contributors to this book do not claim to end this debate, but they do offer a guide to its frontiers that will be of interest to participants and newcomers alike.

In "The Illusion of Learning from Observational Research" Alan Gerber, Donald Green, and Edward Kaplan (GGK hereafter) argue that the only upshot of nonexperimental research is its ability to teach us, when placed side by side with experimental research, how biased nonexperimental work actually is (chapter 1). GGK develop this contentious claim by using a Bayesian framework wherein research is valued according to how dramatically it shifts our prior beliefs about a causal relationship. For them, nonexperimental work has little ability to shift prior beliefs and should, a fortiori, be dropped from the methodological toolbox.

Susan Stokes rejects this logic (chapter 2). She diagnoses the criticisms raised against observational research by GGK and others as part of the worldview of a "radical skeptic"—someone for whom the confluence of events that produce social outcomes is so complex that they can never fully be understood. When confronted with observational work, the radical skeptic is prone to fixate on the potential for omitted variables to sully conclusions, regardless of how sound the theory or how careful the researcher. Stokes argues that such skepticism, if applied evenhandedly to experimental research, would raise similar criticisms of experiments. The radical skeptic would worry, in particular, that heterogeneity among research participants in experimental work complicates interpretations of the average treatment effect. For Stokes, the point could be stated thus: experimentalists should clean their glasses when they read their own work; evenhanded criticism reveals that all methodologies are problematic. Unveiling truths will require more open-minded self-reflection on the part of researchers.

The economists Christopher Barrett and Michael Carter (chapter 3) build on Stokes's framework to address the seemingly infinite ways in which the experimental ideal is violated in practice. Even if we believe that a field experiment would, if properly carried out, get us closer to the truth, in the messy practice of field research some of the assumptions that experiments rely on for sound causal inferences may be violated. For example, in a large-scale experiment a researcher may be unable to verify that the randomization of participants to treatment and control groups was properly carried out. This might happen if an NGO partner doesn't follow instructions, or if someone on the inside thinks some subjects are more deserving or more likely to benefit from receiving the treatment. Further, a researcher who is not on-site might not be able to monitor crossover, that is, people who were assigned to one group but placed themselves in another. Both of these potential problems—imperfect randomization and participant crossover—will bias causal inferences drawn from the field experiment.

Returning to the experimentalists, Abhijit Banerjee and Esther Duflo (chapter 4), prominent development economists at the forefront of the experimental revolution in their field, disregard critiques of experiments because they apply to observational work as well. They review findings from more than ten years of experimental development economics and conclude that, despite the short timeline, experiments have produced hard facts that years of observational research cannot contend with. They argue, moreover, that the common criticism that experiments are unable to answer deep theoretical questions is unfounded: as experiments proliferate in the discipline, scholars, by refining and replicating experiments more carefully suited to the question at hand, will be able to use experimental results to refine theoretical insights.

Departing from purely methodological concerns, I raise several ethical questions about experimental research in chapter 5. When contemplating whether a given methodology is ethical, we must probe the relationship between the researcher and the research subjects. I argue that the crucial distinction between field experiments and observational research is that field experiments, by their very nature, manipulate the real world in the service of research questions. To put this another way, if observational social scientists are spectators of a card game whose hands nature dealt, experimental social scientists have positioned themselves as the dealer. This shift from spectator to dealer changes the relationship of the social scientists to the players, and it begs for an examination of the practices and policies that bind them together. I call for greater attention to be paid to the concerns and needs of study participants and for a no-exceptions policy to individual informed consent in experiments. In closing, I argue for creative thinking in research design, such as the use of placebo groups, to ensure that the spirit of the *Belmont Report*, a foundational document in research ethics, is upheld in all field experimental research.

Chapter 6 reprints, in full, Angus Deaton's "Instruments, Randomization, and Learning About Development," a much-discussed critique of experiments that inspired several of the contributions in this book. Deaton's arguments are many and complex, but they center around two main points. Following Heckman and Smith (1995), Deaton worries that the experimentalist research agenda is too focused on *what* works to the neglect of *why*. An unqualified turn toward field experiments, by this light, would reward scholarship that focuses on small, answerable questions to the neglect of bigger, more profound concerns.

Second, Deaton argues that the "average treatment effect"—the parameter that can be reliably estimated through an experimental design—represents only a small part of what a researcher might want to know. In an experiment that offers cash transfers to the poor in exchange for putting their children in school, we might want to know not only how the average student fared in terms of educational attainment, but also other aspects of the distribution, like the median and the mode. We also might be interested in how the treatment influenced different subgroups of the population, like households with female heads or those that have many children. Deaton reminds us that in order to estimate these quantities a researcher has to rely on the same econometric techniques that experiments were originally employed to avoid, which knocks experiments off their pedestal and brings them back to reality.

Excited by the experimental turn in social science, the statistician Andrew Gelman elaborates the many ways that experimental reasoning has been and can be incorporated into social research (chapter 7). Though they can never fully save us from having to use techniques of observational data analysis, experiments, Gelman claims, are the gold standard for drawing causal inferences. Nevertheless, he worries that the methodology has become synonymous with randomized experiments and argues that other experimental methodologies can be useful for drawing social science inferences. Gelman thus sits at the center of the controversy over whether, moving forward, all forms of nonexperimental inquiry should be abandoned. This question is at the heart of the book, for if the answer is yes, it is hard to draw any other implication than that everything we have learned in the past is wrong.

Kosuke Imai, Gary King, and Elizabeth Stuart try to rescue both experimentalists and observationalists from themselves by helping to explain and troubleshoot common mistakes made by both (chapter 8). The authors highlight the precise advantages and disadvantages of several observational and experimental research designs.[8] By considering different techniques such as "matching," "blocking," and "randomization" the authors show that different research designs can be employed to deal with different sets of problems. They conclude that both experiments and observational work place constraints on what can be known with certainty.

In chapter 9, Ian Shapiro returns to the larger issues at stake in this book: what promises field experiments can deliver on, and where they fall short. He critiques Gerber, Green, and Kaplan's "research allocation theorem," an implication of which is that resources spent on observational research are more likely to be wasted than resources spent on field experimental research, by arguing that the theorem ignores the possibility of diminishing returns to investments in certain types of research methodologies. Experiments might have produced hard facts that change our intuitions about, say, the effect of campaign phone calls versus face-to-face contact on voter turnout, but the rate at which these discoveries are accruing far outpaces their usefulness to the broader goals of social science. In essence, getting more precise answers to the same questions has opportunity costs in terms of foregone research on other topics.

Shapiro notes that while methods can be used to answer questions, they cannot tell us which questions are worth answering. In letting small empirical findings dictate the next set of questions, rather than letting theoretical questions dictate research programs, the agenda of GGK runs the risk of placing social science on a safe path to nowhere. In the end, Shapiro, by stressing the primacy of a good question, advocates a pragmatic approach to methodological choices.

Read together, the chapters in this book offer a fuller account of the uses and abuses of experiments in social science than one would get from simply reading the experimentalists' tracts. A central theme that unites most of the critics is that the choice of methodology depends in large part on what we want to know. When a large body of theoretical work already exists, experiments may be a good method to test competing hypotheses. But experiments may not be best when staking out new terrain, examining politically or personally sensitive issues, or laying out answers to big questions. My hope is that by arraying a diverse set of views in a single forum, readers, too, will be able to decide for themselves.

NOTES

1. Mill (1843: 440).

2. Mill attributes the concept of varying the circumstances to Bacon, without citation.

3. See Rosenbaum (2002) for an explicit treatment of observational analysis.

4. Researchers in lab sciences and clinical medicine believe that experiments offer advantages over observational techniques, but even here there are some challenges. If

a cancer drug is developed and tested on populations of mice that have been bred to have cancer, we might worry that the results, even if strong for the mouse population, will not apply to humans, bringing into question the external validity of the results. If the same drug is tested on human beings with cancer, some of whom are assigned to receive the drug and others that are not, there is still the possibility of human error (if some people don't take the drug as assigned) or of human intrigue (if some people seek out other treatments at the same time). These issues raise the possibility that the experiment is not internally valid, meaning that the experiment was not carried out exactly as it should be for the results to be reliable.

5. See Henrich et al. (2001).

6. The movement of experiments into the mainstream of social science is evidenced by the increasing publication rates of social scientific laboratory experiments (McDermott 2002, Morton and Williams 2008), field experiments in political economy (Palfrey 2009), experiments in the political economy of development (Humphreys and Weinstein 2009), areas of political behavior and collective action (de Rooji et al. 2009), and development economics (Banerjee and Duflo, this book). Behavioral economics, which since the 1970s has relied extensively on laboratory experiments to test the behavioral foundations of neoclassical economics, has also made movements toward laboratory experiments conducted on location. For a review of this approach, see Camerer et al. (2004). Specific examples of this approach can be found in Henrich et al. (2001) and Habyarimana et al. (2009).

7. Two recent textbooks that espouse the experimentalist view are Druckman et al. (2011) and Morton and Williams (2010). For a classic account see Cook and Campbell (1979).

8. *Research design* is used in a technical sense here to mean a strategy for evaluating data that will produce *causal* estimates of the parameters of interest. See Dunning (2008) for an interesting overview of several approaches to design-based inference.

1

—

THE ILLUSION OF LEARNING FROM OBSERVATIONAL RESEARCH

Alan S. Gerber, Donald P. Green, and Edward H. Kaplan

Theory testing occupies a central place within social science, but what kinds of evidence count toward a meaningful test of a causal proposition? We offer two analytic results that have important implications for the relative merits of observational and experimental inquiry. The first result addresses the optimal weight that should be assigned to unbiased experimental research and potentially biased observational research. We find that unless researchers have prior information about the biases associated with observational research, observational findings are accorded zero weight regardless of sample size, and researchers learn about causality exclusively through experimental results. An important implication is that the standard errors conventionally reported by observational researchers may severely underestimate the actual uncertainty surrounding the estimates.

The second result describes the optimal allocation of future resources to observational and experimental research, given different marginal costs for each type of data collection and a budget constraint. Under certain conditions (e.g., severe budget constraints and prohibitive costs of experimental data), it is optimal to allocate one's entire budget to observational data. However, so long as one harbors some uncertainty about the biases of observational research, even an infinite supply of observational data cannot provide exact estimates of causal parameters. In the absence of theoretical or methodological breakthroughs, the only possibility for further learning comes from experiments, particularly experiments with strong external validity.

1. Introduction

Empirical studies of cause and effect in social science may be divided into two broad categories, experimental and observational. In the former, individuals or groups are randomly assigned to treatment and control conditions. Most experimental research takes place in a laboratory environment and involves student participants, but several noteworthy studies have been conducted in real-world settings, such as schools (Howell and Peterson 2002), police precincts (Sherman and Rogin 1995), public housing projects (Katz, Kling, and Liebman 2001), and voting wards (Gerber and Green 2000). The experimental category also encompasses research that examines the consequences of randomization performed by administrative agencies, such as the military draft (Angrist 1990) or the random assignment of judges to cases (Green and Winik 2010). The aim of experimental research is to examine the effects of random variation in one or more independent variables.

Observational research, too, examines the effects of variation in a set of independent variables, but this variation is not generated through randomization procedures. In observational studies, the data generation process by which the independent variables arise is unknown to the researcher. To estimate the parameters that govern cause and effect, the analyst of observational data must make several strong assumptions about the statistical relationship between observed and unobserved causes of the dependent variable (Achen 1986; King, Keohane, and Verba 1994). To the extent that these assumptions are unwarranted, parameter estimates will be biased. Thus, observational research involves two types of uncertainty, the statistical uncertainty given a particular set of modeling assumptions and the theoretical uncertainty about which modeling assumptions are correct.

The principal difference between experimental and observational research is the use of randomization procedures. Obviously, random assignment alone does not guarantee that an experiment will produce unbiased estimates of causal parameters (cf. Cook and Campbell 1979, chapter 2, on threats to internal validity). Nor does observational analysis preclude unbiased causal inference. The point is that the risk of bias is typically much greater in observational research. This chapter characterizes experiments as unbiased and observational studies as potentially biased, but the analytic results we derive generalize readily to situations in which both are potentially biased.

The vigorous debate between proponents of observational and experimental analysis (Cook and Payne 2002; Heckman and Smith 1995; Green and Gerber 2003a; Weiss 2002) raises two meta-analytic questions. First, under what conditions and to what extent should we update our prior beliefs based on experimental and observational findings? Second, looking to the future, how should researchers working within a given substantive area allocate resources to each type of research, given the costs of each type of data collection?

Although these questions have been the subject of extensive discussion, they have not been addressed within a rigorous analytic framework. As a result, many core issues remain unresolved. For example, is the choice between experimental and observational research fundamentally static, or does the relative attractiveness of experimentation change depending on the amount of observational research that has accumulated to that point in time? To what extent and in what ways is the trade-off between experimental and observational research affected by developments in "theory" and in "methodology"?

The analytic results presented in this chapter reveal that the choice between experimental and observational research is fundamentally dynamic. The weight accorded to new evidence depends on what methodological inquiry reveals about the biases associated with an estimation procedure as well as on what theory asserts about the biases associated with our extrapolations from the particularities of any given study. We show that the more one knows ex ante about the biases of a given research approach, the more weight one accords the results that emerge from it. Indeed, the analytics presented below may be read as an attempt to characterize the role of theory and methodology within an observational empirical research program. When researchers lack prior information about the biases associated with observational research, they will assign observational findings zero weight and will never allocate future resources to it. In this situation, learning is possible only through unbiased empirical methods, methodological investigation, or theoretical insight. These analytic results thus invite social scientists to launch a new line of empirical inquiry designed to assess the direction and magnitude of research biases that arise in statistical inference and extrapolation to other settings.

2. Assumptions and Notation

Our analytic framework is based on a Bayesian characterization of how a researcher's prior beliefs are updated in the wake of new evidence, thereby producing posterior beliefs.[1] This framework is designed to be as general as possible, encompassing the more conventional (classical) statistical approach, which ignores prior beliefs and approaches the data *de novo*. The classical approach will be shown to be a special case in the model we present below.

Suppose you seek to estimate the causal parameter M. To do so, you launch two empirical studies, one experimental and the other observational. In advance of gathering the data, you hold prior beliefs about the possible values of M. Specifically, your prior beliefs about M are distributed normally with mean μ and variance σ^2_M. The dispersion of your prior beliefs (σ^2_M) is of special interest. The smaller σ^2_M, the more certain you are about the true parameter M in advance of seeing the data. An infinite σ^2_M implies that you approach the research with no sense whatsoever of where the truth lies.

You now embark upon an experimental study. Before you examine the data, the central limit theorem leads you to believe that your estimator, X_e, will be normally distributed. Given that $M = m$ (the true effect turns out to equal m) and that random assignment of observations to treatment and control conditions renders your experiment unbiased, X_e is normal with mean m and variance $\sigma^2_{X_e}$. As a result of the study, you will observe a draw from the distribution of X_e, the actual experimental value x_e.

In addition to conducting an experiment, you also gather observational data. Unlike randomized experimentation, observational research does not involve a procedure that ensures unbiased causal inference. Thus, before examining your observational results, you harbor prior beliefs about the bias associated with your observational analysis. Let B be the random variable that denotes this bias. Suppose that your prior beliefs about B are distributed normally with mean β and variance σ^2_B. Again, smaller values of σ^2_B indicate more precise prior knowledge about the nature of the observational study's bias. Infinite variance implies complete uncertainty.

Further, we assume that priors about M and B are independent. This assumption makes intuitive sense: there is usually no reason to suppose ex ante that one can predict the observational study's bias by knowing whether a causal parameter is large or small. It should be stressed, however, that independence will give way to a negative correlation once the experimental and observational results become known.[2] The analytic results we present here are meant to describe what happens as one moves from prior beliefs to posterior views based on new information. The results can also be used to describe what happens after one examines an entire literature of experimental and observational studies. The precise sequence in which one examines the evidence does not affect our conclusions (see Gerber, Green, and Kaplan 2003 for a proof), but tracing this sequence does make the analytics more complicated. For purposes of exposition, therefore, we concentrate our attention on what happens as one moves from priors developed in advance of seeing the results to posterior views informed by all the evidence that one observes subsequently.

The observational study generates a statistical result, which we denote X_o (o for observational). Given that $M = m$ (the true effect equals m) and $B = b$ (the true bias equals b), we assume that the sampling distribution of X_o is normal with mean $m + b$ and variance σ^2_{Xo}. In other words, the observational study produces an estimate (x_o) that may be biased in the event that b is not equal to 0. Bias may arise from any number of sources, such as unobserved heterogeneity or errors-in-variables. The variance of the observational study (σ^2_{Xo}) is a function of sample size, the predictive accuracy of the model, and other features of the statistical analysis used to generate the estimates.

Finally, we assume that given $M = m$ and $B = b$, the random variables X_e and X_o are independent. This assumption follows from the fact that the experimental and observational results do not influence each other in any way. In sum, our model of the research process assumes (1) normal and independently distributed priors about the true effect and the bias of observational research and (2) normal and independently distributed sampling distributions for the estimates generated by the experimental and observational studies. We now examine the implications of this analytic framework.

3. The Joint Posterior Distribution of M and B

The central issue to be addressed is how our beliefs about the causal parameter M will change once we see the results of the experimental and observational studies. The more fruitful the research program, the more our posterior beliefs will differ from our prior beliefs. New data might give us a different posterior belief about the location of M, or it might confirm our prior belief and reduce the variance (uncertainty) of these beliefs.

What we want is the posterior distribution of M, given the experimental and observational data. Applying Bayes's rule and integrating over the normal probability distributions, we obtain the following theorem.

Theorem 1: The posterior distribution of M is normally distributed with mean given by

$$E(M \mid X_e = x_e, X_o = x_o) = p_1\mu + p_2 x_e + p_3(x_o - \beta) \qquad (2)$$

and variance

$$\sigma^2_{M|x_e, x_o} = \cfrac{1}{\cfrac{1}{\sigma^2_M} + \cfrac{1}{\sigma^2_{X_e}} + \cfrac{1}{\sigma^2_B + \sigma^2_{X_o}}},$$

where

$$p_1 = \frac{\sigma^2_{M|x_e, x_o}}{\sigma^2_M}, \; p_2 = \frac{\sigma^2_{M|x_e, x_o}}{\sigma^2_{X_e}}, \text{ and } p_3 = \frac{\sigma^2_{M|x_e, x_o}}{\sigma^2_B + \sigma^2_{X_o}}.$$

Proof: See Gerber et al. 2003, which also derives results for the posterior distribution of B and the posterior correlation between M and B.

This theorem reveals that the posterior mean is an average (since $p_1 + p_2 + p_3 = 1$) of three terms: the prior expectation of the true mean effect (μ), the observed experimental value (x_e), and the observational value corrected by the prior expectation of the bias $(x_o - \beta)$. This analytic result parallels the standard case in which normal priors are confronted with normally distributed evidence (Box and Tiao 1973). In this instance, the biased observational estimate is recentered to an unbiased estimate by subtracting off the prior expectation of the bias. It should be noted that such recentering is rarely, if ever, done in practice. Those who report observational results seldom disclose their priors about the bias term, let alone correct for it. In effect, researchers working with observational data routinely, if implicitly, assert that the bias equals zero and that the uncertainty associated with this bias is also zero.

To get a feel for what the posterior distribution implies substantively, it is useful to consider several limiting cases. If prior to examining the data one were certain that the true effect were μ, then $\sigma^2_M = 0$, $p_1 = 1$, and $p_2 = p_3 = 0$. In this case, one would ignore the data from both studies and set $E(M|X_e=x_e, X_o=x_o) = \mu$. Conversely, if one had no prior sense of M or B before seeing the data (or if one approached the data from a classical statistical perspective that ignores prior beliefs), then $\sigma^2_M = \sigma^2_B = \infty$, $p_1 = p_3 = 0$, and $p_2 = 1$, in which case the posterior expectation of M would be identical to the experimental result x_e. In the less extreme case where one has some prior information about M such that $\sigma^2_M < \infty$, p_3 remains zero so long as one remains completely uninformed about the biases of the observational research. In other words, in the absence of prior knowledge about the bias of observational research, one accords it zero weight. Note that this result holds even when the sample size of the observational study is so large that σ^2_{Xo} is reduced to zero.

For this reason, we refer to this result as the Illusion of Observational Learning Theorem. If one is entirely uncertain about the biases of observational research, the accumulation of observational findings sheds no light on the causal parameter of interest. Moreover, for a given finite value of σ^2_B there comes a point at which observational data cease to be informative and where further advances to knowledge can come only from experimental findings.

The illusion of observational learning is typically masked by the way in which researchers conventionally report their nonexperimental statistical results. The standard errors associated with regression estimates, for example, are calculated based on the unstated assumption that the bias associated with a given estimator is known with perfect certainty before the estimates are generated. These standard errors would look much larger were they to take into account the value of σ^2_B.

The only way to extract additional information from observational research is to obtain extrinsic information about its bias. By extrinsic information, we mean information derived from inspection of the observational procedures, such as the measurement techniques, statistical methodology, and the like. *Extrinsic information does not include the results of the observational studies and comparisons to experimental results.* If all one knows about the bias is that experimental studies produced an estimate of 10 while observational studies produced an estimate of 5, one's posterior estimate of the mean will not be influenced at all by the observational results.

To visualize the irrelevance of observational data with unknown biases, consider a hypothetical regression model of the form

$$Y = a + bX + U,$$

where Y is the observed treatment effect across a range of studies, X is a dummy variable scored 0 if the study is experimental and 1 if it is observational, and U is an unobserved disturbance term. Suppose that we have noninformative priors about a and b. The regression estimate of a provides an unbiased estimate of the true treatment effect. Similarly, the regression estimate of b provides an unbiased estimate of the observational bias. Regression, of course, generates the same estimates of a and b regardless of the order in which we observe the data points. Moreover, the estimate of a is unaffected by the presence of observational studies in our data set. This regression model produces the same estimate of a as a model that discards the observational studies and simply estimates

$$Y = a + U.$$

This point warrants special emphasis, since it might appear that one could augment the value of observational research by running an observational pilot study, assessing its biases by comparison to an experimental pilot study, and then using the new, more precise posterior of σ^2_B as a prior for purposes of subsequent empirical inquiry. The flaw in this sequential approach is that, conditional on seeing the initial round of experimental and observational results, the distributions of M and B become negatively correlated (see Gerber et al. 2003). To update one's priors recursively requires a different set of formulas from the ones presented above. After all is said and done, however, a recursive approach will lead to exactly the same set of posteriors.

4. A Numerical Example

A simple numerical example may help fix ideas. Consider two studies of the effects of face-to-face canvassing on voter turnout in a particular election in a particular city. The observational study surveys citizens to assess whether they were contacted at home by political canvassers and uses regression analysis to examine whether reported contact predicts voting behavior, controlling for covariates such as political attitudes and demographic characteristics (Kramer 1970; Rosenstone and Hansen 1993). The key assumption of this study is that reported contact is statistically unrelated to unobserved causes of voting. This assumption would be violated if reported contact were an imprecise measure of actual contact or if political campaigns make a concerted effort to contact citizens with unusually high propensities to vote. The majority of published studies on the effects of voter mobilization uses some version of this approach.

The experimental study of face-to-face canvassing randomly assigns citizens to treatment and control groups. Canvassers contact citizens in the treatment group; members of the control group are not contacted.[3] This type of fully randomized experiment dates back to Eldersveld (1956) and currently enjoys something of a revival in political science (for a review of this literature, see Green and Gerber 2008).

Suppose for the sake of illustration that your prior beliefs about M, the effect of canvassing on voter turnout, were centered at 10 with a variance of 25 (or, equivalently, a standard deviation of 5). These priors imply that you assign a probability of about 0.95 to the conjecture that M lies between 0 and 20. You also hold priors about the observational bias. You suspect that contact with canvassers is measured unreliably, which could produce an underestimate of M, but also that contact with canvassers is correlated with unmeasured causes of voting, which may produce an overestimate of M. Thus, your priors about the direction of bias are somewhat diffuse. Let us suppose that B is centered at 2 with a variance of 36 (standard deviation of 6). Finally, you confront the empirical results. The experimental study, based on approximately 1,200 subjects divided between treatment and control groups, produces an estimate of 12 with a standard deviation of 3. The observational study, based on a sample of 10,000 observations, produces an estimate of 16 with a standard deviation of 1.

With this information, we form the posterior mean and variance for M:

$$E(M \mid X_e = 12, X_o = 16) = p_1(10) + p_2(12) + p_3(16-2) = 11.85$$

$$\sigma^2_{M|x_e, x_o} = \frac{1}{\dfrac{1}{25} + \dfrac{1}{9} + \dfrac{1}{1+36}} = 5.61$$

$$p_1 = \frac{5.61}{25} = 0.23, \ p_2 = \frac{5.61}{9} = 0.62, \ p_3 = \frac{5.61}{36+1} = 0.15.$$

Notice that although the observational study has much less sampling variability than the experimental study, the observational findings are accorded much less weight. Indeed, the experimental study has four times as much influence on the posterior mean as the observational study. The observational study, corrected for bias, raises the posterior estimate of M, while the prior lowers it, resulting in a posterior estimate of 11.9, which is very close to the experimental result. The prior variance of 25 has become a posterior variance of 5.6, a reduction that is attributable primarily to the experimental evidence. Had the observational study contained 1,000,000 observations instead of 10,000, thereby decreasing its standard error from 1 to 0.1, the posterior variance would have dropped imperceptibly from 5.61 to 5.59, and the posterior mean would have changed only from 11.85 to 11.86. A massive investment in additional observational data produces negligible returns.

One interesting feature of this example is that the experimental and observational results are substantively rather similar; both suggest that canvassing "works." Sometimes when experimental results happen to coincide with observational findings, experimentation is chided for merely telling us what we already know (Morton 2002: 15), but this attitude stems from the illusion described above. The standard error associated with the $N=10,000$ observational study would conventionally be reported as 1, when in fact its root mean squared error is 6.1. In this situation, what we "already know" from observational research is scarcely more than conjecture; appearances to the contrary reflect the fact that the nominal standard error of the observational study grossly understates the actual root mean squared error. The posterior variance is four times smaller than the prior variance primarily because the experimental results are so informative.[4]

5. Allocating Resources to Minimize the Posterior Variance of M

Above we considered the case in which a researcher revises prior beliefs after encountering findings from two literatures, one experimental and the other observational. Now we consider a somewhat different issue: how should this researcher allocate scarce resources between experimental and observational investigation?

Suppose the research budget is R. This budget is allocated to experimental and observational studies. The marginal price of each experimental observation is denoted π_e; the price of a nonexperimental observation is π_o. Let n_e be the size of the experimental sample and n_o the size of the observational sample. The budget is allocated to both types of research subject to the constraint $\pi_e n_e + \pi_o n_o = R$.

Let the variance[5] of the experimental study equal $\sigma^2_{Xe} = \sigma^2_e / n_e$, and the variance of the observational study equal $\sigma^2_{Xo} = \sigma^2_o / n_o$. Using the results in Theorem 1, the aim is to allocate resources so as to minimize the posterior variance of M, subject to the budget constraint R.

Theorem 2. The optimal allocation of a budget R, given prices π_e and π_o, disturbance variances σ^2_e and σ^2_o, and variance of priors about observational bias σ^2_B, takes one of three forms depending on the values of the parameters:

Case 1. For $\sigma^2_o (\pi_o / \pi_e) \geq \sigma^2_e$, allocate $n_e = R/\pi_e$ and $n_o = 0$.

Case 2. For $\sigma^2_o (\pi_o / \pi_e) \left(1 + \dfrac{R\sigma^2_B}{\pi_o \sigma^2_o} \right)^2 \geq \sigma^2_e \geq \sigma^2_o (\pi_o / \pi_e)$, allocate $n_o* = \left[\left(\dfrac{\pi_e \sigma_e^2}{\pi_o \sigma_o^2}\right)^{1/2} - 1\right]\left(\dfrac{\sigma_o^2}{\sigma_B^2}\right)$ and $n_e = \dfrac{R - \pi_o n_o*}{\pi_e}$.

Case 3. For $\sigma_e^2 \geq \sigma_o^2 (\pi_o / \pi_e)\left(1 + \dfrac{R\sigma_B^2}{\pi_o \sigma_o^2}\right)^2$, allocate $n_o = R/\pi_o$ and $n_e = 0$.

The implications of the Research Allocation Theorem in many ways parallel our earlier results. When allocation decisions are made based on uninformative priors about the bias ($\sigma_B^2 = \infty$), no resources are ever allocated to observational research. As budgets approach infinity, the fraction of resources allocated to experimental research approaches 1. When σ_B^2 is zero, resources will be allocated entirely to either experiments or observational studies, depending on relative prices and disturbance variances.

The most interesting case is the intermediate one, where finite budgets and moderate values of σ_B^2 dictate an apportioning of resources between the two types of studies. Here, possible price advantages of observational research are balanced against the risk of bias. Particularly attractive, therefore, are observational studies that are least susceptible to bias, such as those based on naturally occurring randomization of the independent variable (Imbens, Rubin, and Sacerdote 2001), near-random assignment (McConahay, 1982), or assignment that supports a regression-discontinuity analysis (Cook and Campbell 1979, chapter 3).

Notice that the allocation decision does not depend on σ_M^2, that is, prior uncertainty about the true causal parameter. How much one knows about the research problem before gathering data is irrelevant to the question of how to allocate resources going forward. Experimentation need not be restricted, for example, to well-developed research programs.

When the price-adjusted disturbance variance in observational research is greater than the disturbance variance in experimental research (see Case 1), all of the resources are allocated to experimental research. Reduction in disturbance variance is sometimes achieved in highly controlled laboratory settings or through careful matching of observations prior to random assignment. Holding prices constant, the more complex the observational environment, the more attractive experimentation becomes.

Conversely, when experiments are prohibitively costly (Case 3) in relation to the payoff from observational research, all resources are committed to the latter. This case comprises situations in which researchers have ready access to reliable observational data as well as situations in which experiments are infeasible. The costliness, both financial and ethical, of changing constitutions, party systems, or political cultures by means of random assignment consigns much of social science to Case 3. The fact that experiments are impractical does not necessarily brighten the prospects for unbiased inference through observational inquiry.

The Research Allocation Theorem provides a coherent framework for understanding why researchers might wish to conduct experiments. Among the leading justifications for experimentation are (1) uncertainty about the biases associated with observational studies, (2) ample resources, (3) inexpensive access to experimental subjects, and (4) features of experimental design that limit disturbance variability. Conversely, (1') budget constraints, (2') the relative costliness of experimental research, and (3') the relative precision of observational models constitute leading arguments in favor of observational research. It should be emphasized, however, that the case for observational research hinges on prior information about its biases.

6. Discussion

In this concluding section we consider the implications of these two theorems for research practice. We consider in particular (i) the possibility of bias in experiments, (ii) the value of methodological inquiry, (iii) the conditions under which observational data support unbiased causal inference, and (iv) the value of theory.

What about bias in experiments? In the preceding analysis we have characterized experiments as unbiased and observational studies as potentially biased. It is easy to conceive of situations where experimental results become potentially biased as well. The external validity of an experiment hinges on four factors: whether the subjects in the study are as strongly influenced by the treatment as the population to which a generalization is made, whether the treatment in the experiment corresponds to the treatment in the population of interest, whether the response measure used in the experiment corresponds to the variable of interest in the population, and how the effect estimates were derived statistically. In the example mentioned above, a canvassing experiment was conducted in a given city at a given point in time. Door-to-door canvassing was conducted by specific precinct workers, using a certain type of get-out-the-vote appeal, and with a rate of contact that reflects the idiosyncrasies of a particular neighborhood. Extrapolating to other times, places, and modes of canvassing introduces the possibility of bias.

A straightforward extension of the present analytic framework could be made to cases in which experiments are potentially biased. Delete the expressions related to the unbiased experiment and replace them with a potentially biased empirical result akin to the observational study. The lesson to be drawn from this type of analysis parallels what we have presented here. Researchers should be partial to studies that raise the fewest concerns about extrapolation bias. The smaller the inferential leap, the better.

This point has special importance for the distinction between laboratory experiments and field experiments. The inferential leap from the laboratory to the outside world increases the risk of bias. Experiments often involve convenience samples, contrived interventions, and response measures that do not directly correspond to the dependent variables of interest outside the lab. These are more serious drawbacks than the aforementioned problems with field experiments. Field experiments may be replicated in an effort to sample different types of interventions and the political contexts in which they occur, thereby reducing the uncertainty associated with generalizations beyond the data. Replication lends credibility to laboratory experiments as well, but so long as the outcome variable observed in the lab (e.g., stated vote intention) differs from the variable of interest (actual voter turnout rates) and so long as there is reason to suspect that laboratory results are specific to the lab setting, the possibility of bias remains acute.

Disciplines such as medicine make extensive and productive use of laboratory experimentation. In basic research, animals such as rats and monkeys are used as proxies for human beings. One might suspect that the idiosyncratic biology and social environments of human beings would render this type of animal research uninformative, but in fact the correspondence between results obtained based on animal models and those based on human beings turns out to be substantial. Even stronger is the empirical correspondence between laboratory results involving nonrandom samples of human subjects and outcomes that occur when medical treatments are deployed in the outside world. As Achen points out, when experience shows that results may be generalized readily from a laboratory setting, "even a tiny randomized experiment may be better than a large uncontrolled experiment" (1986: 7). Our point is not that laboratory experiments are inherently flawed; rather, the external validity of laboratory studies is an empirical question, one that has been assessed extensively in medicine and scarcely at all in political science.

All things being equal, the external validity of field experimentation exceeds that of laboratory experimentation. However, the advantages of field experimentation in terms of external validity may be offset by threats to internal validity that arise when randomized interventions are carried out in naturalistic settings. Heckman and Smith (1995) note that the integrity of random assignment is sometimes compromised by those charged with administering treatments, who deliberately or unwittingly divert a treatment to those who seem most deserving. To this list may be added other sources of bias, such as problems of spillover that occur when a treatment directed to a treatment group affects a nearby control group or the experimenter's failure to measure variations in the treatment that is actually administered (See Brady 2003 for a discussion of the assumptions that underpin experimental inference).

Whether a given field experiment confronts these difficulties depends on the nature of the intervention and the circumstances in which the experiment is conducted. When these threats to unbiasedness do present themselves, valid inference may be rescued by means of statistical correctives that permit consistent parameter estimation. When treatments are shunted to those who were assigned to the control group, for example, the original random assignment provides a valid instrumental variable predicting which individuals in the treatment and control groups actually received the treatment. Despite the fact that some members of the control group were treated inadvertently, consistent parameter estimates may be obtained through instrumental variables regression so long as the assigned treatment group was more likely to receive the treatment than the assigned control group (Angrist, Imbens, and Rubin 1996).[6]

Although statistical correctives are often sufficient to mend the problems that afflict field experiments, certain potential biases can be addressed only by adjusting the experimental design. For example, Howell and Peterson's (2002) experiments gauge the effects of private school vouchers on student performance by assigning vouchers to a random subset of families that apply for them. This design arguably renders a conservative estimate of the effects of vouchers, inasmuch as the competitive threat of a private voucher program gives public schools in the area an incentive to work harder, thereby narrowing the performance gap between the treatment group that attends private schools and the control group that remains in public school.[7] In order to evaluate the systemic effects of vouchers, it would be useful to perform random assignment at the level of the school district rather than at the level of the individual. In this way, the analyst could ascertain whether the availability of vouchers improves academic performance in public schools. This result would provide extrinsic evidence about the bias associated with randomization at the individual level.

Field experiments of this sort are expensive, and they grow more so as researchers attempt to ascertain the general equilibrium effects of a proposed intervention. Difficult as it is to assess, for example, the wage effects of raising a set of individuals' education by one year, it is even more difficult to gauge the effects of raising everyone's education by one year. Extrapolating from a small-scale experiment to a general equilibrium prediction is potentially problematic, particularly if education conveys a market signal that is interpreted in relation to the overall level of education. The costs and potential bias of field experimentation are contingent on the ambitiousness of the research question.

As we point out in our Research Allocation Theorem, however, the uncertainties associated with observational investigation may impel researchers to allocate resources to field experimentation in spite of these costs. Observational inquiry may involve representative samples of the population to which the causal generalization will be applied and a range of real-world interventions, but the knowledge it produces about causality is more tenuous. The abundance of observational research and relative paucity of field experimentation that one currently finds in social science—even in domains where field experimentation is feasible and ethically unencumbered—may reflect excessive optimism about what is known about the biases of observational research.

The value of methodological inquiry. Our analytic results underscore not only the importance of unbiased experimental research but also the value of basic methodological inquiry. To the extent that the biases of observational research can be calibrated through independent inquiry, the information content of observational research rises. For example, if through inspection of its sampling, measurement, or statistical procedures the bias associated with a given observational study could be identified more precisely (lowering σ^2_B), the weight assigned to those observational findings would go up. The same holds for inquiry into the likely sources of bias. By investigating the role of omitted variables and their correlations with the explanatory variables (see Rosenbaum 2002), one may increase one's understanding of bias in observational research.[8]

It should be emphasized that although this type of inquiry is potentially useful, whether it in fact succeeds in reducing uncertainty about bias in observational research remains an empirical question. Even if one correctly discerns the biases associated with all of the confounding factors one can think of, there may remain confounding factors that one has overlooked. The test of whether methodological inquiry succeeds is its ability to correctly anticipate experimental results, because experiments produce unbiased estimates regardless of whether the confounders are known or unknown.

Unfortunately, the ex ante prediction of bias in the estimation of treatment effects has yet to emerge as an empirical research program in the social sciences. To be sure, methodological inquiry into the properties of statistical estimators abounds in the social sciences. A growing body of literature attempts to gauge the biases of observational analysis by comparing it to experimental benchmarks (Arceneaux, Gerber, and Green 2006; Bloom, Michalopolous, Hill and Lei 2002; Glazerman, Levy, and Myers 2002; Heckman, Lalonde, and Smith 1999; Smith and Todd 2001) and finds that observational studies are only occasionally successful in approximating experimental results, even when those results are known to the researchers ahead of time. We know of no study that assesses the degree to which methodological experts can anticipate the direction and magnitude of biases simply by inspecting the design and execution of observational social science research.[9]

Our own experiments on voter turnout have increased our appreciation of how difficult it can be to gauge the severity of bias in observational research. Consider the following question: How much do brief get-out-the-vote calls from commercial phone banks increase turnout? When the question is addressed by using large-scale randomized field experiments, the estimated effect hovers near zero (Arceneaux, Gerber, and Green 2006). Those randomly assigned to receive calls are not significantly more likely to vote than those assigned to the control group. When the same data are analyzed by using observational methods, the results are quite different. Regressing voter turnout on a variable indicating whether one was contacted by the phone bank suggests a strong and statistically significant treatment effect, even after one controls for an enormous list of variables, such as voter turnout in previous elections.

By the usual standards of evaluating observational research, the latter analysis seems very persuasive. It rests on unusually reliable measures of whether people were contacted and whether they voted. The sample comprises hundreds of thousands of subjects. As a result, the observational estimates have a t-ratio of more than 9; by scholarly convention, this finding would warrant at least three and possibly four asterisks. These statistical findings are very robust, with similar findings emerging regardless of whether one analyzes the data by parametric or by nonparametric methods. Moreover, these results are confirmed by other observational studies using different samples of voters. The exemplary methodological credentials of this observational study might entice us to trust its results. Yet the experimental results reveal the observational findings to be highly misleading. Because the right answer is seldom known with precision, methodological arguments in the social sciences are rarely confronted in this way.

When is observational learning not illusory? Sometimes researchers can approximate this kind of methodological understanding by seizing upon propitious observational research opportunities. For example, students of public opinion have for decades charted movements in presidential popularity. As a result, they have a clear sense of how much presidential popularity would be expected to change over the course of a few days. Although the terrorist attacks of September 11, 2001, were not the product of random assignment, we may confidently infer that they produced a dramatic surge in the presidential popularity of George W. Bush from the fact that no other factors can plausibly account for a change of this magnitude and timing. Expressed in terms of the notation presented above, the size of the observational estimate (x_o) dwarfs the bias term (B) and the uncertainty associated with it (σ^2_B), leaving little doubt that the terrorist attacks set in motion a train of events that increased the president's popularity.

Another interesting case is the effect of the "butterfly ballot" on votes cast in Palm Beach County, Florida, during the election of 2000. Using a diverse array of observational evidence, Wand et al. (2001) make a formidable case for the proposition that the unique ballot format used in Palm Beach County cost the Democratic presidential candidate more than 2,000 votes, which was several times larger than his margin of defeat. Wand et al. muster evidence showing that the country-level pattern of votes in this county was the most anomalous of any county in the country, save for one other county in a neighboring state that experienced catastrophic malfunction of its voting machines. The authors bolster this statistical finding with an analysis of precincts within Palm Beach County and an analysis of individual ballots, both of which indicate that Democrats voted for the Reform candidate, Pat Buchanan, by mistake. When these lines of observational inquiry are considered as a package, the uncertainty about bias is dwarfed by the magnitude of the effect.

Notice that the foregoing examples make use of substantive assumptions in order to bolster the credibility of a causal inference. We stipulate the absence of other plausible explanations for the increase in Bush's popularity ratings in the wake of 9/11 or the windfall of votes that Buchanan received in a county where he never campaigned. Were we able to exclude competing explanations routinely in the analysis of observational data, the problems of inference would not be so daunting. Lest one wonder why humans were able to make so many useful discoveries prior to the advent of randomized experimentation, it should be noted that physical experimentation requires no explicit control group when the range of alternative explanations is so small. Those who strike flint and steel together to make fire may reasonably reject the null hypothesis of spontaneous combustion.

When estimating the effects of flint and steel from a sequence of events culminating in fire, σ^2_B is fairly small; but in those instances where the causal inference problem is more uncertain because the range of competing explanations is larger, this observational approach breaks down. Pre-experimental scientists had enormous difficulty gauging the efficacy of medical interventions because the risk of biased inference is so much greater, given the many factors that plausibly affect health outcomes. Consider, for example, inferences drawn about the efficacy of blood-letting during the 1790s. One of the leading physicians of his day, Alexander Gordon,[10] conducted a careful quantitative investigation to determine whether venesection increased the survival rate of women stricken with puerperal fever. As Louden (2000: 27–28) explains,

> Gordon's evidence seems so convincing that, if it were a modern form of treatment that claimed to produce such results in a fatal disease, it would pass today's ethical committees and probably receive a grant for a randomized trial, for he insisted that in the cure of this disease he had been 'much more successful than any other practitioner.' . . . I suspect there are two reasons why Gordon was so certain that bleeding was effective. First, he was sure that bleeding had to be performed very early in the disease. If he bled the patient copiously and she still died, he assumed that it was because the disease had already been too well established; if only he had been called earlier, she would have survived. . . . The second reason was that Gordon did not arrive at his conclusion. . . . until the epidemic was already well established and had been present for several months. It was the nature of all epidemics of puerperal fever that the fatality rate was always highest at the beginning of the epidemic, and declined after the epidemic had been established for some months. Thus most of the cases that Gordon bled copiously were cases late in the epidemic—the very cases most likely to recover in any case.

Gordon's endorsement of bloodletting was not the result of superstition or aversion to rigorous science. Gordon's observational research was executed with great care, and for decades his treatise persuaded leading physicians of the scientific merits of bloodletting. It is only in hindsight that we recognize the biases of his research design.

Between flint-and-steel and bloodletting are examples of observational data that are reliable under certain circumstances, where threats to unbiased inference are relatively small. The analytic framework we present offers an important research principle: In terms of mean-squared error, it may be better to study fewer observations, if those observations are chosen in ways that minimize bias. To see this principle at work, look back at our numerical example and imagine that our complete data set consisted of 11,200 observations, 1,200 of which were free from bias. If we harbor uninformative priors about the bias in the observational component of the data set, the optimal weighting of these observations involves placing zero weight on the 10,000 bias-prone observations and focusing exclusively on the 1,200 experimental observations. The implication for large-N studies of international relations, comparative politics, or public opinion is that it may be better to focus on a narrow but uncontaminated portion of a larger data set.

How can one identify the unbiased component of a larger data set? One way is to generate the data through unbiased procedures, such as random assignment. Another is to look for naturally occurring instances where similar cases are confronted with different stimuli, as when defendants are assigned by lot to judges with varying levels of punitiveness. More tenuous but still defensible may be instances where the processes by which the independent variable are generated have no plausible link to unobserved factors that affect the dependent variable. For example, if imminent municipal elections cause local officials to put more police on the streets, and if the timing of municipal elections across a variety of jurisdictions has no plausible relationship to trends in crime rates, the municipal election cycle can be used as an instrumental variable by which to estimate the effects of policing on crime rates (Levitt 1997, 2002). More tenuous but still arguably more defensible than a blind canvass of all available cases is an attempt to match observations on as many criteria as possible prior to the occurrence of an intervention. For certain applications this is best done by means of a panel study in which observations are tracked before and after they each encounter an intervention, preferably an intervention that occurs at different points in time. These methods are not free from bias, but the care with which the comparisons are crafted reduces some of the uncertainty about bias, which makes the results more informative.

Even when observational research succeeds, it seldom achieves the apparent level of certitude suggested by conventional standard errors. As noted above, these standard errors are calculated based on the assumption of perfect information about B and certainty that σ^2_B is zero.

While sensitivity tests can help ascertain whether alternative estimation approaches would have yielded different observational results, they do not completely eliminate uncertainty about bias. Currently, researchers discuss the sensitivity of their results without venturing precise views about the posterior values of B and σ^2_B derived from this procedure. Providing these values would offer a useful guide to readers trying to convert nominal standard errors into more meaningful root mean squared errors.

The value of theory. The more theoretical knowledge the researcher brings to bear when developing criteria for comparability, the smaller the σ^2_B and the more secure the causal inference. Thus, in addition to charting a new research program for methodologists, our analysis calls attention to an underappreciated role of theory in empirical research. The point extends beyond the problem of case selection and internal validity. Any causal generalization, even one based on a randomized study that takes place in a representative sample of field sites, relies to some degree on extrapolation. Every experiment has its own set of idiosyncrasies, and we impose theoretical assumptions when we infer, for example, that the results from an experiment conducted on a Wednesday generalize readily to Thursdays. Just as methodological insight clarifies the nature of observational bias, theoretical insight reduces the uncertainty associated with extrapolation.

But where does theoretical insight come from? To the extent that what we are calling theories are testable empirical propositions, the answer is some combination of priors, observational data, and experimental findings. Theory development, then, depends critically on the stock of basic, carefully assessed empirical claims. Social scientists tend to look down on this type of science as narrow and uninspiring, grasping instead for weak tests of expansive and arresting propositions. Unlike natural scientists, therefore, social scientists have accumulated relatively few secure empirical premises from which to extrapolate. This lacuna is unfortunate because developing secure empirical premises speeds the rate at which learning occurs as new experimental and observational results become available.

The framework laid out here cannot adjudicate the issue of how a discipline should allocate its resources to research questions of varying substantive merit. Moreover, it leaves open the question of which lines of research are most likely to generate collateral methodological or theoretical advances. But the analytic results presented here do clarify the conditions under which a given research program is likely to make progress. Our ability to draw causal inferences and report accurately the uncertainty associated with these inferences depends on our prior knowledge about the biases of our procedures.

Acknowledgments

The authors are grateful to Henry Brady, Bruce Bueno de Mesquita, Greg Huber, and Doug Rivers for their comments and suggestions. We are indebted as well to the Institution for Social and Policy Studies at Yale University, which provided research support. Comments and questions may be directed to the authors at alan.gerber@yale.edu, donald.green@yale.edu, or edward.kaplan@yale.edu. This article originally appeared as a chapter in *Problems and Methods in the Study of Politics*, ed. I. Shapiro, R. Smith, and T. Masoud, 251–73 (Cambridge University Press, 2004). It has been reproduced and updated slightly with their permission.

NOTES

1. For further discussion of Bayesian approaches to causal inference and statistical reasoning, see Howson and Urbach (1993).

2. This negative correlation results from the fact that the experiment provides an unbiased estimator of M, whereas the observational study provides an unbiased estimator of $M+B$. As we note below, once these findings become known, higher estimates of M from the experimental study imply lower values of B when the experimental result is subtracted from the observational result.

3. As Gerber and Green (2000) explain, complications arise in this type of experiment when canvassing campaigns fail to make contact with those subjects assigned to the treatment group. This problem may be addressed statistically by using instrumental variables regression, although, as Heckman and Smith (1995) note, the external validity of this correction requires the assumption that the canvassing has the same effect on those who could be reached as it would have had among those the canvassing campaign failed to contact. This assumption may be tested by randomly varying the intensity of the canvassing effort. Below, we take up the question of how our conclusions change as we take into account the potential for bias in experimental research.

4. The empirical results also furnish information about the bias associated with the observational data. The posterior estimate of B is 4.1, as opposed to a prior of 2. Because the experimental results tell us a great deal about the biases of the observational

study, the posterior variance of B is 6.3, a marked decline from the prior value of 36. In advance of seeing the data, our priors over M and B were uncorrelated; afterward, the posterior correlation between B and M becomes -0.92. This posterior correlation is important to bear in mind in the event that subsequent evidence becomes available. The estimating equations presented above describe how uncorrelated priors over M and B change in light of all of the evidence that emerges subsequently, regardless of the order in which it emerges. Thus, if a second observational study of 10,000 observations were to appear, we would recalculate the results in this section on the basis of the cumulative N=20,000 observational data set.

5. The notation used in this section has been selected for ease of exposition. When the population variance for the subjects in an experimental study equals v, and n experimental subjects are divided equally into treatment and control groups, the variance for the experiment is $4v/n$. To convert from these units to the notation used here, define π_e as the cost of adding 4 subjects.

6. The interpretation of these estimates is straightforward if one assumes (as researchers working with observational data often do) that the treatment's effects are the same for all members of the population. The instrumental variables regression provides an estimate of the effect of the treatment among Compliers, those who receive the treatment if and only if assigned to the treatment group. Note, however, that the issue of heterogeneous treatment effects is relevant to the issue of external, not internal, validity. Whether bias creeps into an extrapolation to some other population depends on whether effects vary across individuals in different contexts.

7. The magnitude of this bias is likely to be small in the case of the Howell and Peterson interventions, which affected only a small percentage of the total student-age population.

8. A model for this type of literature may be found in survey measurement. The estimation of population parameters by means of random sampling is analogous to the estimation of treatment effects by means of randomized experimentation. Convenience and other nonrandom samples are analogous to observational research. In fields where random sampling methods are difficult to implement (e.g., studies of illicit drug use), researchers make analytic assessments of the biases associated with various nonrandom sampling approaches and test these assessments by making empirical comparisons between alternative sampling methodologies.

9. In the field of medicine, where plentiful experimental and observational research makes cross-method comparisons possible, scholars currently have a limited ability to predict ex post the direction and magnitude of observational bias (cf. Heinsman and Shadish 1996; Shadish and Ragsdale 1996).

10. Gordon is best remembered for his prescient conjecture that hygiene played a role in the spread of disease. That Gordon proved to be right about hygiene but wrong about bloodletting reminds us that observationally derived hypotheses are not doomed to fail. Rather their chances of success or failure are difficult to predict ex ante based on observational methods.

A DEFENSE OF OBSERVATIONAL RESEARCH

Susan C. Stokes

1. Introduction

Experimental research is quickly gaining ground in the social sciences. Building on a rich tradition of experimentation going back to Gosnell's field experiments on voter turnout in Chicago in the 1920s, political scientists have devised laboratory experiments to study (among other topics) media effects on voters, attitudes about race, and distribution rules on collective action, while field experiments cover an increasingly wide range, from voter turnout to voting behavior to corruption and the rule of law. Beginning in the 1990s experimental techniques have become widespread in development and labor economics. Economists have conducted experiments to test the effect of a wide range of interventions, from varying interest rates on the repayment of microloans, to deworming on school attendance, to charging for antimosquito bed nets on the incidence of malaria. Psychology has long been an experimental discipline.[1]

Experiments have contributed to our basic knowledge of causal effects in the social world. When they are feasible, ethically acceptable, and cost-effective they are clearly a valuable research tool. Criticisms of various aspects of experimental research—problems of implementation such as compliance and spillover, problems of external validity, and the scope of the questions that can be addressed—have come from experimentalists and from outsiders. My main objective here is not to criticize social science experimentation. Instead it is to describe and criticize a set of beliefs that a growing number of social scientists hold about observational research. I contend that if these beliefs were applied evenhandedly to experimental studies, we would give up on observation and experiments alike as contributing to the building and testing of theories about the social world.

In the section that follows, I characterize the beliefs entailed in *radical skepticism* of observational research. I do not prove these beliefs to be incorrect, but I do offer reasons why they are unlikely to be warranted. In the section entitled "Radical Skepticism and Experimental Research" I argue that, if one were to embrace radical skepticism and apply it evenhandedly to experimental research, one would despair of the possibility that such research could contribute to the building and testing of social science theories. Yet we should draw back from the abyss and abandon radical skepticism of observational and experimental research. We should replace it with skepticism disciplined by alternative explanations. In the final section, "Observation, Experiments, and Theory," I discuss the relationship of observational and experimental research to the building and testing of theory.

2. Characterizing Radical Skepticism of Observational Research

Fueling the rise of experimental methods in social research has been growing awareness of the pitfalls of observational research. Awareness of these pitfalls is not new; it formed part of the backdrop to the invention of randomized experiments in the 1920s and 1930s.[2] What's new in the social science community is a spreading pervasiveness of radical skepticism about observational studies.[3] This skepticism involves the following logic. Consider a linear model of individual i's outcome on Y:[4]

$$Y_i = \alpha_i + \beta_0 X_{i0} + \sum_{n=1}^{j} \beta_j \mathbf{X}_{ij} + \sum_{m=1}^{k} E_k \mathbf{Z}_{ik} + \mu_i$$

in which (dropping the i subscripts) X_0 is the key explanatory variable. The β_j coefficients relate $n = 1, 2, \ldots, j$ X variables to Y, but these factors are unrelated to X_0. Then $\mathbf{Z}$ represents $m = 1, 2, \ldots, k$ other factors related to Υ and to X_0; these are confounders. μ represents unobserved causes of Υ.[5]

Among the $\mathbf{Z}_k$ confounders, some are not observed at the point at which the research is reported. But assume that some could be observed—if, for instance, the researcher's critics suggested them as confounders—whereas some are unobservable. The confounding variables can be thought of as a set composed of observed, currently unobserved but observable, and unobservable vectors:

$$\mathbf{Z} = \{\mathbf{Z}_{observed}, \mathbf{Z}_{observable}, \mathbf{Z}_{unobservable}\}.$$

The core belief of radical skepticism is that unobservable confounders always exist. $\mathbf{Z}_{unobservable}$ is never itself an empty set. No matter how diligent and inventive the observational researcher, she will never be able to overcome the bias imposed by the presence of unobserved—because unobservable—correlates of the key causal variable. As we shall see, there are two reasons why skeptics conclude that some confounders are likely always to remain unobserved. One has to do with the very large number of ways in which units can vary. This high dimensionality of units, the reasoning goes, means that it is basically impossible for the researcher to consider, much less control for, all confounders. The second reason is that some dimensions of variation are inherently difficult to measure. Given the inevitable existence of unobservable covariates, in the view of radical skeptics, observational researchers will rarely be able to identify, without bias, causal effects. Unobserved heterogeneity inescapably frustrates causal inference from observational data.

Regarding the first reason, one could make sense of the radical skeptic's belief that unobservable confounders always exist by noting the large numbers of ways in which human and social life varies. The social unit, whether a person, an institution, or a case of an event, generally varies on a very large number of dimensions. The dimensions of individuals include their income, schooling, attentiveness, physical characteristics . . . the list could be extended endlessly. So too for other social units. Were this dimensionality much smaller, the problem would appear less intractable. For instance, imagine a study involving people who vary only on three dimensions: income, handedness, and hair color. To test the hypothesis that handedness influences income, the researcher would have to assure himself only that hair color and handedness are unrelated or that hair color exerts no influence on income, and that income has no reciprocal effect on handedness. He would not say to himself that he might be led astray by failing to control for some other confounder; by assumption, in this example, there are no other dimensions along which units vary. The degree of dimensionality of units increases the chances of omitted-variable bias. Because units in the social world tend to have high dimensionality, without a plausibility constraint observational research would indeed be basically incapable of detecting causal effects. Yet, I will argue later, this same high dimensionality would—again, in the absence of plausibility constraints—undermine experimental research as well.

The belief that observational research can never exhaustively introduce controls or make adjustments for all confounding factors tends simply to be asserted. This assertion is in sharp contrast to a more traditional (though embattled) approach. In this approach, the researcher begins with plausible alternative explanations—ones suggested by theory and by logic—that could vitiate his or her causal claim, devises measures of confounders implied by this alternative, and then examines the effect of the key explanatory variable in the presence of controls. A textbook description of such a procedure is offered by King, Keohane, and Verba. They give a hypothetical example in which the investigator seeks to estimate the effect of residential segregation in the Israeli-occupied West Bank on conflict between Israelis and Palestinians. Ideological extremism might be a confounding factor, leading people both to live in segregated communities and to be more prone to conflict. The solution is to control for ideological extremism.

We might correct for the problem here by also measuring the ideology of the residents explicitly and controlling for it. For example, we could learn how popular extremist political parties are among the Israelis and PLO affiliation is among the Palestinians. We could then control for the possibly confounding effects of ideology by comparing communities with the same level of ideological extremism but differing levels of residential segregation.[6]

From the standpoint of radical skeptics, controlling for one potential confounder is not a satisfactory fix. If unobservable covariates always lie just over the horizon, controlling for one or even several does not exhaust the problem of unobserved heterogeneity.

A sense of the intractability of omitted-variable bias in observational research comes through in the methodological reflections of many social scientists. In a thoughtful essay aimed at improving the quality of natural experiments, Dunning writes that "the strong possibility that unobserved differences across groups may account for differences in average outcomes is *always omnipresent* in observational settings."[7] Referring to Posner's study of ethnic relations in Malawi and Zambia, Przeworski writes, "While Posner provides persuasive arguments that members of each of the two groups do not differ otherwise than by being on different sides of the border, rival hypotheses entailing unobserved differences are *always plausible.*"[8]

Gerber, Green, and their coauthors are impressed with the high dimensionality of human and social variation and infer from it that observational research tends to produce biased results. In the first chapter of this book, Gerber, Green, and Kaplan construct a Bayesian framework to compare the increments to knowledge provided by observational and experimental studies.[9] The authors concede that there is a risk of bias in both experimental and observational research but contend that it is typically much greater in observational research.[10]

The main source of bias on which they focus is omitted covariates. Whereas experimental researchers control the assignment of units to treatment and control, in observational studies "the data generation process by which the independent variables arise is *unknown* to the researcher."[11] This ignorance means that the observational researchers can never be confident that an unobserved factor has not shaped both their favored explanatory variable and the outcome. Gerber and coauthors' "Illusion of Observational Learning Theorem" rests on the fact that "if one is *entirely uncertain* about the biases of observational research, the accumulation of observational findings sheds no light on the causal parameter of interest."[12] Though this uncertainty is stated in the conditional tense—"*if* one is entirely uncertain"—the illustrations that Gerber and his coauthors offer represent it as irreducible.

With mediating confounding factors as with other confounders, these skeptics are impressed with their near-limitlessness. Green, Ha, and Bullock write that "as a practical matter, it is impossible to measure all of the possibly confounding mediating variables. Putting measurement aside, it is rare that a researcher will be able to think of all of the confounding mediators."[13]

Like Gerber, Green, and their coauthors, Banerjee and Duflo (chapter 4) view omitted-variable bias as inherent in observational research. And like the political science skeptics, these economists also despair of the possibility of accumulation of knowledge from observational studies:[14] "If we were prepared to carry out enough experiments in varied enough locations, we could learn as much as we want to know about the distribution of the treatment effects across sites conditional on any given set of covariates. In contrast, there is no comparable statement that could be made about observational studies. . . . with observational studies, *one needs to assume non-confoundedness* . . . of all the studies to be able to compare them. If several observational studies give different results, one possible explanation is that one or several of them are biased . . . and another one is that the treatment effects are indeed different."[15]

Do observational researchers "know nothing" about the processes that generate independent variables and are they hence "entirely uncertain" about bias? Is the "strong possibility" of unobserved confounding factors "always omnipresent" in observational research? Are rival hypotheses "always plausible"? Can one do nothing more than "assume non-confoundedness"? To the extent that the answers to these questions are no, radical skepticism is undermined.

Let us consider the first claim, that observational researchers know nothing about the processes that generate their independent variables. The claim elides the undisputed fact that observational researchers do not *control* assignment of units to treatment and controls with the more questionable one that they *cannot understand* the process by which this selection takes place. If nonexperimental researchers can know nothing about the processes that generate their independent variables, they could not take advantage of natural experiments, in which a clearly exogenous event—for example, a natural disaster, a geographic feature, perhaps the drawing of a border—produces "as-if" randomization. Rather than thinking of observational researchers as necessarily in the dark about the processes producing their key explanatory variables, we should think of them as more or less constrained by the fact that they do not control this process. Observational researchers must learn all they can about the process that selects units (individuals, groups, countries) into the kind that will be treated by the presumed cause and about the ways in which this process may also shape the outcome. They must always reassure themselves and their critics that they are dealing adequately with potential confounders and reverse causation.

Turning to the second claim of the omnipresence of unobserved confounding factors, a reason to doubt that they will always undermine observational research is that even though dimensionality of social units tends to be high, the number of plausible alternative explanations for any outcome of interest may not be so large. In fact, the number of plausible rival explanations may, in any given context, be relatively small. But the scope of the problem—are we dealing with myriad possible confounders or a handful?—remains unknown unless the researcher and his critics discuss specific alternative accounts and their plausibility. Instead of offering such specifics, the radical skeptic typically makes a blanket claim of the presence of unobserved covariates. The generality of the claim leaves the often-misleading impression that the number of plausible rival accounts must be very large. And, as Gerber et al. explain (in a paper which, as we have seen, is skeptical of observational research), the smaller the number of plausible rival explanations, the more confident one can be of causal inference in the absence of randomized tests.[16]

A belief in the omnipresence of unobserved confounders informs criticisms of the modeling of observational data. The Neyman model builds on the idea that a treatment effect is the difference in potential outcomes between a unit under treatment and that same unit under control. Though we observe individual units only in one state or the other, an experimental design seeks to ensure that treatment assignment is independent of all baseline variables. When assignment is not random, the researcher attempts to achieve conditional mean independence, which posits that potential outcomes should be, on average, identical between two groups of units under treatment or control, conditional on their having identical covariates. Observational studies, in which the assignment of units is not controlled by the researcher and is often not random, seek to balance units on their *observed* covariates. As Przeworski notes, "Having reached a satisfactory balance, [observational studies] then invoke [the] mean independence assumption, thus assuming either that balancing on the observed

covariates is sufficient to balance on the unobserved ones or that unobserved factors do not affect the outcome."[17] Whether the estimation technique is regression or nonparametric matching, the radical skeptic will be
unsatisfied since there is no matching on unobserved covariates.

The problem may be overstated, for reasons similar to the ones laid out
earlier. To the extent that currently unobserved potential confounders
can be shifted into the category of the observed, the problem is mitigated. We cannot know whether unobservable confounders vitiate causal
inference in any particular case unless we explore plausible rival explanations and seek out additional information and measures that will help us
to evaluate them. What's more, this perspective implies a research process
in which one gathers all information that is readily available about units,
the "low fruit" among covariates, matches on them, and declares the task
complete. A more effective approach is to begin with conjectures about
the causes of an explanandum—conjectures informed both by empirical
observation and by deductive reasoning—observe patterns relating key
causes to the outcome of interest, interrogate oneself and be interrogated
by others about possible confounders or reverse causation, and seek out
information that would allow matching on these covariates, shifting them
from the category of unobserved to observed.

There are plenty of ways in which observational researchers can go
astray, and the challenges are not easy. Yet they appear more insurmount-
able in the abstract than they often prove to be in concrete cases. Observational researchers who self-consciously lay out potential alternative
explanations often find the number of plausible ones to be small and the
confounders that they imply to be observable. The process by which they
present findings and open themselves to alternative explanations is, as
Rosenbaum explains, a crucial part of the research process.[18] They must
take these steps because their interlocutors will suggest alternative explanations, explanations which in turn suggest confounders that must
be taken into account. The researcher will either find that her original
hypothesis survives analyses that take into consideration potential confounders or it does not. Whether plausible rival explanations exist that
would require adjustments for truly unobservable confounders, as opposed to observable ones which the community of researchers has simply
not yet measured, is an open question. In any case, the ratio of unobserv-

able to currently unobserved confounders may be smaller than the radical skeptic supposes.

Rather than indicating specific alternative explanations, thus setting off the effort to shift confounders from the category of unobserved to observed, radical skeptics are prone simply to assert that, in the absence of random assignment of units to treatment and controls, unobserved covariates must be making mischief. Radical skepticism replaces a discussion of specific potential confounders and the alternative explanations to which they are attached with blanket complaints about the absence of an identification strategy. This failure to posit specific rival explanations leaves the impression that myriad alternatives must exist. The lack of specificity often masks the fact that the number of plausible alternatives is tractably small. Radical skepticism thus remains ungrounded, in Wittgenstein's sense.[19] Not the failure to test rival explanations by observing potential confounders, but the failure to randomize assignment to treatment and controls, is what—in the radical skeptic's view—vitiates observational studies.

Przeworski's sense of the intractability of omitted-variable bias stems from the second reason mentioned earlier: that some confounders simply cannot be observed. To illustrate the point, he posits, hypothetically, that democracy promotes economic growth whereas dictatorship slows it. Yet, he claims, any observational study of national growth rates under democracy and dictatorship would be frustrated by an omitted, unmeasurable confounder: the quality of political leadership. But his example of an unobservable confounder seems more illustrative of the wisdom of exploring plausible alternatives than of the inevitable unobservability of confounders:

> Suppose that leaders of some countries go to study in Cambridge, where they absorb the ideals of democracy and learn how to promote growth. Leaders of other countries, however, go to the School of the Americas, where they learn how to repress and nothing about economics. Dictatorships will then generate lower growth because of the quality of leadership, which is "Not Available" [i.e., not measured in this hypothetical exercise and presumably unknowable]. . . . Since this is a variable we *could not observe systematically*, we cannot match on it.[20]

There may be ways of conceptualizing "quality of leadership" that leave it unobservable. But coding the postsecondary educational careers of third world leaders sounds like a laborious task, not an impossible one.

Przeworski laments the "subjectivity" of plausibility assessments of rival hypotheses, seeming to wish for an objective test, a kind of t-test for plausibility. And the language he chooses is heavy with a sense of improvisation and looseness in the absence of random assignment. Evaluating the quality of instrumental variables necessitates "conjuring and dismissing stories" about their effects on outcomes; justifying them entails "rhetoric: one has to tell a story"; the amount of information that can be squeezed out of historical data is "a matter of luck."[21]

The title of his essay is "Is the Science of Comparative Politics Possible?" In light of the difficulty of applying experimental techniques to such questions as do democracies grow economically more rapidly than dictatorships? or do independent central banks promote growth?, his answer is no. Comparative politics is a science if (all) this means is "following justifiable procedures when making inferences and examining evidence" and "agreeing to disagree." We are capable of generating "reproducible results, arrived at through reasonable procedures." But "to identify causal effects, we must rely on some assumptions that are untestable."[22] Here again is the key to his frustration with the limits of comparative politics as a science: the absence of tests for the assumptions we must make.

Yet, as we shall see, to produce meaningful results, experimentalists make assumptions, and some are not testable. We should be wary, furthermore, of a cartoon character of the natural or physical scientist whose work is free of improvisation, intuition, interpretation, and reliance on procedures that are reasonable rather than testable.

None of the foregoing is to say that the problems of unobservable covariates and potential reverse causation are not real—some important covariates simply cannot be observed, proxies are problematic, and good instruments are elusive. But experimental researchers face equivalent sorts of challenges.

3. Radical Skepticism and Experimental Research

Experiments allow us to test the null hypothesis that the average effect of a presumed cause is zero and to estimate the average size of the effect. Random assignment of subjects to treatment and control, with a sufficiently large sample, ensures balance on observable and unobservable covariates, avoiding the problem of omitted-variable bias.[23] Freedman notes that the key parameter of interest is the difference between the average response if all subjects were assigned to treatment and the average response if all subjects were assigned to controls. An unbiased estimator of this difference is the difference between the average response of all subjects assigned to treatment and that of those assigned to the control.[24]

Experimental researchers are well aware of a number of problems that can afflict their work. My focus here is on the phenomenon of subsets of experimental subjects' responding differently to a treatment, known as an *interaction* (i.e., the treatment interacts with traits of subjects) or as a *heterogeneous treatment effect*.

The history of medical research is littered with examples of interactions. Consider recent research into the effectiveness of cholesterol-lowering drugs on heart attacks. It was well established that low-density lipids (LDL) increased the risk of coronary events and that statin therapy lowered both LDL levels and the risk of these events. Additional research suggested health benefits from statin therapy even among subjects with LDL levels considered normal. But researchers suspected an interaction: that statin therapy improved health among people whose LDL level was normal but whose level of c-reactive protein (CRP), a marker for inflammation, was elevated, while having little beneficial effect among those with normal levels of both.[25] The public health implications were important: not all people with normal LDL levels, only those with elevated CRP, would benefit from statin therapy. It is not hard to find less innocuous examples of drugs whose beneficial average effect masks small benefits for a majority of the sample and highly deleterious ones for a subpopulation.[26]

Interactions do not threaten the step from experimentally uncovered average treatment effects to causal inference. If an experimental study is large, well designed, and well implemented, random assignment of units to treatment and control allows one to infer that the treatment is the cause of any observed average difference in outcomes between treatment and control groups.[27] Experimental design ensures that no unobserved covariate is the real cause in differences in outcomes and that apparent differences are not the result of reverse causation. These are no mean feats. The problem posed by interactions is that they can change the meaning of experimental results in a broader sense.

For example, consider Wantchekon's field experiment on clientelism in Benin.[28] With the cooperation of four major political parties in the run-up to a national election in 2001, he studied the impact of alternative campaign strategies in eight of Benin's eighty-four electoral districts. In each of the eight districts he selected one noncompetitive village to receive a "clientelist" treatment and one a "public policy" treatment; the remaining villages were controls.[29] In the clientelist treatment, campaign workers promised local public goods or trade protections for local producers, should their party be elected. In the public policy treatment, campaign workers made promises that were national in scope: alleviating poverty, advancing national unity, and eradicating corruption, among others.[30] Wantchekon then compared aggregate voting patterns in the following election across treatment and control villages and conducted a postelection survey in which respondents were asked how they voted.

Wantchekon finds that the average effect of the clientelist treatment was to increase electoral support for the party associated with this message. The average effect of the public policy message was to reduce support. In the villages of one district, however, there was no positive effect of the clientelism treatment, and in the villages of two districts there was no negative effect of the public policy treatment. It is not clear from Wantchekon's presentation whether the reported average treatment effects are across the full sample.

The results indicate many and complex interactions. Viz: "there is a significant and negative public policy treatment effect for northern candidates, regional candidates, and incumbent candidates. By contrast, there is a positive treatment effect for southern candidates. A direct comparison of the treatment effects—that is, of clientelism versus control . . . reveals that clientelism is more effective for northern candidates."[31] Wantchekon also uncovers interactions between gender and the treatments, with women on average responding more favorably than men to the public policy treatment and men more favorably than women to the clientelism treatment (though here again he cites a somewhat dizzying set of caveats related to the region and incumbency status of the candidate).

The author makes a vigorous effort to explain these interactions, perhaps less so to use them to evaluate theories of clientelism. As mentioned, from his presentation it is not entirely clear whether the average treatment effect holds even without controls for interacting variables or whether positive (clientelism) or negative (public policy) average treatment effects emerge only when one disregards the regions in which these effects were missing. Assuming the latter is the case, we would have no average treatment effects but potentially theoretically relevant interactive effects of treatment with region, incumbency status of candidates, and gender. Should the big news of this study be "Clientelism has no significant effect on voting behavior?" or should it be (for example) "Men are more susceptible to clientelist appeals than women?"

Note, furthermore, that units have not been randomly assigned to values of the interacting factors. Individuals whom Wantchekon surveyed were not randomly assigned to gender, region, or—for candidates—incumbency status; nor could they be. Without follow-up studies, a version of the unobserved heterogeneity problem creeps back in. For instance, is it women who are more susceptible to public policy appeals? or people engaged in interregional trade, who hence have wider exposure to national problems? (Most such people, Wantchekon notes, are women.)

In light of suspected interactions, researchers can undertake a number of research design fixes and statistical adjustments. With a sufficiently large sample, they can calculate the difference between treatment and control groups within the relevant subsample. But with small samples and multiple interactions, the number of units will be used up quickly. Other strategies are statistical, such as regressing the outcome variable on the assignment variable (a dummy registering assignment to treatment or control groups), a control for the trait in question, and an interaction between these two main effects.[32] Research design can be crafted with an eye toward suspected interactions; for instance, researchers can randomize within strata of observable factors that are suspected to interact with the treatment. Hence medical researchers who suspect that cholesterol-lowering drugs have a differential impact on people with high and low levels of c-reactive protein can conduct a new study, this time of people with high levels of CRP, randomly assigning them to treatment and control groups.[33] Wantchekon or others could undertake a follow-up study exclusively of women, assigning them randomly to clientelism and public policy treatments and to a control group; presumably long-distance traders and nontraders would be balanced among the groups.

But from the standpoint of the radical skeptic, no research design can dispose of all potential interactions. Setting plausibility aside, if units have high dimensionality and if some confounders are unmeasurable, some unobserved trait is always likely to interact with the treatment. Faced with an experimental study that uncovers a causal effect, the radical skeptic should posit some unspecified subset of units whose response to treatment is at odds with the average response, potentially changing the theoretical implications of the study's findings. If interactions can change the interpretation of experimental results, then the radical skeptic should be unnerved by their implication for experimental research. Because one can test only for interactions between treatments and *observed* factors, ungrounded skepticism implies that we will remain in the dark regarding the real findings of experimental studies.

Unobserved interactions play—or ought to play—the same role in the radical skeptic's view of experimental results as do unobserved covariates in her view of observational research: both are omnipresent and inevitably limit the contribution of research to knowledge. We may be able to rule out (or in) the possibility that not just people with high CRP levels but other subpopulations who differ on some other dimension, specified or not, will be helped by drugs, or that not just women and southerners but some other subpopulation is resistant to clientelism. But if some key traits (like some covariates) will always remain unobservable, then additional experiments and statistical adjustments cannot fix the problem.

To see the parallels between the problem of unobserved confounders and unobserved heterogeneous treatment effects, consider a model of an experimental subject's response on outcome Y:

$$Y_i = \alpha + \beta_0 T_i + \sum_{n=1}^{j} \gamma_j \mathbf{Z}_{ij} + \sum_{n=1}^{j} \theta_j \mathbf{Z}_{ij} * T_i + \mu_i,$$

β_0 relates an assignment variable, T_i, indicating treatment status, to the expected outcome for individual i. The $\mathbf{Z}$ matrix represents $n = 1, 2, \ldots, j$ traits particular to each observational unit (gender, age, race, income, regime type, what have you). γ_j coefficients relate these traits to the dependent variable (the main effect); with random assignment and large samples, we expect these traits to be balanced, whether or not the researcher observes them. $\mathbf{Z}_{ij}$ picks out the ith row of the $\mathbf{Z}$ matrix, that is, the set of j characteristics for person i. θ_j coefficients relate the effects of treatment, conditional on these traits: the effect, for instance, of a drug on mortality among people with higher or lower levels of a blood protein or of the region a person lives in on their susceptibility to electoral appeals.

As with confounding covariates, the Z traits can be conceived as a set composed of observed, unobserved but observable, and unobservable elements:

$$Z = \{Z_{observed}, Z_{unobserved}, Z_{unobservable}\}.$$

The radical skeptic should believe that the set of unobservable interacting factors is never empty. Her keen sense of human and social variability and hence of the high dimensionality of units, as well as of the unmeasurability of some of these key dimensions, should lead her to believe that unobservable interactions always threaten the meaningfulness of causal inference based on experimental data.

The case of statin therapy illustrates the difficulties experimental researchers would face if radical skepticism were warranted. First, note that detailed biochemical knowledge, not prior double-blind testing, led researchers to suspect that CRP played an interactive role between statin therapy and health outcomes. Second, the interacting trait (elevated levels of CRP) was readily observable: experimental subjects could be given a simple test to detect its level. Had either ingredient been missing—had researchers been unaware of a likely interaction or had they been aware of it but unable to measure levels of CRP—they would not have been able to assess the difference between the statin treatment's effect on the average recipient and on those with elevated CRP. As a consequence, they would have been led far astray in their assessment of the health benefits of statin therapy on people with normal cholesterol levels.

Another example, this one also from a study of voter mobilization, illustrates how radical skepticism challenges the meaningfulness of experimental research. To gauge the impact of norms of civic duty and social pressure on electoral participation, Gerber, Green, and Larimer conducted an ingenious field experiment on a sample of 180,000 people registered to vote in Michigan in 2006.[34] They mailed letters containing messages intended to elicit shame and, they conjectured, to induce higher rates of turnout to four treatment groups. The outcome variable was turnout in the primary election in August of that year. The difference in turnout rates between the control group, who received no mailing, and the treatment group that received the strongest shaming cue was 8.1 percentage points—37.8 percent for the treatment versus 29.7 percent for the control.[35]

The authors tested for two kinds of interactions. One was between a person's internalized sense of civic duty and the social shaming treatment. Their measure of civic duty was the individual's voting propensity. Their likelihood-ratio test for the interactions failed to reject the null hypothesis of equal treatment effects among high- and lower-propensity voters.[36] They also tested for interactions between treatments and the probability of voting Democratic, which they estimated with demographic information. They found no evidence of interaction. Because the authors had excluded most Democratic voters from the experimental sample, this test is less persuasive.[37] Hence the study's findings can be summarized in this way: among some categories of registered voters in Michigan—and probably more broadly—shame increases turnout. Shame has the same effect across registered Michigan voters with varying levels of civic duty and (perhaps) partisan orientations.

There are other interactions that a student of political mobilization might reasonably want to consider, particularly in light of the implications that Gerber, Green, and Larimer draw from their experimental results. Perhaps not people (or Michigan residents) in general but those already involved in organizations are primed to suffer such shame. A follow-up study that stratified by level of organizational participation might lead to a fairly substantial revision of the study's results, viz: in Michigan and probably more broadly social shame encourages turnout among organizationally active citizens but not among nonparticipants.

More generally, one would like to know not just the average effect of treatment but its heterogeneous effects on subpopulations because these parameters can change the interpretation of why a treatment has the effect it does, with implications for theory. If people from all regions of Benin are susceptible to clientelist mobilization, the explanation might be that clientelism boosts consumption, the marginal utility of consumption diminishes as income rises, and Benin is a poor country.[38] Yet if mainly men were persuaded by such offers, perhaps not poverty but particular labor market experiences and, behind them, a parochial versus national perspective drive voters' responses to clientelist electoral appeals. If U.S. voters in general are susceptible to shaming, the implication is that very basic social sensibilities to shame induce people to undertake costly behavior such as voting. If only people already involved in organizations are susceptible, the implication might be that a susceptibility to shame needs to be elicited by experiences outside of the political sphere, as in, say, religious communities or unions, before it is available for political activists to take advantage of. In the latter settings, contacts tend to be more intimate and ongoing than in party politics in advanced democracies. Heterogeneous treatment effects imply quite different theories of electoral participation.

On the radical skeptic's view, one could not hope to test all such hypotheses. The problem could not be fixed by piling experiment upon experiment, as in Banerjee and Duflo's contention that "if we were prepared to carry out enough experiments in varied enough locations, we could learn as much as we want to know about the distribution of the treatment effects across sites conditional on any set of covariates."[39] Green, Ha, and Bullock's less sanguine view is more consistent with the implications of radical skepticism. Regarding the problem posed by interactions, they write, "The bottom line is that when subjects are governed by different causal laws, analyses that presuppose that the same parameters apply to all observations may yield biased results. . . . a single experiment is unlikely to settle the question of heterogeneous treatment effects. In order to ascertain whether different subjects transmit the causal influence of X in different ways, multiple experiments—maybe decades' worth—will be necessary."[40] Yet if, like unobserved confounders, unobserved interactive traits always lie just over the horizon, in fact we could never learn as much as we want to know from more experiments. The truly consistent radical skeptics' position would be that the diversity of human and social units makes the observation of all interactions impossible; hence there can be no stopping rule, no point at which one has tested for all possible interactions.

Of course, observational researchers cannot be complacent in the presence of unobserved interactive effects. Imagine that we were to gather data on vote shares in response to clientelist appeals, without random assignment to treatment and control. Imagine, furthermore, that measures were readily available of all plausible covariates, and that an effect of higher vote shares survived the introduction of these controls. If, nevertheless, we suspected an interactive effect of some other factor, and if this factor were unmeasurable, we could not be confident of our causal inferences about the effect of the campaign strategy.

I have made the case that radical skepticism implies equally devastating consequences for observational and experimental research. Yet the implications are not identical. Assume for the sake of argument that the radical skeptics are right. What are the consequences? The observational researcher could never be certain that a putative causal effect in fact operates. We could never be sure that A causes B, rather than C causing both A and B; there will always be some unobserved C's out there that may actually be explaining the apparent causal effect. Or, in the presence of ungrounded doubt, we can never be certain that A causes B rather than B causing A. For experimental research, confidence remains high that, on average, A causes B; random assignment, given a sufficient sample size, ensures balance on all covariates, the observed, the unobserved, and the unobservable.[41] And well-designed experiments also dispose of the problem of reverse causation. Yet, if the radical skeptic is both right and consistent in her criticisms of observational and experimental research, we must always doubt whether the experimentally elicited response of some subgroups is very different from that of others. If so, the average treatment effect may mislead us as to the study's meaning and theoretical implications.

Radical skeptics might reject the equating of unobserved covariates and unobserved interactions on the following grounds. At least the finding of a significant average treatment effect tells us that a causal effect is present. Follow-up studies can always be conducted to refine our understanding of any interactive effects, whereas one cannot be sure that an observational study has identified any real effect.

But if we really believe that some unknown and unobservable factor could be interacting with the treatment, we should always be uncertain about the meaning of experimental results. The Benin example points to the possibility of false negatives: experimental evidence against any effect when in fact there are significant and theoretically meaningful effects on subpopulations. Or, returning to the study of shaming and turnout, imagine that in reality shaming increased the probability of voting only among people who are already involved in organizations, whereas those not involved were not affected by it. And imagine that researchers carried out an experiment like the shaming study but did not entertain the possibility that organizational involvement was a required condition for shaming to boost turnout. The average effect of the treatment could be entirely due to its very large impact on the organizationally active. The researchers would draw the wrong conclusion from the study: that shame has a universal effect on people, whereas in fact it has an effect only on organizational participants. The theoretical implications are quite different.

In sum, even when experiments turn up significant treatment effects, if we really believe that some crucial interacting factor remains unobserved, then our explanation of this effect is unlikely to be accurate or complete. A causal effect that cannot be explained cannot be identified, in any meaningful sense of that term.

Yet radical skepticism of experimental research is unwarranted, just as it is unwarranted of observational research; and for similar reasons. The range of plausible interactions is not infinite but finite. Blanket challenges such as "there is undoubtedly, among the population sampled, some heterogeneity that makes the average treatment effect irrelevant" are unpersuasive. More persuasive are concrete challenges of the form, "Is it not likely that subgroup X responds in a distinctive way to this intervention?" especially when knowledge of subgroup X and its reactions motivates the question. To be more concrete, returning to the turnout study, a blanket claim of unobserved interactions should give way to conjectures such as "It may be that organizationally active people react to shaming cues by turning out more, but the uninvolved won't be responsive or might even turn out less." In sum: challenges to both observational and experimental research need to be disciplined by specific and reasonable alternatives accounts.

Are heterogeneous treatment effects a potential challenge to internal validity or to external validity? The answer is, both. We saw in the voter mobilization studies that uncertainty about the effects of treatments on subsamples opened up a great deal of ambiguity about the fundamental findings that particular experiments had unearthed and potentially undercut their role in constructing and testing theory. These are problems of internal validity. But interactions are probably also a common obstacle to external validity. Consider a hypothetical randomized experiment that reveals an average treatment effect of β_t, but—unbeknownst to the researcher—the treatment interacts with variable X_j in such a way that, for a small subpopulation with high values on X_j, the average (subgroup) treatment effect is $\beta_j = -\beta_t$. If the identical experiment were repeated in another location in which a majority of the population had high values on X_j, we would expect the average treatment effect to be very different from that of the original study.

These are the kinds of problems that lead Rodrik, Deaton, and other development economists to doubt that individual studies close the case on the effectiveness of policy interventions. Rodrik's example is research into the effectiveness of various methods for distributing insecticide-treated bed nets, which are helpful in preventing malaria infection. The debate is whether free distribution or charging a nominal price for the nets is more effective in getting people to use them. A single study that strongly favored free distribution, carried out in western Kenya, would not necessarily generalize to other African settings because the treatment might have interacted with factors specific to this region, such as a lot of prior social marketing of the nets.[42] Interactions are not the only hindrance to generalizability or external validity, but they are an important one.

4. Observation, Experiments, and Theory

A central role of social science is the building and testing of broad theories of social phenomena. A powerful role that experiments can play is to test whether basic causal claims that theories rely on or imply in fact can be sustained, especially when there are good reasons to think that observational research is hobbled by endogeneity problems (good specific reasons, not ungrounded skepticism).

Skeptics are sometimes tempted to set aside not just all prior (observationally based) causal claims but all received theories. They argue for a tabula rasa. Their reasoning is that observational research produces unreliable causal claims, and these causal claims are the foundation of much theory. Gerber, Green, and their coauthors sometimes advocate for this tabula rasa stance, such as when they write,

Lest one wonder why humans were able to make so many useful discoveries prior to the advent of randomized experimentation, it should be noted that physical experimentation requires no explicit control group when the range of alternative explanations is so small. Those who strike flint and steel together to make fire may reasonably reject the null hypothesis of spontaneous combustion. When estimating the effects of flint and steel from a sequence of events culminating in fire, σ^2_B [the uncertainty associated with the degree of bias] is fairly small; but in those instances where the causal inference problem is more uncertain because the range of competing explanations is larger, this observational approach breaks down.[43]

Green, Ha, and Bullock are more strident, arguing in favor of "black box experimentation," by which they mean experimental studies that do not attempt to explain why a cause has the effect it does:

> Experimenters have good reason to be cautious when encouraged to divert attention and resources to the investigation of causal mechanisms. First, black box experimentation as it currently stands has a lot going for it. One can learn a great deal of theoretical and practical value simply by manipulating variables and gauging their effects on outcomes, regardless of the causal pathways by which these effects are transmitted. Introducing limes into the diet of seafarers was an enormous breakthrough even if no one at the time had the vaguest understanding of vitamins or cell biology. Social science would be far more advanced than it is today if researchers had a wealth of experimental evidence showing the efficacy of various educational, political, or economic interventions—even if uncertainty remained about why these interventions work.[44]

The idea that theories, in social or natural sciences, are built inductively from the accumulation of shreds of cause-and-effect relationships is a misconception. Theory building always involves a great deal of deduction as well as inductive testing. The late-eighteenth-century innovation of feeding foods rich in ascorbic acid to sailors was an "enormous breakthrough" in public health but not, on its own, in biological science. The discovery—supported, in fact, with experimental evidence—of dietary means to fight scurvy, along with other like innovations, certainly contributed to biological theory but so did deductive reasoning and observational investigations.

Indeed, in contemporary medical practice the vast majority of accepted treatments and procedures have never been subjected to double-blind clinical trials. Among them are appendectomies for appendicitis, cholecystectomy for gallstones, penicillin for tuberculosis, and diuretics for heart attack patients.[45] Doctors use these treatments even though they have never been and are unlikely ever to be tested experimentally. In this connection, critics of the evidence-based medicine movement argue for a restored sense of the value of clinical experience and biochemical research as sources of objective evidence on which medical practice is based. Perhaps, one might counter, doctors persist in these untested practices even though the evidence in their favor is indeed weak only because it would be ethically unacceptable to expose appendicitis patients, for example, to the risk of foregoing an appendectomy. Yet, as Worrall points out, if we really believe that the evidence is weak, we would not be convinced that the risk is great.[46] Though one can cite many examples of treatments thought to be therapeutic and turning out not to be, in the history of medicine most have been abandoned on the grounds of nonexperimental evidence—think bloodletting.

Social scientists should resist the temptation to cast all nonexperimental research as flawed, to reject all prior theorizing as based on flawed evidence, and to conceive of theory building as the incremental accretion of shreds of knowledge about cause-and-effect relations, narrowly construed. We need rich and variegated evidence, rigorously developed and analyzed, and considered in light of theories—which, as in all fields of science, are in part deductive in nature—if we are to gain knowledge about the workings of the social world.

Acknowledgments

I am grateful to Chris Achen, Thad Dunning, Don Green, William Hennessey, Gary King, Matt Kocher, Noam Lupu, Steve Pincus, Frances Rosenbluth, Ian Shapiro, and Dawn Teele for their comments.

Notes

1. For experiments on voters, see Iyengar and Kinder (1987) and Ansolabehere and Iyengar (1995); and on voting behavior Wantchekon (2003). For attitudes about race, see Nelson, Sanbonmatsu, and McClerking (2007) and Valentino, Hutchings, and White (2002). On distribution rules on collective action, Dawes et al. (1986). On corruption and the rule of law, see Fried et al. (2010). For recent reviews, see Druckman et al. (2006) and Humphreys and Weinstein (2009). For an account of early political science field experiments, see Green and Gerber (2003b). Brady (2009) and Brady, Collier, and Box-Steffensmeier (2009) review experiments in the broader context of political science methodologies. For experiments in labor economics, see Sackett et al. (2000). Experiments on microloans, Karlan (2005). On deworming on school attendance, Miguel and Kremer (2004); and on bednets and malaria, see Cohen and Dupas (2007). For recent reviews of experimental research in development economics, see Imbens and Wooldridge (2009) and Banerjee and Duflo (2009). For recent critical assessments of experimentation in development economics, see Deaton (chapter 6 in this book) and Rodrik (2009). See Morton and Williams's (2010) discussion of disciplinary shifts to experimentalism.

2. See Fisher (1925). Rosenbaum (2002) and Freedman (2006) provide historical background to this development.

3. By no means are all experimentally oriented social scientists radical skeptics. Morton and Williams (2010), for instance, are much more circumspect in their criticisms of observational research.

4. In this illustration the effects are assumed to be constant, but the same point holds with nonlinear effects.

5. Even if all factors systematically related to Y were measured, we might expect unexplained variation in Y, due to fundamentally unexplainable variability.

6. King, Keohane, and Verba (1994: 95).

7. Dunning (2008: 289), emphasis added.

8. Przeworski (2007: 287). His reference is to Posner 2004. Referring to an earlier draft of Dunning 2008, Przeworski adds that rival hypotheses "may be more or less plausible but, as Dunning [2005] emphasizes, assessments of their plausibility are inevitably subjective" (2007: 153–54). In fact, Dunning seems less troubled than Przeworski about the "subjectivity" entailed in posing and evaluating alternative explanations. About Posner's same study, Dunning writes that his "investigation of the plausibility of the relevant counterfactuals provides an example of 'shoe leather' research (that is, walking from house to house to find nuggets of evidence and rule out alternative explanations)" (2007: 287).

9. Gerber, Green, and Kaplan (chapter 1 in this book, p. 12).

10. Ibid.

11. Ibid., p. 10, emphasis added.

12. Ibid., p. 15, emphasis added.

13. Green, Ha, and Bullock (2010: 203). The context of this discussion is mediating variables, ones that transmit the causal effects of other variables. Confounding

mediating variables covary with the variable which the researcher believes is the key mediator.

14. Banerjee and Duflo (chapter 4 in this book, p. 94)

15. Ibid.

16. Gerber, Green, and Kaplan (chapter 1 in this book, p. 28).

17. Przeworski (2007: 153).

18. Rosenbaum (2002).

19. Wittgenstein (1969).

20. Przeworski (2007: 161), emphasis added.

21. See ibid., 162, 163, 167.

22. Ibid., 169.

23. It is relatively straightforward to show that observed covariates are balanced across treatment and control groups, but some philosophers of science question whether randomization ensures balance on unobserved covariates. See Urbach (1985).

24. Freedman 2006. Cook and Campbell recommend that researchers report their results in a cautious manner, such as that, in this test, a given effect was found to be of magnitude X and "in tests similar to the one conducted, the effect in 95 percent of the cases would be an increase" of this same magnitude. But they lament the general lack of circumspection. Cook and Campbell (1979: 41).

25. And further clinical trials showed that people with elevated CRP levels benefited from statin therapy, independent of the therapy's effect on LDL levels; see Ridker et al. (2005).

26. Worrall (2007b: 995) discusses clinical trials of benoxaprofen, developed to treat arthritis, in which the subjects included only eighteen to sixty-five year olds. The drug was approved for the market but later was associated with kidney failure among elderly patients, leading to a number of deaths. In this case, the treatment seemed to interact with a factor (age) in a nonlinear fashion, and the experimental sample excluded subjects with values of this factor over which the interaction occurred. In this case the average treatment effect was probably biased by the exclusion of part of the relevant population, at least if the outcome variable included overall quality of health rather than, narrowly, a relief of pain from arthritis.

27. Large sample size is important, Urbach (1985) reminds us, because small samples may produce imbalance in unobserved covariates, simply by chance.

28. Wantchekon (2003).

29. It is not clear from Wantchekon's report whether the sets of villages were randomly assigned to treatments or control groups.

30. There is a tension between the construct of clientelism used by most theorists and Wantchekon's treatment. The former stresses parties' distribution of minor material goods to voters, whereas Wantchekon's treatment entails promises of local public goods.

31. Wantchekon (2003: 413–14).

32. Some are queasy about estimating multivariate regression models with experimental data. Freedman explains that in a regression model of the outcome variable,

the error term is not a random variable but is fixed by assignment to treatment or control; the only random variable in the model is the assignment variable. Hence "the assignment variable . . . and the error term in the model will generally be strongly related" (2008: 2). For a response, see Green (2009). Furthermore, the inclusion into successive regression specifications of controls for covariates (subgroup identifiers) and interaction terms raises questions of data mining.

33. Ridker et al. (2008).

34. Gerber, Green, and Larimer (2008).

35. The strongest, "neighbors" treatment was a letter reminding them of their own voting history and reporting that of their neighbors.

36. Gerber, Green, and Larimer (2008: 39).

37. Only 2.7 percent of their sample was composed of Democrats. The remaining Democrats, what's more, were ones who lived in households with likely Republicans. The reason for the exclusion was that there were no competitive Democratic races; therefore Democratic voters would be unlikely to open campaign mailings.

38. See, e.g., Dixit and Londregan (1996).

39. Banerjee and Duflo (chapter 4 in this book).

40. Green, Ha, and Bullock (2010: 206.)

41. However, random assignment does not ensure the identification of an average treatment effect in the experimental population that is an unbiased estimate of the average effect in populations not included in the experiment. For this we need random sampling from the broader population of interest into the experimental subject population.

42. Rodrik (2009). The study he discusses is by Cohen and Dupas (2007)

43. Gerber, Green, and Kaplan (chapter 1 in this book, p. 27).

44. Green, Ha, and Bullock (2010: 207–8)

45. These and other examples are offered by Worrall (2007b: 986).

46. Ibid., 986–87.

A RETREAT FROM RADICAL SKEPTICISM: REBALANCING THEORY, OBSERVATIONAL DATA, AND RANDOMIZATION IN DEVELOPMENT ECONOMICS

Christopher B. Barrett and Michael R. Carter

1. Introduction

Not so long ago the typical empirical development economics seminar reached a moment of specific or structural skepticism in which attendees theorized about specific omitted or ignored structural factors that might plausibly bias reported estimates of the coefficients of interest. The speaker responded with detailed comments on the data generation process, perhaps convincing attendees that their specific concerns were ill-founded. Attendees departed, mentally recentering reported confidence intervals up or down depending on the nature of the plausible bias, expanding the girth of those same intervals, and doing a Bayesian merger of the adjusted results into their understanding of the preexisting literature. When the seminar went poorly, the skewered speaker would fall fitfully asleep that night, wishing surveys had measured confounding variables, perhaps later dreaming of random variation in key policy variables or in the instruments that predict their uptake or placement.

While few would dispute the usefulness of random variation in key variables, the meteoric rise over the past decade or so of randomization methods in development economics has replaced structural skepticism with a generalized skepticism, or what Stokes (chapter 2 in this book) calls radical skepticism. Following Stokes, radical skepticism imagines a world in which the number of potentially confounding and omitted factors is unmanageably large or even unknowable. In this world, the burden of proof falls uniquely on the researcher to establish the independence of key variables to the unknown universe of potentially confounding factors. Skepticism becomes generalized, and the only defensible identification strategy is random allocation of the key independent variable across the population of interest. Seminar attendees can intone stock phrases about identification rather than theoretically grounded concerns specific to the problem at hand. Discussion of causal pathways becomes secondary to concerns about the indisputably exogenous assignment of households (or firms or areas) to treatment and control groups. The unbiasedness of point estimates, rather than their mean squared error, becomes the central statistical preoccupation, and Bayesian learning from imperfect evidence seems to be replaced by a binary division of evidence into that which meets a purported statistical gold standard and that which does not. Skewered seminar speakers still do not sleep well at night.

While this shift from structural to radical skepticism may make for less interesting seminars, it bespeaks a more fundamental problem. As Stokes points out, if radical skepticism is correct, it not only undermines research based on observational data but also poses an intractable problem of essential heterogeneity to randomized controlled trials (RCTs). If we cannot count, model, and potentially measure factors that might be spuriously or otherwise correlated with key variables in observational data, then we can similarly never know if a universe of unknowable factors mediates the effects of even randomly distributed treatments. Well-identified local average treatment effects become data-weighted averages of multiple response regimes with unknowable dimensionality. Generalization to other populations, where the relative preponderance of the regimes may be different, becomes indefensible. Radical skepticism thereby destroys in equal measure the internal validity of observational studies and the external validity of RCTs. One cannot invoke one without unleashing the other.

Ironically, by generalizing the researcher's natural, healthy skepticism about new findings and divorcing it from specific, theoretically grounded concerns, radical skepticism drives a wedge between the use of RCTs in development economics and its use in the agricultural and biomedical disciplines from whence RCTs originate and draw much of their inspiration.

Bhargava (2008) and Stokes (chapter 2) give examples from coronary medicine in which theoretically grounded causal models identify specific confounding factors (coronary artery dimension and c-reactive protein levels) that mediate the treatment impacts of cholesterol-lowering drugs. If what economists call the policy-relevant treatment effect is to be inferred, measurement of these confounders is of equal importance irrespective of whether one is examining observational or RCT data.

We development economists might benefit from greater fidelity to the biological scientists' approach. That is, we might integrate in a more balanced fashion the experimental testing of hypotheses about effects associated with specific causal pathways with the theory and insights from observational data that yield those hypotheses and that enable us to generalize from necessarily small samples to the broader development experience. This requires a retreat from radical to structural skepticism and a rebalancing of the roles of theory, observational data, and randomization in development economics research. Such a move will not only make for more meaningful RCTs but also reopen the door to measuring heretofore unobservables and (skeptically) learning from observational data. The latter is especially important because the understandable excitement about the statistical power of RCTs can blind us to its pitfalls in economic applications. Because of these limitations, we continue to need analysis based on observational data.

In the remainder of this chapter, we will first look at four problems that limit what we can (or should) learn about economics from RCTs:

1. ethical constraints;
2. faux exogeneity of uncontrolled treatments;
3. measuring efficacy rather than effectiveness; and
4. scale and temporal limits to randomization.

We will then close by returning to the issue of rebalancing theory, measurement, and randomization in order to obtain internally and externally valid understandings of the development economics process.

2. Ethical Constraints

Experimental research involving any sort of researcher-managed intervention requires safeguards to protect the rights and welfare of humans participating as subjects in the study. Four broad classes of ethical dilemmas nonetheless routinely arise in experiments conducted by development economists. While these dilemmas have commonalities with the dilemmas that confront, say, medical trials, many are specific to social and economic interventions. These dilemmas receive distressingly little attention in graduate training and in the literature. They are of concern not only because they violate ethical principles sacrosanct to all serious research, but also because they commonly lead subjects, implementers, or both to actively circumvent the research design, thereby undercutting the statistical raison d'être of the initial randomization. While ethical issues are uncomfortable to discuss, raising them now seems preferable to waiting for a major disaster to occur that would undermine the research agenda.

The first and most obvious class of ethical dilemma revolves around the unintended but predictable adverse consequences of some experimental designs. The do no harm principle is perhaps the most fundamental ethical obligation of all researchers. Most universities and serious research organizations have institutional review boards established to guard against precisely such contingencies. Nonetheless, many highly questionable designs make it through such reviews, and the results have been published by leading economists in reputable journals. As but one prominent example involving widely respected scholars, Bertrand et al. (2007) randomized incentives for subjects in India who did not yet possess a driver's license, so as to induce them to bribe officials in order to receive a license without having successfully completed the required training and an obligatory driver safety examination. The very predictable consequence of such an experiment is that it imperils innocent nonsubjects—not to mention the subjects themselves—by putting unsafe drivers on the road illegally. This is an irresponsible research design, yet the study was published in one of the profession's most prestigious journals. Such research plainly signals insufficient attention paid to fundamental ethical constraints on field experimentation within economics.

Another example illustrates the challenges of anticipating harm from an intervention. Gugerty and Kremer (2008) evaluate the impact of NGO assistance to women's groups in Kenya. While the intervention was designed to improve the groups, the study finds the opposite and the 2005 working paper version frames the research as a test of the "Rockefeller

Effect," the idea, attributed to John D. Rockefeller, that too many resources will harm groups. While the published version of this work drops the Rockefeller Effect framing, the study indeed reports that the intervention had negative impacts on group composition and leadership. While this research offers real social insight—it is indeed useful to know if and when too much help is bad—it illustrates the complexities associated with protection of human subjects under socioeconomic interventions. It would seem in retrospect that the risks associated with the intervention were neither fully understood by the researchers and implementers nor communicated to the research subjects so that the latter could make informed participation decisions. In this context of unanticipated harm, presumably the data were also not monitored during the course of the study, making it impossible to follow the standard human subjects protection rule to cease an intervention discovered to cause harm.

A third example illustrates how attempts to experimentally vary the economic fundamentals of individual behavior can introduce risks of harm to human subjects that do not exist in observational studies. Jensen (2010) gave students at randomly selected schools information on the estimated returns to schooling that exceeded the students' prior, preintervention beliefs. Through this experimental intervention, Jensen hoped to show that perceptions artificially depress educational attainment, a hypothesis that would be challenging to test using observed variation in students' prior beliefs, as these beliefs would surely be endogenous to a range of child and parental attributes. To be sure, this is a research and policy question of first-order importance, so there is merit to trying to obviate the endogeneity of prior perceived returns to education. The problem is that researcher-provided information on the returns to education might itself be wrong and mislead the subject to, say, overinvest in schooling.

In his paper Jensen includes a healthy discussion of this ethical issue (see especially footnote 23), and his protocol included a warning that the estimated returns to education provided by the research team may be inaccurate predictors of individual outcomes. Somewhat ironically, Jensen relies on observational data to estimate expected returns to education, despite the fact that a standard skeptical perspective might see those estimates (drawn from those who endogenously chose to complete higher levels of schooling) as upwardly biased for those who, without the informational intervention, would have chosen not to complete secondary schooling. Moreover, all students in the Jensen study were given the same unconditional estimate of returns to schooling, rather than conditional estimates adapted to the student's circumstance (for example, a rural resident with poor local schools). As Jensen observes, provision of this sort of systematic misinformation would not be harmful if we knew that the subjects, preintervention, were underinvesting in education.

While that condition may be true, it is also the fundamental issue being studied. Absent that condition, we find ourselves looking at an experimental information treatment that predictably misinforms at least some parents and children with the specific intent of inducing behavioral change. For some students, the information provided was likely much closer to the (unknown) truth than were the subjects' prior beliefs, generating gains for the subject. But for some others, it misled them into overinvestment in education at nontrivial cost relative to the resource allocation they would have chosen under their uninformed prior. And the researcher cannot even identify the subjects harmed by the experiment, so it is infeasible even to make amends through compensation.

A fourth and final example further illustrates the ethical dilemmas that are specific to efforts to answer core economic questions that are intertwined with purposeful human behavior. In an effort to determine the impact of capital access on the capital constrained, Karlan and Zinman (2010) worked with a South African paycheck lender to "de-ration" a randomly selected subset of loan applicants whose credit scores deemed them credit-unworthy. De-rationed individuals included those marginally below the credit score threshold as well as some individuals well below that threshold. The research design aimed to compare postloan outcomes of the de-rationed with the non-de-rationed potential borrowers.

While promising as an approach, the Karlan-Zinman (2010) study illustrates several intrinsic ethical difficulties of implementing RCTs with real economic institutions. Unlike studies that randomly gift people with liquidity increments,[1] the Karlan-Zinman (2010) study created real debt for the randomly de-rationed, exposing them not only to the benefits of liquidity but also to the penalties of prospective default. Given that the lender's scoring model predicted repayment difficulties for the de-rationed, ethical concerns are important here. From a human subjects'

protection perspective, implementing such experiments would thus require full disclosure to the de-rationed and an ability to compensate them
for any harm caused for the sake of experimental learning. However, ful-
filling these standard human subjects requirements (e.g., by telling a de-
rationed study participant that a lender's credit scoring model predicts
they will fail, but that the study will restore their reputation and collateral
should they default) would obviously change behavioral incentives and
destroy the internal validity of the experiment. This underscores how researchers' ethical obligations often confound the purity of experimental
research design.

The second class of ethical problem emergent in many development
experiments revolves around the suspension of the fundamental principle of informed consent. This raises the subtle but important distinction between treating human beings as willful agents who have a right
to participate or not as they so choose versus treating them as subjects
to be manipulated for research purposes. To avoid the various endogenous behavioral responses that call into question even the internal validity of experimental results (due to Hawthorne effects and the like),
many prominent studies randomize treatments in group cluster designs
such that individuals are unaware that they are (or are not) part of an experiment. The randomized rollout of Progresa in Mexico is a well-known
example for development economists (Schultz 2004). Even when the
randomization is public and transparent, cluster randomization maintains
the exogeneity of the intervention, but at the ethically questionable cost
of sacrificing the well-accepted right of each participant to informed consent as well as the corresponding obligation of the researcher to secure
such consent. Biomedical researchers have given this issue much thought
(e.g., Hutton 2001), but we have yet to see any serious discussion of this
issue among development economists.

Informed consent becomes a more serious concern as development
agencies push for ever-greater "ownership" of development policies and
projects by target populations and their political leaders. In order for communities to own the results of a study, they must understand and trust
the study design and its implementers. But blinding research subjects to
the details of their treatment condition, which is commonly necessary in
RCTs—such as Karlan and Zinman (2010) and Jensen (2010)—requires

expressly withholding information from them. That is hardly a strategy for building trust between researchers and the subject communities that we then hope will internalize and act on the research findings. Thus, in addition to the ethical concerns of strategically underinformed consent, practical concerns arise that experimental treatment may subtly undermine subject communities' willingness to adopt results as their own and to subsequently act as those more-statistically-pure estimates suggest.

A third class of problem revolves around the role of blindedness in experiments. In most natural sciences, the entire response of physical material can be attributed to the treatment to which it has been subjected. But when humans are the subjects, response is a complex product of both the treatment itself and the perceived difference in treatment between oneself and other subjects. Hence the importance of blinding subjects—and, in best practice, double blinding researchers as well—regarding their placement within a study's control or treatment group. But whereas biomedical researchers can commonly develop and distribute to a control group a placebo identical to the experimental treatment medicine, few RCTs make any effort to blind subjects. Indeed, in many cases it would be infeasible to do so, as the economic treatment of interest involves obviously differential exposure to a new product, institution, technology, or resource.

This matters for both ethical and statistical reasons. The well-known placebo effect associated with treatment has an important corollary, in other words, that those who know themselves to be in a control group may suffer emotional distress when subjected to discernibly different treatment and that such distress can have adverse biophysical consequences that exaggerate the differences between control and treatment groups. Clinical researchers are deeply divided on the ethics of unblinded research.[2]

Moreover, the emotional suffering inflicted by unblinded treatments often induces active efforts to undo the randomized assignment. Subjects have been known to enroll themselves in multiple trials until they get a lucky assignment draw as part of the treatment cohort, and implementers discreetly violate the assignment rules as a merciful response to randomly assigned emotional and physical suffering. In this way ethical dilemmas quickly turn into statistical problems as well; human agency intended to overcome the perceived inequity of differential treatment randomization compromises clean identification.

The fourth class of ethical dilemma arises from abrogating the targeting principle upon which most development interventions are founded. Given the scarce resources and fiduciary obligations of donors, governments, and charitable organizations entrusted with resources provided (voluntarily or involuntarily) by others, there is a strong case to be made for exploiting local information to improve the targeting of interventions to reach intended beneficiaries (Alderman 2002; Conning and Kevane 2002). The growing popularity of community funds and community-based targeting involves exploiting precisely the asymmetric information that randomization seeks to overcome.

By explicitly refusing to exploit private information held by study participants, randomized interventions routinely treat individuals known not to require the intervention instead of those known to be in need, thereby predictably wasting scarce resources. Indeed, in our experience the unfairness and wastefulness implied by strict randomization in social experiments often sow the seeds of some implementers' breach of research design. Field partners less concerned with statistical purity than with practical development impacts commonly deem it unethical to deny a control group the benefits of an intervention strongly believed to have salutary effects, or to knowingly treat one household instead of another when the latter is strongly believed likely to gain and the former not. Well-meaning field implementers thus quietly contravene the experimental design, compromising the internal validity of the research and reintroducing precisely the unobserved heterogeneity that randomization was meant to overcome.

3. The Faux Exogeneity of Uncontrolled Treatments

The core purpose of RCTs is to use random assignment in order to ensure that the assumption of no confounds essential to identifying an average treatment effect holds (Imbens 2010). In the abstract, this is a strong argument for the method. Problems arise, however, when pristine asymptotic properties confront the muddy realities of field applications, and strict control over fully exogenous assignment almost inevitably breaks down, for any of a variety of reasons discussed below or in the preceding section on ethical dilemmas. The end result is that the attractive asymptotic properties of RCTs often disappear in practice, much like the asymptotic properties of other instrumental variables (IV) estimators. We term this the faux exogeneity problem.

In retrospect, the seminal deworming study carried out by Miguel and Kremer (2004) may have misdirected subsequent researchers in that it was based on a medical treatment in which it was possible to know exactly what had been given *and received* by the treated subject.[3] However, when randomization is used for larger, economics-oriented topics (for example, changing agents' expectations by offering them new contract terms or technologies), the true treatment received by subjects becomes harder to discern. Subjectively perceived treatments are likely to be nonrandomly distributed among experimental subjects whose capacities to comprehend and to act vary in subtle but substantive ways. Unobservable perceptions of a new product, contract, institutional arrangement, information, technology, or other intervention vary among participants and in ways that are almost surely correlated with other relevant attributes and expected returns from the treatment.

An obvious example is the previously mentioned study of perceived returns to education (Jensen 2010). The experimenter knows the information provided to treated subjects but cannot possibly know what change, if any, this information induced in their prior beliefs. Another example of this problem can be found in Karlan and Zinman's (2008) effort to determine price elasticity of credit demand using randomly distributed price variation in an established paycheck lending market. In this study, researchers surprised randomly selected loan applicants by offering them loans at rates other than the usual market rate. In analyzing the resulting data on loan uptake, Karlan and Zinman find a kink in the demand at the existing market interest rate. Increases above that level reduced demand, but reductions do not symmetrically increase it. A possible interpretation of this odd finding is that potential borrowers did not find the announcement of a price below the usual market price to be credible ("there must be something in the fine print"). While a medical experiment can largely control the treatment (for example, so many milligrams of a drug injected into the bloodstream), manipulating prices and other phenomena is more complex. Although the price announcement was randomized, we really do not know what the treated subjects effectively perceived. Some may have reacted suspiciously to a seemingly good deal (after all, there is supposed to be no free lunch), and others (perhaps those able to read loan contract language) may have received the intended treatment, acting as if the market price really had decreased. This uncontrolled treatment (some treatment group subjects received the intended treatment, others did not, and which was which was likely correlated with subjects' education and sophistication) can result in what we called faux randomization and raises a serious issue of interpretation. Unlike medical trials, human agency and understanding can confound the use of RCT to study economic problems.

As this example illustrates, the correlation between treatment (lower interest rates) and confounding factors (borrower sophistication) that one seeks to remedy through randomization can creep back in (Heckman, Urzua, and Vytlacil 2006; Heckman 2010). In our view it is far better to be aware of and explicit about likely bias due to unobserved heterogeneity than to hide it under the emperor's clothes of an RCT that does not truly randomize the treatment to which agents respond; this is crucially distinct from the treatment the experimenter wishes to apply.

Note that this unobservable heterogeneous treatment problem differs from the well-recognized compliance problem, which induces the important distinction between the average treatment effect (ATE) in the population of interest and the local average treatment effect (LATE) that is identified only for the subpopulation which complies with the treatment (Angrist, Imbens, and Rubin 1996). Proponents of LATE estimates—which are not specific to RCTs but are more general to all IV estimators—routinely argue that LATE is the policy-relevant parameter because monitoring compliance is difficult and ineffective. This is true. But in the presence of unobservable heterogeneous treatments within the compliant subpopulation, even the LATE estimate becomes uninformative. Using the "intent to treat" approach to return to the ATE among subjects who comply likewise fails to overcome the problem. This point obviously applies generally, not solely to RCTs. In our experience, however, random assignment too often fosters overconfidence such that claims of clean identification blind the researcher to this problem.

A somewhat similar problem can result from the so-called encouragement design—the use of side payments designed to bolster the voluntary uptake of a new program within a treatment group. While such payments may be absolutely essential if an RCT is to achieve any measure of statistical power, in the presence of essential heterogeneity (in other words, some agents will benefit more than others from an intervention) encouragement designs can result in a different population, with different expected benefits, than the population that would eventually take up the intervention absent the subsidy built in to the experiment to encourage uptake of the treatment condition.

Note that this is a fundamentally different problem than medical researchers confront when employing payments to encourage participation. Participants in medical studies presumably have no idea whether their particular biological system will respond more or less favorably to a treatment than the system of the average person. We would not therefore expect that higher payments would bring in people who know that they will benefit less from the treatment. In contrast, many economic interventions (e.g., access to a new financial contract or technology) depend precisely on participants' understanding and evaluating the returns to the new treatment. Mullally et al. (2010) illustrate this problem and the bias it imparts on estimated average treatment effects using an encouragement design employed to evaluate an agricultural insurance program in Peru. The fact that bias may creep in need not obviate the study. Indeed, by specifically modeling the bias, Mullally et al. show that at reasonable sample sizes, the biased estimator is more informative in the mean square error sense than is the unbiased estimator obtainable without encouragement. They make, in other words, the very old-fashioned point that biased estimators can be more informative and useful than noisy, unbiased estimators, a point to which we return in the conclusion to this chapter.

Another source of faux exogeneity arises due to the challenges of implementing RCT designs in the field. Intended random assignments are commonly compromised by field teams implementing a research design, especially when government or NGO partners have nonresearch objectives for the intervention that must be reconciled with researchers' aims to cleanly identify causal effects. The ethical concerns raised in the preceding section are but one common source of conflicting aims. Corruption, incomplete comprehension of research methods, logistical complications, etc. also lead to imperfect implementer compliance with the intended research design, and thus to sampling bias.

Note that this compliance problem differs from the problem of non-compliant subjects that partly motivates IV estimation of LATE. This problem creeps in earlier in the research, routinely emerging when implementers select survey respondents for observational studies, thus compromising the claimed integrity of the data collection. In the pre-RCT research environment, this was (at least) an equally commonplace but less fatal flaw than when true randomization is itself the source of identification. In the natural sciences the exact details of experiments are systematically recorded and shared with reviewers and made publicly available to readers for the purpose of exact replication. But in social scientific papers that employ experimental methods these crucial details of how design deviates from implementation are almost never reported.[4] Indeed, when research is subcontracted to implementing partners, study authors commonly do not even know if such sampling bias exists in the data.

Unobservable heterogeneous treatments, encouragement bias, and sampling bias in economic studies undercut the gold standard claim that RCTs reliably identify the (local) average treatment effect for the target population (in other words, that RCT estimates have internal validity). Just as the original (monetary) gold standard depended on a range of strong assumptions, so the claim of internal validity depends on multiple, strong, often-contestable assumptions. As in studies based on conventional, observational data, the development economics community needs to interrogate the underlying identifying assumptions before accepting RCT results as internally valid.

The preceding general point is not novel. Heckman (1992, 2010), Deaton (chapter 6 in this book), and Leamer (1983, 2010) discuss a variety of statistical limitations to the internal validity of RCT estimates that merit brief mention. One that we specifically highlight, because we find it such a commonplace problem, is that randomization bias is a real issue in the typically small samples involved in RCTs. The identical equivalence of control and treatment subpopulations is an asymptotic property only.

The power calculations now routine in designing experimental studies necessarily tolerate errors in inference just as nonexperimental studies do. And, unlike many quasi-experimental studies, such as those that rely on propensity score matching, RCT studies frequently fail to confirm that control and treatment groups exhibit identical distributions of observable variables. This problem is easily fixed, and the best RCT studies carefully check for balance. But the frequency with which this is ignored in RCT-based studies today betrays a dangerous overconfidence that pervades much of the RCT practitioner community today.

Given the likelihood of randomization bias in small samples, experimental approaches must take special care to balance control and treatment groups based on observables. But there is no standard practice on how to best do this, and not all methods of randomization perform equally well in small samples. Bruhn and McKenzie (2009) find that pairwise matching and stratification outperform the most common methods used in RCTs in smaller samples. As a result, standard errors reported in RCT studies that do not control for the used randomization method are commonly incorrect, leading researchers to incorrect inferences regarding treatment effects.

In summary, RCTs are invaluable tools for biophysical scientists, where the mechanisms involved are more mechanical than is the case in behavioral and social sciences and where virtually all conditions can be controlled in the research design. Human agency complicates matters enormously, as is well known in the agricultural and medical literatures on experiments. It is often unclear what varies beyond the variable the researcher is intentionally randomizing. Hawthorne effects are but one well-known example. As a result, impacts and behaviors elicited experimentally are commonly endogenous to environmental and structural conditions that vary in unknown ways within a necessarily highly stylized experimental design. This faux exogeneity undermines the claims of clean identification due to randomization. In our experience, this is the rule in RCTs, not the exception. As Leamer (2010: 33) vividly writes, "You and I know that truly consistent estimators are imagined, not real. . . . [But some] may think that it is enough to wave a clove of garlic and chant 'randomization' to solve all our problems just as an earlier cohort of econometricians have acted as if it were enough to chant 'instrumental variable.'"

4. Measuring Efficacy Rather than Effectiveness

The aim of most RCTs is to eliminate the endogeneity that commonly plagues explanatory variables of interest in observational data. But it is by no means clear that purging agents' endogenous behavioral response is always desirable. Often the question of greatest interest is what will happen as a result of real people's nonrandom responses to the introduction of a policy, project, or technology. Precise answers to the wrong question are not always helpful. Put differently, when we impose exogenous allocations we do not, in fact, replicate real human behavior. Indeed, we violate the most fundamental proposition of microeconomics: resource allocation is endogenous.

The crucial distinction between the impact of an exogenously imposed treatment and of a treatment allowing for full endogeneity is reflected in the epidemiology and public health literature as the difference between *efficacy* (the study of a treatment's capacity to have an effect, as established under fully controlled, ideal conditions) and *effectiveness* (the study of induced change under real-life conditions, as in clinical practice). Economists who seek to inform agents making real decisions in the real world ultimately need to be able to address questions of effectiveness, not merely of efficacy. The latter is a first, not the final, step toward scientific demonstration of interventions that work and are ready for widespread promotion.

The biomedical sciences clearly recognize this, as reflected, for example, in the Society for Prevention Research's formal standards of evidence, meant to "provide guidance for the research community to generate and test evidence-based prevention programs to improve the public health" (Flay et al. 2005: 152). These standards explicitly note that "effective programs and policies are a subset of efficacious interventions" (Flay et al. 2005: 1). Once again, greater fidelity to the literature of the biophysical sciences that have more developed experimental traditions would induce development economists to retreat from radical skepticism and to more creatively balance observational and experimental data, both informed by precise structural theories of change. Overcorrection for endogeneity may, ironically, render findings that are unbiased but irrelevant to the real-world questions concerning the intervention under study.

5. Scale and Temporal Limits to Randomization

As noted by other commentators, one shortcoming of experimental methods is that only a nonrandom subset of relevant topics is amenable to investigation via RCTs. For example, macroeconomic and political economy questions that many believe to be of first-order importance in development are clearly not candidates for randomization (Basu 2005; Deaton, chapter 6 in this book; Rodrik 2009; Shapiro, chapter 9 in this book); nor are infrastructure issues or any other meso- or macro-scale intervention that cannot be replicated in large numbers. Furthermore, the placement of these issues is necessarily and appropriately subject to significant political economy considerations (Ravallion 2009). As one moves from smaller scale, partial equilibrium questions (for example, Which type of contract generates a greater response from a microfinance institution's clientele?, or What is the marginal effect of cash versus food transfers on recipients' nutritional status?) to larger scale, general equilibrium and political economy questions, RCTs necessarily become less useful.

The fact that RCTs are not appropriate for all questions is not a criticism of the methodology per se. However, it becomes a serious problem when RCTs are seen as *the* way of knowing, and the applicability of the RCT method, rather than the importance of the question being asked, seems to drive research agendas. While it would be unfair to single out individual papers, most readers of development economics literature can easily recall papers that, in their zealous quest for exogenous variation, prove points utterly obvious to laypersons. More worrisome is when leading development economists tell policymakers that the questions they ask which are not amenable to analysis by RCTs are the wrong questions, or that economists know nothing until an RCT has been implemented and has generated a point estimate.

To reiterate, these observations are not an argument against RCTs. Instead, they are an argument for rebalancing the research agenda and recognizing the complementarity of different ways of knowing. Even questions apparently amenable to exclusively RCT analysis may be less amenable than they seem at first glance. An example from the evaluation of Mexico's well-known Progresa program may help clarify this point.

Given the amount of time required to accumulate and realize returns to human capital, exclusive reliance on RCTs to evaluate a program like Progresa can be problematic. The RCT analysis of the Progresa cash transfer program identified a statistically significant increase of 0.7 years of schooling (Schultz 2004). However, inferring the (long-run) economic significance of this increase was inevitably left to other methodologies that assembled best estimates of the long-term earnings impact of this additional schooling, an exercise necessarily requiring a series of assumptions, including those of a general equilibrium nature (e.g., Behrman, Sengupta, and Todd 2005). The point is that the best research recognizes and exploits the fundamental complementarities among methods.[5] No method has a unique claim to being able to answer the most important questions on its own.

RCTs can in principle be exploited over a long-term time horizon, as shown by the recent follow-up to the early 1970s INCAP study of childhood nutritional intervention in Guatemala (Hoddinott et al. 2008; Maluccio et al. 2009). While the ability to observe adult earnings (and other outcomes) forty years after the intervention is striking, the unavoidably large attrition rate (and the assumptions therefore required to make inference) placed this study into the Bayesian hopper as one further, important piece of (quasi-experimental) evidence that needed to be mixed with the extensive research on education in developing countries using nonexperimental methods in order to generate important, highly policy-relevant findings.[6]

6. Finding Our Balance in Development Economics

The limits to RCTs in development economics by themselves mandate a return to methodological pluralism if we are continue to answer the important questions. That said, there is a large class of economic development problems whose answers can be ethically and feasibly pursued using randomization methods. RCT studies focus on generating consistent and unbiased estimates of treatment effects of development interventions. In the biophysical sciences from which the RCT tradition arises, this often works because basic physio-chemical laws ensure a certain degree of homogeneity of response to an experiment. But in the behavioral sciences, such as economics, there is even less reason to believe in homogeneity of response to a change in environmental conditions. Furthermore, there is such heterogeneity of microenvironments that one has to be very careful about model mis-specification. These concerns apply to all research but seem especially overlooked in the current RCT fashion.

These observations relate closely to what is perhaps the most widespread critique of experimental evidence, namely that RCT estimates lack external (out of sample) validity. There are two dimensions to this external validity critique. The first dimension is that unobservable and observable features inevitably vary at the community level and cannot be controlled for in experimental design due to contextual issues (see, for example, Acemoglu 2009; Deaton, chapter 6 in this book; Ravallion 2009; Rodrik 2009). For example, is an agency that is willing to implement an experimental design for a pilot program likely to be representative of other agencies that might implement it elsewhere? Probably not, and in ways that almost surely confound the measurable impacts of the experiment.

The second dimension of the external validity critique postulates the existence of treatment effects that vary systematically with unobserved individual heterogeneity within the sample (Heckman, Urzua, and Vytlacil 2006). As discussed above, in this context, RCTs generate point estimates that are unknown, data-weighted averages across subpopulations of multiple types with perhaps zero population mass on the weighted mean estimate. As is true of any research method that pools data from distinct subpopulations, there is a nontrivial probability that no external population exists to whom the results of the experiment apply on average. Collecting the data experimentally does not solve this problem. If the inferential challenge largely revolves around essential heterogeneity rather than around endogeneity, experiments that address only the latter issue can at best claim to solve a problem of second-order relevance.

Ironically, these critiques of unobserved and unknown confounds are the very same ones used by some RCT advocates to delegitimize learning from observational data. To slightly misquote Shakespeare's *Hamlet*, radically skeptical RCT engineers have been hoisted with their own petard. While one conclusion might be to retreat entirely from empirical economic research, a more promising path is to retreat from radical skepticism and let theory and careful observation—what Frank (2007) terms "economic naturalism"—guide an understanding of the causal process and name the potential confounds that can cripple inference from both observational data and from RCTs.

As we have argued in a companion paper, advances in behavioral economics that render observable measures of key sources of economically relevant heterogeneity (such as degrees of risk aversion and time preferences) hold out promise for studies using both experimental and observational data (Barrett and Carter 2010). Of course, in the end, no measures are beyond reproach. We need to treat them all with healthy, structural skepticism and retreat from the radical skepticism that prevails in much of economics today. Rebalancing the mix of theory, observational data, and randomization in development economics will not deliver an elusive gold standard. But it just might return us to the humility of Bayesian learning and the relentless pursuit of, not unbiasedness per se, but of confidence intervals that are sufficiently narrow to reliably guide policy advice and the design of development interventions that can improve the human condition without predictably harming those whom we hope will benefit from our research.

Acknowledgments

Portions of this chapter are reproduced with permission from Oxford University Press from our 2010 paper "The Power and Pitfalls of Experiments in Development Economics: Some Non-random Reflections," *Applied Economic Perspectives and Policy* 32(4): 515–48. Several sections are new to this version.

NOTES

1. De Mel, McKenzie, and Woodruff (2009) give away random amounts of liquidity, but at the cost of failing to distinguish liquidity-constrained from liquidity-unconstrained households, as Barrett and Carter (2010) discuss.

2. See Harmon (2010) for an example from a current controversy in oncology research.

3. Even in the Miguel and Kremer (2004) case, incomplete treatment due to non-random school attendance on days in which treatments were administered leads to bias of unknown sign. The authors report incomplete uptake but never fully explore its implications.

4. An important exception is the Karlan and Zinman (2009) study discussed below.

5. One of us learned this lesson the hard way when a Finance Ministry official greeted evidence that cash transfers seem to statistically significantly increase height by two centimeters with the dreaded question, "So what?"

6. A forty-year wait for an answer is, of course, often not practical. The INCAP studies are rare examples.

4

THE EXPERIMENTAL APPROACH TO DEVELOPMENT ECONOMICS

Abhijit V. Banerjee and Esther Duflo

Randomized experiments have become a popular tool in development economics research and have been the subject of a number of criticisms. This chapter reviews the recent literature and discusses the strengths and limitations of this approach in theory and in practice. We argue that the main virtue of randomized experiments is that, owing to the close collaboration between researchers and implementers, they allow the estimation of parameters that would not otherwise be possible to evaluate. We discuss the concerns that have been raised regarding experiments and generally conclude that, although real, they are often not specific to experiments. We conclude by discussing the relationship between theory and experiments.

1. Introduction

The past few years have seen a veritable explosion of randomized experiments in development economics. At the fall 2008 meeting of the North East Universities Development Consortium (NEUDC), a large conference in development economics attended mainly by young researchers and doctoral students, 24 papers reported on randomized field experiments, out of the 112 papers that used microeconomics data (laboratory experiments excluded). This is up from 4 in 2004. At the fall 2008 Bureau for Research and Economic Analysis of Development (BREAD) conference, the premier conference on development economics, 4 of the

8 papers invited were randomized field experiments. Three out of the 6 papers using microeconomic data from developing countries published in 2008 or forthcoming in the *Quarterly Journal of Economics* involve randomized assignment. The enthusiasm is not limited to academia. At the World Bank there are 67 ongoing randomized evaluations (out of 89 ongoing program evaluations) in the African region alone.

Perhaps inevitably, this progress has generated a rising tide of criticism. Almost all of the criticism is well meant, recognizing the benefits of such experiments while suggesting that we not forget that there are a lot of important questions that randomized experiments cannot answer. Much of it is also not new. Indeed, most of the standard objections (and some not so standard ones) may be found in a single seminal piece written by James Heckman more than a decade ago (Heckman 1992).

Much of this criticism has been useful—even when we do not entirely agree with it—both in helping us define the strengths and limitations of randomized experiments and in clarifying where the field needs to go next. However, we argue that much of this criticism misses (or at least insufficiently emphasizes) the main reasons why there has been so much excitement surrounding experimental research in development economics. We then return to the various criticisms, in part to clarify and qualify them and to argue that, because of an imperfect recognition of what is exciting about the experimental agenda, there is a tendency to set up false oppositions between experimental work and other forms of research.

2. The Promise of Experiments

Experimental research in development economics, like earlier research in labor economics, health, and education, started from a concern about the reliable identification of program effects in the face of complex and multiple channels of causality. In general, participants to a program differ from nonparticipants in many ways, and we have no information on how they would have fared had they not been participating. This makes it difficult to separate the causal effect of the program (i.e., for a given participant, the difference between the outcome he experienced under the program and the outcome he would have experienced if he had not been participating) from other factors. A central problem is selection, the fact that participants may be systematically different from nonparticipants. Although the treatment effect for each person cannot be identified, experiments make it possible to vary one factor at a time and therefore provide internally valid estimates of the average treatment effect for a population of interest. (For detailed discussions of the evaluation problem, see Heckman and Vytlacil 2008a; Imbens and Wooldridge 2009.)

The experimental work in the mid-1990s (for example, Glewwe et al. 2004, 2009; Banerjee et al. 2005) was aimed at answering very basic questions about the educational production function: Does better access to inputs (textbooks, flipcharts in classes, lower student-teacher ratios) matter for school outcomes (attendance, test scores), and if so, by how much? The motivating theoretical framework was thus very simple, but this research produced a number of surprising results, both negative and positive. For example, improving access to textbooks from one per four or more students to one per every two does not affect average test scores (Glewwe et al. 2009); halving the teacher-student ratio also had no effect (Banerjee et al. 2005). However, a study of treatment for intestinal worms in schools in Kenya (Miguel and Kremer 2004) showed that a deworming treatment that costs 49 cents per child per year can reduce absenteeism by 25 percent. In part, this is because of externalities: worms are transmitted when children walk barefoot in places where other children who are infected by worms have defecated. As a result, in terms of increasing attendance, deworming is nearly twenty times as effective as hiring an extra teacher (the cost for an extra child-year of education was $3.25 with deworming, whereas the cost was approximately $60 for the extra teacher program, despite the fact the extra teacher was paid only $25 or so a month), even though both "work" in the sense of generating statistically significant improvements.

What this research was making clear is that, at the level of the efficacy of individual ingredients of the educational production function, our intuition (or economic theory per se) was unlikely to be very helpful—how could we possibly know, a priori, that deworming is so much more effective than hiring a teacher? More generally, a bulletin of the Abdul Latif Jameel Poverty Action Lab (2005) compares the cost per extra child-year of education induced across an array of different strategies. The costs vary widely, between $3.50 per extra child-year for deworming and $6,000 per extra child-year for the primary education component of Progresa, the Mexican Conditional Cash Transfer Program. Some of these programs (such as the Progresa programs) may have other objectives as well, but for those whose main goal is to increase education, it is clear that some are much cheaper than others. Even excluding Progresa, the cost per extra year of education induced ranges from $3.25 to more than $200. Thus, even when comparing across programs to achieve the same goal, the rates of returns of public investment are far from being equalized.

Moreover, it became clear that economists were not the only people who were clueless; implementing organizations were not much better informed. For example, the nongovernmental organization (NGO) that financed the deworming intervention was also initially enthusiastic about giving children school uniforms, even though a randomized evaluation showed that the cost of giving children a free uniform worked out to be $100 per extra child-year of schooling.

Several important conclusions emerged from this experience. First, effective policymaking requires making judgments about the efficacy of individual program components—without much guidance from a priori knowledge. Second, however, it is also difficult to learn about these individual components from observational (in other words, nonexperimental) data. The reason is that observational data on the educational production function often come from school systems that have adopted a given model, which consists of more than one input. The variation in school inputs we observe therefore comes from attempts to change the model, which, for good reasons, involves making multiple changes at the same time. Although there are exceptions, this means that a lot of the policy-relevant knowledge that requires observing the effects of variation in individual components of a package may not be available in observational data. This provides a first motivation for experiments.

One of the immediate implications of this observation is that, given the fixed cost of organizing an experiment and the fact that experiments necessarily require some time when program implementation has to be slowed down (to make use of the results), it is worth doing multiple experiments at the same time on the same population to evaluate alternative potential variants of the program. For example, the World Bank provided money to school committees to hire extra teachers on short contracts to reduce grade 1 class sizes in Kenya. When researchers worked with the school system to set up an evaluation of the program, they did not just assign the entire program to the randomly selected treatment schools (Duflo et al. 2008a). Instead, they introduced two additional dimensions of variation: (a) training of the school committee that received the money to monitor the extra teacher and (b) tracking by prior achievement. Using this design, researchers can estimate the impact of class-size reduction without changing pedagogy; the relative merit of young, extra teachers on short contracts versus regular, experienced, civil servant teachers; the role that suitably empowered school committees can play; and the impact of tracking by achievement in primary school. As in Banerjee et al. (2005), albeit in a different context, the study did not find that reducing class size without any other changes has a significant impact. However, it showed a strong positive impact of switching from the regular teacher to a contract teacher, a positive and significant impact of class-size reduction when coupled with school committee empowerment, and, for a given class size, strong benefit of tracking students both for the weaker and the stronger students. Other "multiple treatment experiments" include Banerjee et al. (2007) (remedial education and computer-assisted learning), Duflo et al. (2006), and Dupas (2007) (various HIV-AIDS prevention strategies among adolescents), Banerjee et al. (2010a) (information and mobilization experiments in primary schools in India), Banerjee et al. (2010b) (demand and supply factors in improving immunization rates in India), and Giné et al. (2010) (two strategies to help smokers quit smoking).

A related observation is that, from the point of view of building a usable knowledge base, there is a need for a process of dynamic learning because experimental results are often surprising and therefore require further clarification. Duflo et al. (2008c, d) reflects exactly such an iterative process, where a succession of experiments on fertilizer use was run over a period of several years. Each result prompted the need to try out a series of new variations to better understand the results of the previous one.

In addition, from the point of view of optimal learning, it is often worth testing a broad intervention first to see whether there is an overall effect and then, if it is found to work, delving into its individual components to understand what part of the broad program works.[1] Policy experiments often stop at the first step. One example is the popular Progresa–Oportunidades program in Mexico, which combined a cash transfer to women in poor families that was conditional on "good behavior" (e.g., investments in education and preventive health) and some upgrading of education and health facilities. The program has been replicated in many countries, often along with a randomized evaluation (Fizbein and Schady 2009). However, only an ongoing study in Morocco formed and compared different treatment groups so that researchers could evaluate the importance of the much-praised conditionalities. In this experiment, one group of villages receives a purely unconditional transfer, one group receives a weak conditionality transfer (e.g., attendance requirements are verified only by teachers), and two groups receive stricter variants of the conditionality (in one group, children's attendance is supervised by inspectors; in the other, it is verified daily with a fingerprint recognition device).

Although all this seems obvious in retrospect, it was only after the first few experiments that both researchers and the implementing organizations fully appreciated the significance of such a design. From the point of view of the organizations, it became clear that there was value in setting up relatively long-term relationships with researchers, so that the experimentation could constitute a process of ongoing learning and multiple experiments of mutual interests could be designed. In other words, there was less emphasis on one-off evaluations, where the researcher is brought in to evaluate a specific program that the organization has already decided to evaluate. This is a difference with the evaluation literature in the United States or Canada, where, with a few important exceptions (for example, Angrist, Lang, and Oreopoulos 2009), the programs to be evaluated are mainly chosen by the implementing agencies, and the researchers are evaluators only.

From the point of view of the researchers, this design offered the possibility of moving from the role of the evaluator to the role of a co-experimenter, which included an important role in defining what gets evaluated. In other words, the researcher was now being offered the option of defining the question to be answered, thus drawing on his knowledge of what else was known and the received theory. For example, when Seva Mandir, an NGO in Rajasthan, India, with whom we have had a long-standing relationship, was interested in improving the quality of their informal schools, their initial idea was to implement a teacher incentive program based on test scores. However, they were persuaded by the results from Glewwe et al. (2003) that showed that teacher incentives could result in teaching to the test or other short-run manipulations of test scores. They then decided to implement an incentive program based on teacher presence. To measure attendance in very sparsely populated areas where schools are difficult to access, Duflo and Hanna (Duflo et al. 2007) proposed the use of cameras with date and time stamps. Although Seva Mandir was initially surprised by the suggestion, they agreed to try it out. In program schools (the "camera schools"), teachers took a picture of themselves and their students twice a day (morning and afternoon), and their salary was computed as a (nonlinear) function of the number of days they attended. The results were striking (Duflo et al. 2007): teacher absence dropped from 40 percent to 20 percent while students' performance improved.

Seva Mandir was convinced by these results and decided to continue the program. However, they did not give up on the hope of improving the teachers' intrinsic motivation. Instead of extending the camera program in all of their schools immediately, they decided to continue it in the schools where it had already been introduced and spend some time experimenting with other programs, both in schools with cameras and in schools without. With Sendhil Mullainathan, they brainstormed about ways to motivate teachers. One idea was to give every child a diary to write in every day based on work done in school. On days when the student or the teacher was absent, the diary was to remain blank or the date was to be crossed out. Parents were supposed to look at the diary every week. The hope was that they would register the extent of teacher and child absence. This approach, it turned out, did not succeed: parents started with such a low opinion of school that the diary tended to persuade them that something was happening, regardless of number of absences. Indeed, parents of diary schools had a higher opinion than did those of nondiary schools, and there was no impact on teacher presence. However, the diaries were popular with both students and teachers, and their use induced teachers to work harder. Test scores improved in the diary schools. It thus appears that the diaries failed as a tool to improve teacher presence but succeeded as a pedagogical tool. However, because this was not a hypothesis put forward in the initial experimental design, it may just be a statistical accident. Thus, Seva Mandir will now put cameras in all schools (after several years, they continue to have a large impact on presence and tests scores), while they also conduct a new diary experiment to see if the results on pedagogy persist.

One important consequence of this process has been the growing realization in the research community that the most important element of the experimental approach may lie in the power (when working with a friendly implementing partner) to vary individual elements of the treatment in a way that helps us answer conceptual questions (albeit policy-relevant ones) that could never be reliably answered in any other way.[2] One telling example is Berry (2008). While incentives based on school participation and performance have become very popular, it is not clear whether the incentives should target children (as in the programs evaluated in Angrist et al. 2008 and Angrist and Lavy 2009) or parents (as in Kremer et al. 2009). If the family were fully efficient, the choice of the target should not make a difference, but otherwise it might. To answer this question, Berry designed a program in the slums of Delhi in which students (or their parents) were provided incentives (in the form of toys or money) based on the child's improvement in reading. He found that, for initially weak students, rewarding the child is more effective than rewarding the parents in terms of improving test scores, whereas the opposite is true for initially strong students. The ability to vary who receives the incentives within the same context and in the same experiment is what made this study possible.

Experiments are thus emerging as a powerful tool for testing theories. Although the theories to be tested are different, the motivation of the recent literature in experimental development economics is similar to that of the first generation of experiments in the United States, which were designed to identify well-designed parameters (in other words, income and substitution effect in the negative income tax experiments, moral hazard in the Rand health insurance experiment, etc.). Interventions are being designed and evaluated not only to show the average treatment effect for a particular policy or program, but also to allow identification of specific economic parameters. One example is a project conducted by

Karlan and Zinman (2005) in collaboration with a South African lender that gives small loans to high-risk borrowers at high interest rates. The experiment was designed to test the relative weights of ex post repayment burden (including moral hazard) and ex ante adverse selection in loan default. Potential borrowers with the same observable risk are randomly offered a high or a low interest rate in an initial letter. Individuals then decide whether to borrow at the solicitation's offer rate. Of those who apply at the higher rate, half are randomly offered a new lower contract interest rate when they are actually given the loan, whereas the remaining half continue at the offer rate. Individuals did not know ex ante that the contract rate could differ from the offer rate. The researchers then compared repayment performance of the loans in all three groups. The comparison of those who responded to the high offer interest rate with those who responded to the low offer interest rate in the population that received the same low contract rate allows the identification of the adverse selection effect; comparing those who faced the same offer rate but differing contract rates identifies the repayment burden effect.

The study found that women exhibit adverse selection but men exhibit moral hazard. The fact that this difference was unexpected poses something of a problem for the paper (is it a statistical fluke or a real phenomenon?) but its methodological contribution is undisputed. The basic idea of varying prices ex post and ex ante to identify different parameters has since been replicated in several studies. Ashraf et al. (2010) and Cohen and Dupas (2010) exploit it to understand the relationship between the price paid for a health protection good and its utilization. Raising the price could affect usage through a screening effect (those who buy at a higher price care more) or a "psychological sunk cost effect." To separate these effects, they randomize the offer price as well as the actual paid price. The effect the offer price has on keeping the actual price fixed identifies the screening effect, whereas the variation in the actual price (with a fixed offer price) pins down the sunk cost effect. Ashraf et al. (2010) studied this for a water purification product, whereas Cohen and Dupas (2010) focused on bed nets. Neither study shows much evidence of a psychological sunk cost effect. The experimental variation was key here, and not only to avoid bias: In the world, we are unlikely to observe a large number of people who face different offer prices but the same actual price. These types of experiments are reminiscent of the motivation of the early social experiments (such as the negative income tax experiments) that aimed to obtain distinct wage and income variations to estimate income and substitution effects that were not available in observational data (Heckman 1992).

Other examples of this type of work are the experiments designed to assess whether there is a demand for commitment products, which could be demanded by self-aware people with self-control problems. Ashraf et al. (2006) worked with microfinance institutions in the Philippines to offer their clients a savings product that let them choose to commit not to withdraw the money before a specific time or amount goal was reached. Giné et al. (2010) worked with the same organization to invite smokers who wanted to quit to put a "contract" on themselves: money in a special savings account would be forfeited if they failed a urine test for nicotine after several weeks. Both cases were designed by the economists to solve a real-world problem, but they also came with a strong theoretical motivation. The fact that these were new ideas that came from researchers made it natural to set up a randomized evaluation: because the cases were experimental in nature, the partners were happy to try them out first with a subset of their clients/beneficiaries.

These two sets of examples are focused on individual behavior. Experiments can also be set up to understand the way institutions function. An example is Bertrand et al. 2010, who set up an experiment to understand the structure of corruption in the process of obtaining a driving license in Delhi. They recruited people who are aiming to get a driving license and set up three groups, one that receives a bonus for obtaining a driving license quickly, one that gets free driving lessons, and a control group. They found that those in the bonus group get their licenses faster, but those who get the free driving lessons do not. They also found that those in the bonus group are more likely to pay an agent to get the license (who, they conjecture, bribes someone). They also found that the applicants who hired an agent were less likely to have taken a driving test before getting a driving license. Although they did not appear to find that those in the bonus group who get licenses are systematically less likely to know how to drive than those in the control group (which would be the litmus test that corruption does result in an inefficient allocation of driving licenses), this experiment provides suggestive evidence that corruption in this case does more than "grease the wheels" of the system.

The realization that experiments are a readily available option has also spurred creativity in measurement. In principle, there is no automatic link between careful and innovative collection of microeconomic data and the experimental method. And, indeed, there is a long tradition in development economics to collect data specifically designed to test theories, and both the breadth and the quantity of microeconomic data collected in development economics have exploded in recent decades, not only in the context of experiments.

However, the specificity that experiments have, which is particularly prone to encourage the development of new measurement methods, is high take-up rates and a specific measurement problem. In many experimental studies a large fraction of those who are intended to be affected by the program are actually affected. This means that the number of units on which data need to be collected to assess the impact of the program does not have to be very large and that data are typically collected especially for the purpose of the experiment. Elaborate and expensive measurement of outcomes is then easier to obtain than in the context of a large multipurpose household or firm survey. By contrast, observational studies must often rely for identification on variations (policy changes, market-induced variation, natural variation, supply shocks, etc.) that cover large populations, requiring the use of a large data set often not collected for a specific purpose. This makes it more difficult to fine-tune the measurement to the specific question at hand. Moreover, even if it is possible ex post to do a sophisticated data collection exercise specifically targeted to the question, it is generally impossible to do it for the preprogram situation. This precludes the use of a difference-in-differences strategy for these types of outcomes, which again limits the incentives.

Olken (2007) is one example of the kind of data that were collected in an experimental setting. The objective was to determine whether audits or community monitoring were effective ways to curb corruption in decentralized construction projects. Getting a reliable measure of actual levels of corruption was thus necessary. Olken focused on roads and had engineers dig holes in the road to measure the material used. He then compared that with the level of material reported to be used. The difference is a measure of how much of the material was stolen or never purchased but invoiced and thus was an objective measure of corruption. Olken then demonstrated that this measure of "missing inputs" is affected by the threat of audits, but not, except in some circumstances, by encouraging greater attendance at community meetings.

Another example of innovative data collection is found in Beaman et al. (2009). The paper evaluates the impact of mandated political representation of women in village councils on citizens' attitude toward women leaders. This is a natural randomized experiment in the sense that villages were randomly selected (by law) to be "reserved for women": in the "reserved" villages, only women could be elected as the village head. To get a measure of "taste" for women leaders that would not be tainted by the desire of the respondent to please the interviewer, the paper implements "implicit association tests" developed by psychologists (Banaji 2001). Although those tests are frequently used by psychologists, and their use has also been advocated by economists (Bertrand et al. 2005), they had not been implemented in a field setting in a developing country, and there had been almost no studies investigating whether these attitudes are hard wired or can be affected by features of the environment. The study also used another measure of implicit bias toward women, inspired by political scientists. The respondents listen to a speech, supposedly given by a village leader and delivered by either a male or female voice, and are asked to give their opinion of it. Respondents are randomly selected to receive either the male or the female speech. The difference in the ratings given by those who receive male versus female speeches is a measure of statistical discrimination. The paper then compares this measure of discrimination across reserved and unreserved villages.

These are only two examples of a rich literature. Many field experiments embed small lab experiments (dictator games, choices over lotteries, discount rate experiments, public good games, etc.). For example, in their evaluation of the Columbia Conditional Cash Transfer Program, the team from the Institute for Fiscal Studies included public goods, risk sharing, and coalition formation games as part of the data collection (Attanasio et al. 2008a).

3. Concerns About Experiments

As we mentioned above, the concerns about experiments are not new. However, many of these concerns are based on comparing experimental methods, implicitly or explicitly, with other methods for trying to learn about the same thing. The message of the previous section is that the biggest advantage of experiments may be that they take us into terrain where observational approaches are not available. In such cases, the objections raised by critics of the experimental literature are best viewed as warnings against overinterpreting experimental results. There are, however, also cases where both experimental and observational approaches are available in relatively comparable forms, where there is, in addition, the issue of which approach to take. Moreover, there are concerns about what experiments are doing to development economics as a field. The rest of this section lists these objections and then discusses each one. Note that, although some of these issues are specific to experiments (we point these out along the way), most of these concerns (external validity, the difference between partial equilibrium and market equilibrium effects, nonidentification of distribution of effect) are common to all microevaluations, both with experimental and nonexperimental methods. They are more frequently brought to the forefront when discussing experiments, which is likely because most of the other usual concerns are taken care of by the randomization.

3.1. Environmental Dependence

Environmental dependence is a core element of generalizability (or external validity). It asks the question, Would we get the same result if we carried out the same experiment in a different setting, or, more exactly, would the program that is being evaluated have the same effect if it were implemented elsewhere (not in the context of an experiment)?

These are actually two separate concerns. First, and most obviously, we may worry about the impact of differences in the environment where the program is evaluated on the effectiveness of the program. One virtue of experiments is that they allow us to evaluate the mean effect of the program for a specific population without assuming that the effect of the program is constant across individuals. But if the effect is not constant across individuals, it is likely to vary systematically with covariates. For example, school uniforms will surely not have the same impact in Norway (where every child who needs one no doubt has one) that it has in Kenya. The question is where to draw the line: is Mexico, for example, more like Norway or more like Kenya? The same issue also arises within a country. Clearly, a priori knowledge can help us here only to some extent—simple economics suggests that uniforms will have an effect only in populations where the average wage is not too high relative to the price of uniforms, but how high is too high? If our theories are good enough to know this, or we are willing to assume that they are, then we probably do not need experiments anymore. Theory may then be good enough to give us a sense of who tends to get a uniform, and who does not, and we could use this restriction to convincingly estimate structural models of the impact of school uniforms. In other words, without assumptions, results from experiments cannot be generalized beyond their context; but with enough assumptions, observational data may be sufficient. To argue for experiments, we need to be somewhere in the middle.

Second, and more specific to experiments in development economics, which have often been conducted with NGOs, is the issue of implementer effects. That is, the smaller the implementing organization, the greater the concern that the estimated treatment effect reflects the unique characteristics of the implementer. This problem can be partially mitigated by providing detailed information about the implementation in the description of the evaluation, emphasizing the place of the evaluated program within the overall action plan of the organization (e.g., how big was the evaluated piece relative to what they do? how was the implementing team selected? what decided the choice of location?). Clearly, for the results to be anything more than an initial "proof of concept," the program must come from a program that is sufficiently well defined and well understood so that its implementation routinely gets delegated to a large number of more or less self-sufficient, individual implementing teams.

All of this, however, is very loose and highly subjective (what is large enough? how self-sufficient?). To address both concerns about generalization, actual replication studies need to be carried out. Additional experiments have to be conducted in different locations with different teams. If we have a theory that tells us where the effects are likely to be different, we focus the extra experiments there. If not, we should ideally choose random locations within the relevant domain.

Indeed, there are now a number of replication studies. The supplemental teaching (*balsakhi*) program evaluated by Banerjee et al. (2007) was deliberately carried out simultaneously in two separate locations (Mumbai and Vadodara), working with two separate implementing teams (both from the Pratham network but under entirely separate management). The results turned out to be broadly consistent. Similarly, Bobonis et al. (2006) obtained an impact of a combination of deworming and iron supplementation on school attendance in north India similar to what Miguel and Kremer (2004) found in Kenya. Likewise, Bleakley (2007) found similar results using natural data from the southern United States in the early part of the twentieth century using a natural experiment approach. The Progresa–Oportunidades program was replicated under different names and with slight variations in many countries, and in several of them (Colombia, Nicaragua, Ecuador, and Honduras; Morocco is under way) it was accompanied by a randomized evaluation. (For a discussion of the original Progresa evaluation and subsequent replications, see Fizbein and Schady 2009.) The results, analyzed by different teams of researchers in different countries, were consistent across countries.

Other results turn out not to be replicable: An information campaign that mobilized parents' committees on issues around education and encouraged them to make use of a public program that allows school committees to hire local teachers where the schools are overcrowded had a positive impact on learning outcomes in Kenya but not in India (Banerjee et al. 2010a; Duflo et al. 2008a). A similar intervention that sought to energize Health Unit Management Committees in Uganda also reported a massive impact on hard-to-affect outcomes such as infant mortality (Bjorkman and Svensson 2009).

In addition to pure replication, cumulative knowledge is generated from related experiments in different contexts. The analytical review by Kremer and Holla (2008) of sixteen randomized experiments of price elasticity in health and education is a good example. We return to these results in more detail below, but the key point here is that these experiments cover a wide range of education and health goods and services in several countries. A strong common thread is the extremely high elasticity of the demands for these goods relative to their price, especially around zero (both in the positive and negative direction). Although they are not strictly replications of each other, this shows the value of cumulative knowledge in learning about one phenomenon.

However, more replication research is needed. Some worry that there are few incentives in the system to carry out replication studies (because journals may not be as willing to publish the fifth experiment on a given topic as the first one), and funding agencies may not be willing to fund them either. The extensive use of experiments in economics is a recent development, so we do not know how big a problem this may be, but given the many published estimates of the returns to education, for example, we are not too pessimistic. The good news is that several systematic replication efforts are under way. For example, a program of asset transfers and training targeted to the ultra-poor, originally designed by the Bangladeshi NGO BRAC (described in detail below), is currently being evaluated in Honduras, Peru, Karnataka, West Bengal, Bangladesh, and Pakistan. Each country has a different research team and a different local implementation partner. Studies of interest rate sensitivity replicating Karlan and Zinman (2008) are currently under way in Ghana, Peru (in two separate locations with two different partners), Mexico, and the Philippines (in three separate locations with two different partners). Microcredit impact evaluations are happening simultaneously in Morocco, urban India, the Philippines (in three separate locations), and Mexico. Business training is being evaluated in Peru, the Dominican Republic, urban India, and Mexico. Similar programs to encourage savings are being evaluated in Peru, the Philippines, Ghana, and Uganda. It thus seems that there is enough interest among funding agencies to fund these experiments and enough willing researchers to carry them out. For example, in the case of the several ongoing ultra-poor experiments, the Ford Foundation is funding all of them, in an explicit attempt to gain a better understanding of the program by evaluating it in several separate locations. Innovations for Poverty Action, an NGO founded by Dean Karlan, which has been leading the effort for many of these replications, is hosting the grant, but the research teams and the implementation partners are different in each country. The different research teams share evaluation strategies and instruments to make sure that different results represent differences in the contexts rather than in evaluation strategies.

Those studies are still ongoing, and their results will tell us much more about the conditions under which the results from programs are context dependent. Systematic tests on whether the results differ across sites will be needed. The insights of the literature on heterogeneous treatment effects, which we discuss below, can be applied here: first, the different site dummies can be treated as covariates in a pooled regression; nonparametric tests of heterogeneity (e.g., Crump et al. 2008) can be performed. If heterogeneity is found, a more powerful test would be whether heterogeneity still remains after accounting for the heterogeneity of the covariates. Another way to proceed is to test whether the treatment effect conditional on the covariates is equal for all the site dummies (Heckman et al. 2010). The point is not that every result from experimental research generalizes, but that we have a way of knowing which ones do and which ones do not. If we were prepared to carry out enough experiments in varied enough locations, we could learn as much as we want to know about the distribution of the treatment effects across sites conditional on any given set of covariates.

In contrast, no comparable statement can be made about observational studies. Although identifying a particular quasi-experiment that provides a source of identification for the effect of a particular program may be possible, it seems highly unlikely that such a quasi-experiment could be replicated in as many different settings as one would like. Moreover, with observational studies, one needs to assume nonconfoundedness (i.e., that the identification assumptions are valid) of all the studies to be able to compare them. If several observational studies give different results, one possible explanation is that one or several of them are biased (this is the principle behind an overidentification test), and another explanation is that the treatment effects are indeed different.

However, it is often claimed—see Rodrik (2009), for example—that environmental dependence is less of an issue for observational studies because these studies cover much larger areas, and as a result the treatment effect is an average across a large number of settings and therefore more generalizable.[3] In this sense, it is suggested, there is a trade-off between the more "internally" valid randomized studies and the more "externally" valid observational studies, yet this is not necessarily true. A part of the problem comes down to what it means to be generalizable: it means that if you take the same action in a different location you would get the same result. But what action and what result? In cross-area studies that compare, say, different types of investments, the fact that the action was the same and that the results were measured in the same way must be taken on faith, a decision to trust the judgment of those who constructed the data set and pooled a number of programs together under one general heading. For example, "education investment" could mean a number of different things. The generalizable conclusion from the study is therefore, at best, the impact of the average of the set of things that happened to have been pooled together when constructing the aggregate data.

There is also a more subtle issue about generalizations that arises even when we evaluate well-defined individual programs. The fact that a program evaluation uses data from a large area does not necessarily mean that the estimate of the program effect that we get from that evaluation is an average of the program effects on all the different types of people living in that large area (or all the people who are plausible program participants). The way we estimate the program effect in such cases is to try first to control for any observable differences between those covered by the program and those not covered (for example, using some kind of matching) and then to look at how those in the program perform relative to those not in the program. However, once we match like with like, either almost everyone who is in a particular matched group may be a program participant or everyone may be a nonparticipant. There are several methods to deal with this lack of overlap between the distribution of participants and nonparticipants (Heckman et al. 1997a, 1998; Rubin 2006—also see a review in Imbens and Wooldridge 2009), but in all cases the estimate will be entirely driven by the subgroups in the population where, even after matching, there are both enough participants and nonparticipants, and these subgroups could be entirely nonrepresentative. Even though we can identify the observable characteristics of the population driving the estimate of the treatment effect (though this is rarely done), we have no way of knowing how they compare to the rest of the population in terms of unobservables. In the words of Imbens and Wooldridge (2009), "a potential feature of all these methods [that improve overlap between

participants and nonparticipants] is that they change what is being estimated. . . . This results in reduced external validity, but it is likely to improve internal validity." Thus, the trade-off between internal and external
validity is also present in observational studies. By contrast so long as the
compliance rates among those chosen for treatment in an experiment are
high, we know that the affected population is at least representative of the
population chosen for the experiment. As is well known (see Imbens and
Angrist 1994), the same point also applies to instrumental variables estimates: The "compliers" in an IV strategy, for whom the program effect is
identified, may be a small and unrepresentative subset of the population
of interest.

Randomization bias is one issue regarding the ability to generalize that
is specific to evaluation: the fact that the program is evaluated using a
randomized evaluation changes the way that actors behave in the experiment. One form of randomization bias is the Hawthorne effect or the
John Henry effect: The behavior of those in the treated or the control
group changes because they know the program is being evaluated, so although the estimate of the effect of the program is internally valid, it has
no relevance outside of the experiment (Heckman and Vytlacil 2008b).
Hawthorne effects are, in principle, a problem in any setting where participants are studied and are not specific to a given experiment.[4] Social scientists worry about reporting bias (for example, because people want to
give a certain impression of themselves to a field officer). However, in an
experiment, subjects who know they are being studied may purposefully
try to make the treatment a success or a failure. (We discuss Hawthorne
effects in more detail below.)

Another, more subtle form of randomization bias is discussed by Heckman (1992). He points out that, in the Job Training Partnership Act
(JTPA) experiment, not every site agreed to participate, and, in particular, some sites specifically refused because there was a randomization.
Those sites may be different and have unique treatment effects. Experiments in development economics tend to be conducted with a variety of
partners, but it is true that not every NGO or government is willing to
participate in a randomized evaluation. If randomized evaluations can be
carried out only in very specific locations or with specific partners, precisely because they are randomized and not every partner agrees to the

randomization, replication in many sites does not get rid of this problem. This is a serious objection (closely related to the compliance problem, which we discuss below)—i.e., compliance at the level of the organization—and one that is difficult to refute, because no amount of data could completely reassure us that this is not an issue. Our experience is that, in the context of developing countries, this is becoming less of an issue as randomized evaluations gain wider acceptance. Evaluation projects have been completed with international NGOs, local governments, and an array of local NGOs. This situation will continue to improve if randomized evaluation comes to be recommended by most donors, as the willingness to comply with randomization will then be understood not to set organizations apart.

That is already happening. In particular, many World Bank researchers and implementers are working with developing-country governments to start an ambitious process of program evaluation.[5] For example, the Africa Impact Evaluation Initiative is supporting (with money and technical capacity building) a number of African governments to start randomized evaluation on various topics in Africa. Currently, sixty-seven randomized evaluations are ongoing within this program, covering five themes: education, malaria, HIV-AIDs, accountability, and transport. An evaluation recently completed under this umbrella, the AGEMAD, a school reform initiative in Madagascar (World Bank 2008), demonstrates the willingness and ability of a ministry of education to implement a randomized evaluation project, when given the necessary support and encouragement by a major donor.

A more serious issue, in our experience, is the related fact that what distinguishes possible partners for randomized evaluations are competence and a willingness to implement projects as planned. These may be lost when the project scales up. It is important to recognize this limit when interpreting results from evaluations: finding that a particular program, when implemented somewhere, has a given mean effect leaves open the problem of how to scale it up. Not enough effort has been made so far in trying medium-scale evaluation of programs that have been successful on a small scale, where these implementation issues would become evident.

That said, this problem is not entirely absent from observational studies either, especially in developing countries. Not all programs can be convincingly evaluated with a matching study. Large data sets are often required, especially if one wants to improve external validity by focusing on a large area. In some cases data are collected specifically for the evaluation, often with the assistance of the country's statistical office. In this case the country needs to accept the evaluation of a large program, which is politically more sensitive to evaluate than pilot programs, because the former is usually well publicized, so countries may be strategic with respect to the choice of programs to evaluate. In other cases, regular, large-scale surveys (such as the National Sample Survey in India, the Susenas in Indonesia, etc.) can be used. But not all developing countries have them, though data sets such as the Demographic and Health Surveys, which are available for many countries, have certainly ameliorated the issue. Thus, a potential bias, although distinct from that of randomized evaluation, also exists in the types of countries and programs that can be evaluated with observational data. The point here is not that generalizability is not an issue for the experimental/quasi-experimental approach, but that it is not obviously less of an issue for any other approach.

3.2. Compliance Issues

Above, we make the point that a high compliance rate makes it easier to interpret the instrumental variables estimate of the "treatment on the treated" estimates and, therefore, to generalize the results to other environments. The experiments in development economics have often been carried out by randomizing over a set of locations or cluster (villages, neighborhoods, schools) where the implementing organization is relatively confident of being able to implement. At the location level, the take-up rate is high, often 100 percent. It should be emphasized that this means only that the treated sample is likely to be a random subset of the set of locations that were selected for the program. The actual individuals who benefited from the treatment are not guaranteed to be a random subset of the population of those locations, but it is assumed that the selection at this level mirrors the selection an actual program (i.e., not just under experimental conditions) would induce and that the treatment on the treated parameter of an IV estimate using a "treatment" village as the instrument is the policy parameter of interest.

Heckman (1992) was specifically concerned with the interpretation of the results of randomized experiments in the United States in which individuals were offered the option to participate in a job training program. The fact that take-up was low and potentially highly selected implies that comparing those who were offered the option to participate in a training program to those who were not correctly identifies the effect of offering people such an option. Thus, the IV estimate using the intention to treat as an instrument correctly estimates the average of the impact of this program on the people who chose to participate. However, this fact does not provide information on the average impact of a training program that was made compulsory for all welfare recipients. To find this out, one would need to set up an experiment with compulsory participation (an interesting outcome would be whether or not people decide to drop out of welfare).

Similar issues arise in some of the developing-country experiments. For example, the study by Karlan and Zinman (2010) of the effect of access to consumer credit starts from a population of those whose loan applications were rejected by the bank. Then they asked the loan officers to identify a class of marginal rejects from this population and randomly "unrejected" a group of them. However, the loan officers still had discretion and used it to reject approximately half of those who were unrejected. The experiment identifies the effect of this extra credit on the population of those who remained unrejected: it appears to have raised the likelihood that the person remains employed as well as their incomes. However, while this experiment provides very valuable evidence that consumer credit may be good for some people, given the unusual nature of the treated population (the twice unrejected), some concern remains that the estimate of the effect of getting a loan in this sample is not representative of this experience for those who are accepted for the loan or for those who are definitely rejected.

Another point made by Heckman is that randomized evaluations are not the best method to study who takes up programs once they are offered to them and why. However, such a concern is not always valid, as randomization can be used precisely to learn about selection issues. As we discuss above, several studies have been conducted in which the randomization is specifically designed to measure the selection effect, which would be difficult to do in any other way (Karlan and Zinman 2005; Ashraf et al. 2010; Cohen and Dupas 2010). To learn more about selection, Cohen and Dupas (2010) collected hemoglobin levels of women who purchased bed nets at different prices. They were interested in whether women who obtain nets only when they are offered for free are less likely to be anemic. In other studies, although the evaluation is not specifically designed to capture selection effect, the take-up among those offered the program is of special interest, and baseline data are specifically collected to study this effect. For example, one important outcome of interest in Ashraf et al. (2006) regards who takes up a self-control device that helps people save.

In other cases take-up is not an issue because the treatment is in the nature of a pure gift, unlike the offer of training, for example, which is worthless unless someone is prepared to put in the time. For example, de Mel et al. (2008) studied the effect of offering each firm in their Sri Lankan sample approximately $200 in the form of additional capital. They found a large impact on the revenue of the firm, equivalent to a 5–7 percent return on capital. McKenzie and Woodruff (2008) repeated the same experiment in Mexico and found larger returns (20–35 percent). In both these cases the fact that the target firms were small was crucial: the size of the grant ensured that almost everyone was interested in participating in the program (even with gifts there is always some cost of participation) and allowed such a small gift (which is all they could afford) to have a discernable impact.

However, sometimes even a gift may be refused, as we discovered to our surprise while working with the microfinance institution Bandhan to evaluate its programs designed to help the ultra-poor (one of the several evaluations of this program mentioned above) (A. Banerjee, R. Chattopadhyay, E. Duflo, and J. M. Shapiro, unpublished results). Under the Bandhan program, villagers who are too poor to be brought into the microfinance net are identified through participatory resource assessments and other follow-up investigations and then offered an asset (usually a pair of cows, a few goats, or some other productive asset) worth between $25 and $100 with no legal strings attached but with the expectation that they will take care of the asset and there will be some follow-up, as well as a weekly allowance and some training. The goal is to see if access to the asset creates a long-term improvement in their standards of living or whether they simply sell the asset and exhaust the proceeds quickly. The evaluation design assumed that everyone who is offered the asset will grab it, which turned out not to be the case. A significant fraction of the clients (18 percent) refused the offer. Some were suspicious because they thought it was part of an attempt to convert them to Christianity; others thought it was a trick to get them into a debt trap—that eventually they would be required to pay back. Others did not doubt the motives of Bandhan, but they did not feel capable of doing a good job taking care of the asset and did not want to feel embarrassed in the village if they lost it.

3.3. Randomization Issues

The Bandhan study offers an example of randomization bias, i.e., the Hawthorne effect: being part of an experiment and being monitored influence behavior. The fact that these villagers were not accustomed to having a private organization go around and give away assets certainly contributed to the problem. However, Bandhan may not have put in the kind of public relations effort to inform the villagers about why the program was being conducted, precisely because they were not planning to serve the entire population of the very poor in each village.

Most experiments, however, are careful to avoid the potential of creating bad feeling due to the randomization. Location-level randomization is justified by budget and administrative capacity, which is precisely why the organizations often agree to randomize at that level. Limited government budgets and diverse actions by many small NGOs mean that villages or schools in most developing countries are used to the fact that some areas receive certain programs whereas others do not, and when an NGO serves only some villages they see it as a part of the organization's overall strategy. When the control areas are given the explanation that the program has enough budget for a certain number of schools only, they typically agree that a lottery is a fair way to allocate those limited resources. They are often used to such arbitrariness, and so randomization appears both transparent and legitimate.

One issue with the explicit acknowledgment of randomization as a fair way to allocate the program is that implementers may find that the easiest way to present it to the community is to say that an expansion of the program is planned for the control areas in the future (especially when such is indeed the case, as in phased-in design). This may cause problems if the anticipation of treatment leads individuals to change their behavior. This criticism was made in the case of the Progresa program, where control villages knew they would eventually be covered by the program.

When it is necessary for the evaluation that individuals not be aware that they are excluded from the program, ethics committees typically grant an exemption from full disclosure until the end-line survey is completed, at least when the fact of being studied in the control group does not present any risk to the subject. In these cases participants at the ground level are not told that randomization was involved. This happens more often when randomization takes place at the individual level (though some individual-level randomizations are carried out by public lottery). In such cases the selected beneficiaries are informed only that, for example, they received a loan for which they had applied (Karlan and Zinman 2010) or that the bank had decided to lower the interest rate (Karlan and Zinman 2005).

3.4. Equilibrium Effects

A related issue is what is usually and slightly confusingly called general equilibrium effects (we prefer the term *equilibrium effects* because general equilibrium is essentially a multimarket concept). Program effects found in a small study may not generalize what will happen when the program is scaled up nationwide (Heckman et al. 1999; Abbring and Heckman 2008). Consider, for example, what would happen if we tried to scale up a program that shows, in a small-scale experimental implementation, that economically disadvantaged girls who get vouchers to go to private schools end up with a better education and higher incomes. When we scale up the program to the national level, two challenges arise: crowding in the private schools (and potentially a collapse of public schools) and a decline in the returns to education because of increased supply. Both challenges could prompt the experimental evidence to overstate the returns to a nationwide vouchers program.

This phenomenon of equilibrium effects poses a problem that has no perfect solution. Fortunately, in many instances the phenomenon does not present itself. For example, if we want to determine which strategy for promoting immunization take-up (reliable delivery or reliable delivery plus a small incentive for the mother to remember to immunize her child on schedule) is more cost effective in raising immunization rates and by how much (as in Banerjee et al. 2010b), the experimental method poses no problem. The fact that immunizing the entire district would not require that many extra nurses helps us here because we can assume that the price of nurses would not increase much, if at all. In another example, although learning that those who received vouchers in Colombia do better in terms of both educational and life outcomes is useful (see Angrist et al. 2002, 2006), it is hard to not worry about the fact that an increase in the overall supply of skills brought about by the expansion of the vouchers program will lower the price of skills. After all, this concern is precisely one of the reasons why the government may want to carry out such a program. A similar issue arises in the evaluation of training programs. For example, Attanasio et al. (2008b) used randomized allocation of applicants to the job-training program Jóvenes en Acción in Colombia to evaluate its impact. They found that the program had a large effect on the employment rate after graduation. However, because the training program offered placement aid, it may have also helped the trainees jump the queue to get a job. Although part of the impact of a relatively small program, this effect could be muted or entirely disappear once all the youth in a city benefit from the program.

Equilibrium effects offer the one clear reason to favor large studies over small ones. That does not necessarily mean cross-country-style regressions—which often conflate too many different sources of variation to be useful in making causal claims—but rather micro studies using large-scale policy shifts. Even though they are typically not randomized, micro studies still offer the opportunity to be careful about causality issues as well as equilibrium effects, many of which become internalized. A good example of this kind of research is the work of Hsieh and Urquiola (2006), who use a quasi-experimental design to argue that a Chilean school voucher program did not lead to an overall improvement in the skill supply, though it changed sorting patterns across schools. Other studies specifically designed to evaluate potential market equilibrium effects of policies include Acemoglu and Angrist (2001) and Duflo (2004a).

It is possible to check if the results from quasi-experimental area-level study are consistent with experimental evidence. For example, in the case of vouchers, we expect the equilibrium effects to dampen the supply response and therefore expect larger quasi-experimental studies to generate smaller effects than those found in experiments. If we find the opposite, we may start worrying about whether the larger study is reliable or representative. In this sense, experiments and nonexperimental studies may be complements rather than substitutes.

Another approach is to try to estimate directly the size of the equilibrium effect using the experimental method. In ongoing research M. Kremer and K. Muralidharan (unpublished results) study the effect of a vouchers program using a double randomization: they randomize villages where the vouchers are distributed as well as the individuals who receive vouchers within a village. By comparing the estimates they will get from the two treatments, they hope to infer the size of the equilibrium effect. This approach deals with only one level of equilibration—people can move to the village from outside and leave the village to find work, in which case estimating what is happening to the supply of education rather than to the price of skills may be a better approach—but it is clearly an important start.

An alternative approach is to combine the results from different experiments by using one experiment (or, more plausibly, quasi-experiment) to estimate the elasticity of demand for skills, another to estimate the supply of quality teaching, and a third to estimate how much vouchers contribute to skill building. This style of work requires taking a more structural approach because we need to identify the relevant parameters. Yet it has the potential to bridge the gap between the micro and macro worlds and addresses the criticism that experiments may get the right answer to minor questions but fail to address the big questions of interest (as seen in some of the comments to Banerjee's piece in the Boston review, for example, published in Banerjee [2007]). As we discuss above, experiments can help us estimate economic parameters (such as the returns to capital for small firms, the labor supply elasticity, individual returns to education, etc.), which can then be used in combination with microfounded equilibrium models (Heckman et al. 1999 developed and exposed this method for tuition policy). There is a small but growing literature in development economics, associated in particular with Robert Townsend and his collaborators, that attempts to integrate microestimates into calibration of growth models with credit constraints.[6] Clearly, much work remains to be done in this area.

3.5. Heterogeneity in Treatment Effects

Most evaluations of social programs focus exclusively on the mean impact. In fact, one of the advantages of experimental results is their simplicity: They are easy to interpret because all you need to do is compare means, a fact that may encourage policymakers to take the results more seriously (see, e.g., Duflo 2004b; Duflo and Kremer 2004). However, as Heckman et al. (1997b) point out, the mean treatment effect may not be what the policymaker wants to know: exclusive focus on the mean is valid only under specific assumptions about the form of the social welfare function. Moreover, from the point of view of the overall intellectual project, restricting the analysis to the naive comparison of means does not make sense.

Unfortunately, the mean treatment effect (or the treatment effect conditional on covariates) is also the only conventional statistic of the distribution of treatment effects that is straightforward to estimate from a randomized experiment without the need for additional assumptions (Heckman 1992). Of course, we can always compare the entire distribution of outcomes in treatment with that in control: tests have been developed to measure the equality of distributions as well as stochastic dominance (see Abadie 2002). For example, Banerjee et al. (2007) showed that the distribution of test scores among the students who study in schools that received a *balsakhi* (in other words, "child's friend" or tutor) first-order stochastically dominates that of the treatment group, and most of the gains are seen at the bottom. This finding is important because, in the program classrooms, the children at the bottom were pulled out and given remedial teaching, whereas those at the top remained in the classroom. We would therefore expect different effects on the two groups, and justifying the program would be difficult if it helps only those at the top. Duflo et al. (2007) also looked at how the camera-based teacher incentive program discussed above affects the entire distribution of absence among teachers, and they found first-order stochastic dominance.

However, comparing these distributions does not inform us about the distribution of the treatment effect per se because the differences in quantiles of a distribution is not the quantile of the difference.

In their excellent review of the recent econometric literature on program evaluation, including the technical details behind much of the material covered here, Imbens and Wooldridge (2009) make the case that the distribution of the outcome in treatment and in control (which is always knowable) is all that we could possibly want to know about the program, because any social welfare function should be defined by the distribution of outcomes or by the distribution of outcomes conditional on observable variables. However, it is not clear that this is entirely correct. The planner may care about the percentage of people who benefit from a treatment, which is not identified by experiments (or any other evaluation method) without further assumption. To see the issue in its starkest form, consider the following example: there is a population of three people, and we know their potential outcomes both with and without treatment. If not treated, A's potential outcome is 1, B's is 2, and C's is 3. If treated, A's potential outcome is 2, B's outcome is 3, and C's outcome is -4. What should we think of this program? Both in terms of the mean treatment effect and in terms of the overall distribution, the treatment failed: the distribution 1, 2, 3 of the potential outcome nontreated first-order dominates the distribution -4, 2, 3 of the potential outcome treated. Should we therefore conclude that a policymaker should always favor control over treatment? Not necessarily, because the treatment benefits a majority, and the policymaker may care about the greatest good for the greatest number. And even if we disagree with the policymaker's preferences here, it is hard to argue that the evaluator should dictate the choice of the objective function.

Once we recognize the potential value of identifying the set of people (from an ex ante undifferentiated group) who moved up or down owing to the treatment, a problem arises: extracting this information from the distribution of outcomes in treatment and in control is impossible. The problem here is logical and not a function of the experiments per se or any other specific estimation strategy—the relevant information is simply not there. In the setting of a randomized social experiment, Heckman et al. (1997b) show that the introduction of additional behavioral assumptions (in effect, modeling the decision to participate as a function of the potential outcomes under treatment and nontreatment) allows estimation of precise bounds on features of the distribution of the treatment effect. Abbring and Heckman (2008) provide a detailed treatment of methods to estimate the distribution of treatment effects. These techniques also apply in nonexperimental settings, but the authors point out that they may be particularly useful with experimental data both because one "can abstract from selection problems that plague non-experimental data" and because the experimental setting guarantees balance in the support of the observable variables, something on which the techniques rely.

Our view is that experimental research would benefit by engaging more with this body of research. Reporting additional "assumption-dependent" results along with the more "assumption-free" results that are usually reported in experiments (and making the necessary caveat emptor) can only enrich experimental work. However, experiments still have the advantage over methods that, with few assumptions, one can know important aspects of impact of the treatment (such as the mean for any subgroup). The fact that we may want to go beyond these measures, and to do so we may need to invoke assumptions that make random assignment less important, cannot possibly be counted in favor of methods not based on random assignment

Moreover, a lot of the heterogeneity that features prominently in people's objective functions (as opposed to heterogeneity that drives economic outcomes) is not about unobserved differences in people's characteristics, but about potentially observable differences. For example, in the *balsakhi* experiment (Banerjee et al. 2007) we observed not only that the distribution of test scores in treatment first-order stochastically dominated that in control, but also that those who had low baseline scores gained the most. From the point of view of the implementing organization, Pratham, this was what mattered, but we could know this only because we had baseline test scores. In other words, we need to start the experiment with clear hypotheses about how treatment effects vary based on covariates and collect the relevant baseline data.

Fortunately, recent econometric research can help. Crump et al. (2008) developed two nonparametric tests of whether heterogeneity is present in treatment effects: one to determine whether the treatment effect is zero for any subpopulation (defined by covariates) and another for whether the treatment effect is the same for all subpopulations (defined by covariates). Heckman et al. (2006) and Heckman and Vytlacil (2008a, b) discuss the implication of treatment heterogeneity in terms of both observables and nonobservables.

In addition, treatment effects can be estimated for different subgroups. One difficulty here is that if the subgroups are determined ex post, there is a danger of "specification searching," where researchers and policymakers choose ex post to emphasize the program's impact on one particular subgroup. As in the application by Heckman et al. (1997b), theory can help by telling us what to expect. Specifying ex ante the outcomes to be observed and what we expect from them (as is encouraged in the medical literature) is another possibility. Should we still want to try to learn from possibly interesting but ex ante unexpected differences in the treatment effect, replication can help. When a second experiment is run, it can be explicitly set up to test this newly generated hypothesis. For example, both Karlan and Zinman (2010) and de Mel et al. (2009) found different results for men and women. These differences were not expected, and they are difficult to reconcile. But once the study is replicated elsewhere, these differences can form the basis of a new set of hypotheses to be tested. (See Duflo 2007 for a more detailed discussion of these and other design issues.)

Finally, some recent literature (Manski 2000, 2002, 2004; Dehejia 2005b; Hirano and Porter 2005) seeks to make all of this less ad hoc. The authors want to integrate the process of evaluation and learning into an explicit framework of program design. They therefore try to put themselves explicitly in the shoes of the policymaker who is trying to decide not only whether or not to implement a program, but also how to implement it (should the program be compulsory? should the administrator be given some leeway on who should participate?). They allow the policymaker to be concerned not only with expected income gain, but also with expected utility gain (taking into account risk aversion), and hence with potential increase or decrease in the variability of the outcome with the treatment status. The policymaker has access to covariates about potential beneficiaries as well as to the results from randomized experiments. This literature tries to develop a theory of how the administrator should decide, taking into account both heterogeneity and uncertainty in program benefits conditional on covariates. As far as we know, these tools have not been used in development economic research. This is a fruitful avenue for future work.

3.6. Relationship with Structural Estimation

Most of the early experimental literature focused on reduced-form estimates of the program effect. However, there is no reason not to use those data to extract structural parameters wherever possible. Although doing so will require us to make more assumptions, the structural estimates can be used to cross-check the reduced-form results (for example, are the results reasonable if they imply an elasticity of labor supply of x or an expected return on schooling of y?) and more generally to bolster their external validity. Moreover, if we are comfortable with the assumptions underlying the estimates, it is possible to derive policy conclusions from them that go well beyond what is obtained from the reduced form.

Early examples of this method in development include Attanasio et al. (2001) and Todd and Wolpin (2006), both of which use Progresa data. Attanasio et al. (2001) were interested in evaluating the program's impact while allowing, for example, for anticipation effects in the control (which cannot be done without making some additional assumptions). They found no evidence of anticipation effects. Todd and Wolpin (2006) wanted to use the experiment as a way to validate the structural model: they estimated a structural model outside the treated sample and checked that the model correctly predicts the impact of the treatment. Another example of the potential of marrying experiments and structural estimation is Duflo, Hanna and Ryan (2007). After reporting the reduced-form results, the paper exploits the nonlinear aspect of Seva Mandir's teacher incentive schemes (teachers received a minimum wage of $10 if they were present less than ten days in the month and a bonus of $1 for any extra day above that) to estimate the value of teachers' absences and the elasticity of their response with respect to the bonus. The model is extremely simple: by coming to school in the early days of the months, the teacher is building up the option of getting $1 extra per day by the end of the month, thereby giving up a stochastic outside option of not going to school this day. Yet this model also gives rise to interesting estimation problems once we try to introduce heterogeneity and serial correlation in the shock received by the teacher on the outside option in a realistic way. As with Todd ad Wolpin (2006), this paper then compares the predictions of various models to both the control and a "natural experiment" when Seva Mandir changed their payment rules (after the experiment period was over). This exercise shows that accounting for heterogeneity and serial correlation is important because only those simulations come close to replicating the control group means and the distribution of absence under the new rules.

In principle, it ought to be possible to exploit even further the complementarity between structural estimation and experiments. As mentioned above, one advantage of experiments is their flexibility with respect to data collection and the choice of treatments (within the limits of ethical rule and human subject reviews and what partners are willing to and capable of implementing). It should be possible to design the experiment to facilitate structural estimation by ensuring that the experiment includes sources of variation that would help researchers identify the necessary parameters and collect the appropriate data. Experiments in development economics increasingly involve complex designs and many treatment groups, demonstrating the feasibility of introducing variation that could help identify structural parameters of interest. One could also estimate a structural model from baseline data before the experimental results are known in order to perform a "blind" validation of the structural models. However, we have yet to see examples of this kind of work: the examples we discuss exploit ex post variation in the way the program is implemented rather than introducing it on purpose.

3.7. Relation to Theory

We have argued that experiments can be and have been useful for testing theories (see Banerjee 2005 and Duflo et al. 2006 for a longer treatment of these issues). The fact that the basic experimental results (e.g., the mean treatment effect) do not depend on the theory for their identification means that a clean test of theory (i.e., a test that does not rely on other theories too) may be possible. This understanding has prompted us to rethink some basic elements of demand theory. A number of independent randomized studies on the demand for so-called health protection products consistently found that the price elasticity of demand around zero is huge. In Kenya, Kremer and Miguel (2007) found that raising the price of deworming drugs from 0 to 30 cents per child reduced the fraction of children taking the drug from 75 percent to 19 percent. Also in Kenya, Cohen and Dupas (2010) found that raising the price of insecticide-treated bed nets from 0 to 60 cents reduces the fraction of those who buy the nets by 60 percent. In Zambia, raising the price of water disinfectant from 9 to 24 cents reduces the fraction of people who take up the offer by 30 percent (Ashraf et al. 2010). Similar large responses are also found with small subsidies: in India, Banerjee et al. (2010b) found that offering mothers one kilogram of dried beans (worth approximately 60 cents) for every immunization visit (plus a set of bowls for completing immunization) increases the probability that a child is fully immunized by 20 percent. Most remarkably, a reward of 10 cents got 20 percent more people in Malawi to pick up the results of their HIV test (Thornton 2007).

Reviewing this evidence (and several papers on education with similar conclusions), Kremer and Holla (2008) conclude that these demand elasticities cannot come from the standard human-capital model of the demand for better health, given the importance of the issue at hand. For example, one can imagine that either conventionally rational economic agents decide to get an HIV test (knowing their status could prolong their life and that of others) or they decide against getting it (the test may be extremely stressful and shameful). What is more difficult to predict is that so many of them change their minds, for a mere 10 cents, about something that has a good chance of entirely transforming their lives.

Kremer and Holla (2008) suggest that this pattern of demand is more consistent with a model in which people actually want the product but are procrastinating; it is tempting to delay paying the cost given that the benefits are in the future. However, if people really want to buy bed nets or want to know their test result but are perpetually unable to do so, then, given the potential lifesaving benefits that these offer, they have to be extraordinarily naive. In terms of financial products, the (experimental) evidence argues against their being that naive. Ashraf et al. (2006) found that those who show particularly hyperbolic preferences are also particularly keen to acquire commitment devices to lock in their savings, indicating a high degree of self-awareness. Duflo et al. (2008c, d) found that farmers in Kenya who complain of not having enough money to buy fertilizer at planting time are willing to commit money at harvest time for fertilizer to be used several months later. Moreover, when given ex ante (before the harvest) the choice about when vendors should come to sell fertilizer, almost half the farmers request that the vendors come right after harvest rather than later when the farmers will need fertilizer, because the farmers know they will have money after the harvest. Their request for fertilizer to be delivered to them right away suggests that the farmers have enough self-control to keep fertilizer at home and not resell it. This finding further suggests that the theory may extend beyond the now-standard invocation of self-control problems as a way of dealing with all anomalies.

Sometimes experiments throw up results that are even more troubling to the existing body of theory (see Duflo 2007 for a longer discussion). Bertrand et al. (2010) provide one striking example that fits no existing economic theory: they found that seemingly minor manipulations (such as the photograph on a mailer) have effects on take-up of loans as large as meaningful changes in interest rates.

In all of this literature, field experiments play the role traditionally played by lab experiments, but perhaps with greater credibility. The goal is better theory, but can theory help us design better experiments and interpret experimental results for better policy design? One possible direction, discussed above, is to use experimental results to estimate structural models. However, we also want theory to play a more mundane but equally important role: we need a framework for interpreting what we find. For example, can we go beyond the observation that different inputs into the educational production function have different productivities? Is there any way to group the different inputs into broader input categories on a priori grounds, with the presumption that there should be less variation within the category? Or, on the outcome side, can we predict which outcomes of the educational system should covary more closely than the rest? Or is every experimental result sui generis?

A useful theory for this purpose is unlikely to be particularly sophisticated. Rather, it would provide a convenient way to reduce dimensionality on the basis of a set of reasonable premises. Banerjee et al. (2010a) attempted such an approach for the local public action, but their effort is, at best, partially successful. More work along these lines will be vital.

4. Conclusion

We fully concur with Heckman's (1992) main point: to be interesting, experiments need to be ambitious and need to be informed by theory. At this convergence point is also, conveniently, where they are likely to be the most useful for policymakers. Our view is that economists' insights can and should guide policymaking (see also Banerjee 2002). Economists are sometimes well placed to propose or identify programs that are likely to make big differences. Perhaps even more important, they are often in a position to midwife the process of policy discovery, based on the interplay of theory and experimental research. This process of "creative experimentation," where policymakers and researchers work together to think out of the box and learn from successes and failures, is the most valuable contribution of the recent surge in experimental work in economics.

Acknowledgments

We thank Guido Imbens for many helpful conversations and James J. Heckman for detailed comments on an earlier draft. The original version of this chapter appeared in the *Annual Review of Economics* (2009) 1:151–78. It has been reprinted with the journal's permission.

NOTES

1. The opposite approach, i.e., going from one intervention at a time to the full package, also makes sense when your priors are that some combination will work, whereas the alternate is better when you are generally skeptical.

2. This flexibility is, of course, not boundless. Ethical concerns (supervised by universities' internal review boards) and the constraint of working with an implementing organization do limit the set of questions you can ask, relative to what one can do in a lab experiment. Not everything can be tested, and not everyone wants to be experimented on. However, the extra realism of the setting is an enormous advantage. It should also be noted that the lower cost of the programs and working with NGO partners greatly expand the feasible set of experiments in development, compared with what has been feasible in the United States.

3. Note that not all randomized experiments are small scale. For example, the mandated representation programs we mention above were implemented nationwide in India. Whereas Chattopdhyay and Duflo (2004) originally looked at only two (very different) states, Topalova and Duflo (2003) extended the analysis to all the major Indian states.

4. In fact, the original Hawthorne effect happened during "experiments" in workplace conditions that were not randomized.

5. Francois Bourguignon and Paul Gertler, when they were the chief economist and the chief economist of the human development network at the World Bank, respectively, played key roles in encouraging evaluations.

6. We discuss this literature in Banerjee and Duflo (2005). See also Banerjee (2009) for a detailed response to the argument that researchers should give up micro-estimates because the only thing that matters is growth and that the use of aggregate data is the only way to estimate what drives growth.

5

REFLECTIONS ON THE ETHICS
OF FIELD EXPERIMENTS

Dawn Langan Teele

1. Introduction

Throughout this book we have considered whether field experiments offer the best way forward for social scientific research. This question has been asked from multiple methodological and epistemological viewpoints, and the chapters reveal considerable disagreement among distinguished social scientists. One issue that has not been raised systematically concerns the ethical implications of running experiments in the spaces where real people live out their lives. By definition, these environments are not wholly controlled by the researcher. Because we, as citizens, might be wary of scientists who, clipboards in hand, descended upon our neighborhoods in order to set up new institutions, start traditions, or change discourses, as social scientists we should be aware of the real-life impacts of field experimental research.

In this chapter I ask whether and how research participants and their communities can be treated ethically in the course of social scientific field experiments. I first establish that by their very natures, experimental and observational studies beget distinctive relationships between study participants and researchers. Both methods raise ethical challenges, but I argue that the ethical hurdles for experimental work are higher than those for observational work. This is because experiments alter the setting, scenery, and sometimes life chances of individuals who are either directly or indirectly involved. Well-known scandals brought these concerns to the fore in medical research, leading to the development of thorough guidelines for medical research. So far, however, social scientists have assumed that good intentions and an Institutional Review Board's seal of approval suffice to ensure that the dignity and autonomy of research participants are respected.

A critic might respond, even at this early point in the chapter, that the ethics of field experimentation are beside the point, since there is no alternative to field experiments if (1) experimental research is the only way to ensure valid causal inference and rigorous policy evaluations; and (2) the policies being evaluated experimentally would be implemented anyway, but without any sort of evaluation or, worse, with mere observational evaluation. This book contains arguments sufficiently compelling to cast doubt on the first proposition; indeed, the jury is still out as to whether experiments are the only way or the best way to tell us all we need to know about a policy intervention. As to the second point, while it is true that policy interventions should be evaluated so that donors and governments can know whether their resources are being spent effectively, it is misleading to claim that this argument provides an ethical defense of field experimentation as it is practiced today. Not only do researchers often engage in independent experimental projects, without any connection to governments or NGOs, but also they are increasingly engaged in bringing policy ideas to governments and think tanks to be tried out in real-world settings. I don't want to criticize these practices; I think scholars should engage in independent research unconnected to policy evaluation, and that social scientists should play an active role in policymaking, but this means that the ethical implications of field experiments cannot be dismissed by saying that all we are doing is evaluating policies that are going to be implemented anyway.

More generally, although though this chapter raises some ethical issues surrounding the treatment of subjects in field experimental research, it in no way endorses a ban on their use. In what follows we will not encounter any "smoking gun" experiments that cast the method in inexorable doubt. This is attributable to the commendable efforts of Institutional Review Boards in protecting human subjects and to the responsible choices of journal editors in shelving submissions based on ethically questionable research. But the absence of a smoking gun should be celebrated cautiously, because, as will be shown below, in the writings of the preeminent experimenters a plea can be heard for the prerogatives of research to be placed before the rights of research participants, with some experimenters going as far as to endorse covert experimentation or the deliberate misinforming of human subjects as critical for clean identification strategies.[1] This is particularly troubling given the noble inspiration of many research agendas that employ the experimental method. Research that seeks to learn how citizens can be encouraged to express themselves politically, or that tries to understand how villagers can pull themselves out of poverty, is fundamentally and sincerely concerned with improving lives and welfare. If the method used to address these questions involves misleading potential participants and ignoring the sometimes diffuse risks that experiments pose to communities in a research site, it undermines the very ideals that originally inspired its pursuit. For this reason it is imperative that the question of experimental ethics be brought into what is all too often an entirely technical methodological discourse.

The chapter is organized as follows: section 2 argues that the entry of researchers into real-world settings and the manipulation of subjects in these environments, which distinguishes field experiments from other research methodologies, raise specific ethical dilemmas and increase the ethical burden of justification for field experimental researchers. Section 3 describes and applies the principles of the *Belmont Report*, developed to guide medical research, to field experimentation in the social sciences. It demonstrates that the spirit of these principles has been violated in the writings of some prominent experimenters. In conclusion, section 4 discusses prescriptions and suggestions for how field experimental practices could be made to comply with ethical principles. I suggest that informed consent and a more thoroughgoing evaluation of the downstream and community-level risks that stem from field experiments must guide all research if it is to be ethical. Where scholars are worried that informed consent will change the behavior of participants and thereby interfere with the estimators of causal relationships, I suggest that placebo group designs will help the research remain inside the bounds of acceptable treatment of human subjects.

2. What Makes the Field Experimental Method Different from Any Other?

How do field experiments differ from other research methodologies that involve studying people—cataloging their responses, measuring their movements, and interpreting these data? The most basic difference is that whereas observational research hopes to make causal inferences by measuring and analyzing variation in the world, field experiments induce the variation whose outcomes will later be studied. In a classic article on causal inference, Holland (1986: 959) famously writes, "No causation without manipulation," implying that a researcher cannot claim that a causal relationship exists between a catalyst and an outcome unless the catalyst is set into motion by an experiment. Though the use of the term *manipulation* seems rather anodyne, manipulation of the research environment is precisely what makes field experiments different from, and potentially more ethically dubious than, observational work. To illustrate this point: if observational social scientists are spectators of a card game whose hands nature dealt, experimental social scientists have positioned themselves as the dealer. This shift from spectator to dealer changes the relationship of the social scientists to the players, and it begs for an examination of the practices and policies that bind them together.

Table 1 makes this distinction clearer; it catalogues two dimensions of social science research: *Field* (on the vertical axis) and *Intervention* (on the horizontal access). Elizabeth Wood (2007) defines field research as research that is "based on personal interaction with research subjects in their own setting" (123). Thus *Field* in this table signifies whether, in order to carry out a project, a researcher must join the "setting" of the research participants. Research that does not involve joining someone else's setting includes the use of data that can be downloaded from official websites, the collection of records from archives, and research in a laboratory environment.

Intervention, the variable along the horizontal axis, signifies whether the researcher purposively manipulates the research context in some way, for example, by randomly assigning participants to treatment and control groups. A heuristic for understanding this dimension is the answer to the question, Does the research itself alter the environment in which the

Table 5-1. Classifying Social Science Research by Intervention and Entry

	Intervention: No	Intervention: Yes
Field: No	Archival or library work	Lab experiments
Field: Yes	Field surveys, ethnographic work	Field experiments

participants are active? Or, perhaps more accurately, Does the research *intentionally* alter the environment in which the participants are active? The answer to these questions is clearly no for work with national accounts data and archival research and for surveys carried out in the field (even surveys that randomize the order of questions). The answer is also no for ethnographic work, in which a cardinal rule is for the researcher to avoid actively influencing events.[2] To sum up, the answer to the question of whether intentional alteration occurs, in other words, manipulation of the research environment, is yes for social science experiments carried out in the lab and also for those carried out in the field.

The point I wish to highlight from table 5-1 is that moves down and to the right increase the burden on the researcher to question whether the research comports with ethical principles. Research that moves down the vertical axis of *Field* must be subject to more critical scrutiny because interacting with research participants in their own setting can exacerbate existing power dynamics because of the often large cultural, educational, and socioeconomic differences between the researcher and the participant. Ethnographers in particular are sensitive to these power dynamics. Standard practice in research that employs the tool of participant observation mandates that certain groups must be studied with care: the participation of those who are economically vulnerable, mentally handicapped, socially deviant (Thorne 1980) or who live under authoritarian regimes (Goduka 1990) has been given considerable attention by ethnographic methodologists. Wood (2006) summarizes a basic message from this literature as doing no harm, meaning that the researcher has to anticipate and be attentive to the ways in which the research itself might complicate the lives and practices of the people being studied. To put it another way, the consensus among those who employ the techniques of participant observer conceive of ethical field research as similar to deep woods camping: the research itself should leave no trace.

Research that moves across the horizontal axis of *Intervention* also requires greater ethical scrutiny because, by definition, it undermines the leave-no-trace maxim. Indeed, experimental intervention intentionally alters the participant's environment and can produce unintended and unforeseen consequences. Unforeseen consequences have typically been examined in the context of deception: the famous psychological experiments by Stanley Milgram (1974) first inspired inquiries into whether deception is an ethical practice in social research, and later works by Baumrind (1985), Geller (1992), and Bonetti (1998) have followed up on the negative outcomes from experimental deception.

Milgram was interested in understanding how seemingly decent people could, under the sway of an authority figure, be persuaded to inflict pain upon another person.[3] He devised an experiment wherein one research participant acted as a "teacher" who was to help another participant, the "student," learn a list of words. If the student answered the teacher's prompt incorrectly, the teacher was to administer an electric shock to the student with increasingly higher voltage as the total number of wrong answers increased. Two things were key in this experiment; first, the teacher could hear but not see the student, who was strapped to a chair, with electrodes attached to his wrists, in a separate room. Second, a "medical doctor," who served as the experiment's authority figure, was present in the same room as the teacher. The doctor encouraged the teacher to keep administering electric shocks to the student when the latter produced the wrong answer. Milgram's experiment revealed that most of the teachers, despite voicing concerns and hesitating to administer electric shocks, continued to issue the shocks when the doctor encouraged them to do so. Many even continued to shock the student until the maximum voltage was reached.

The reaction to the Milgram experiment was visceral. Many questioned the ethical validity of the experiment on the grounds that the deception involved in the experimental protocol inflicted an unusual amount of stress on the research participants (Baumrind 1985). Alternatively, Patten (1977) argues that Milgram's experiment was unethical because the researchers claim that the stress to the participants was *unintended*, when, insofar as the participants had to believe they were inflicting real pain for inferences to be valid, the very nature of the experiment depended on this discomfort.[4]

Two issues spring from the Milgram debate that are relevant to our purposes here. The first is that experiments can inflict undesirable consequences on participants, in this case stress and anguish. The second issue is that some of these consequences will be unforeseen by the researcher. It is precisely these negative consequences, both foreseen and unforeseen, that increase the burden on the experimenter to scrutinize the ethics of the intervention.

What differentiates the field experimental method from any other, and which is revealed by its location in the bottom right quadrant of table 5-1, then, is that the method raises ethical concerns both by entering into a research participant's setting and by intentionally manipulating the research environment. The ethical terrain is therefore complicated by the very nature of the method.

Despite this, even as field experimentation became more common in social science, there has not been much discussion of its ethical requirements. Most papers promoting the method contain some statement that experiments are the ideal method, provided they are ethical (Banerjee and Duflo, chapter 4 in this book; Humphreys and Weinstein 2009), but only few actually describe the nature of this responsibility (for an exception, see Barrett and Carter, chapter 3 in this book). Further, while there are well-developed standards for reporting measurement strategies and estimation protocols, there are no current standards for reporting on the ethical challenges involved in the research process.

To get some traction on these issues, I provide below a nuanced reading of a foundational document in the ethics of human subjects' research, the *Belmont Report*, and pinpoint places in which the report's three principles—*respect for persons, beneficence*, and *justice*—have been undermined in the new experimental social science. The *Belmont Report* is a foundational document because it is cited in the bibliographies of most guidebooks for institutional review of human subjects' research. A cursory survey of the institutional review documents at fifteen top research universities—including, inter alia, Yale, Harvard, Cornell, Stanford, and Northwestern—reveals that every one of these universities lists the *Belmont Report* in either the mission statement or the opening page of their human subjects' manuals. Thus, the report is a useful launching pad for my discussion of experimental ethics.

3. Implications of the *Belmont Report* for Field Experiments

Experiments have been a tool of medical research dating back to the second century A.D., and many medical innovations, including the development of the invaluable smallpox vaccination, might not have been possible without some form of experimental science (Ivy 1948). Nevertheless, unpalatable choices have been made in the course of experimental science, causing the professions that utilize this technique to exert a considerable and commendable effort to outline and enforce the ethical and legal limits of this type of research.

An infamously unpalatable example that led directly to the construction of ethical codes for human subjects' research is the Tuskegee Syphilis Study, which was carried out by the U.S. Public Health Service from 1932 to 1970. The experimental population was composed of 399 black men, 199 of whom had syphilis, from very poor rural areas near Tuskegee, Alabama. In exchange for routine checkups and regular blood work, participants in the experiment were given access to clinical care unrelated to the disease, were fed warm meals on days that they went to the lab, and were promised a stipend to defray the costs of burial in the event of death. The purpose of the research was to study untreated syphilis as it progresses, and all members of the treatment group were in late stages of the disease.

There are several ethical problems embedded in the Tuskegee study. To begin with, participants were not told they were being called on to study syphilis, a disease which many of them did not know they had. Rather, participants were told that they had "bad blood," a colloquial term for syphilis, that the doctors wanted to test, and some participants actually believed they were being treated for bad blood rather than contributing to the study of syphilis (Jones 1981). Despite the emergence of penicillin (a reliable cure for the disease) in the 1940s, none of the study's participants were actually administered treatment for syphilis. Years of investigation revealed that the scientists in the Tuskegee study deliberately withheld information about the disease and possible treatments in order to study its effects as it progressed (ibid.).

As documented by Jones, when the American public was informed about the Tuskegee study in 1972, the overwhelming response was outrage. The U.S. government, which should actively protect its vulnerable citizens, had instead inflicted a considerable amount of pain and harm on them. Moreover, it could hardly escape notice that the study's subjects were members of a marginalized racial minority that was largely illiterate and extremely poor. This aroused suspicions that the study was carried out on those who would not know that their rights were being trod upon and who were likely to feel grateful for whatever remuneration they were offered. In other words, the researchers in the Tuskegee study chose their study population precisely because, due to their marginalized social and economic status, subjects were unlikely to learn about the nature and treatment of their disease and, in the event they did, were unlikely to take action against the researchers. Jones writes, "The ultimate lesson that many Americans saw in the Tuskegee Study was the need to protect society from scientific pursuits that ignored human values" (1981: 14). Though not the first and clearly not the last time that the rights of minority citizens would be violated in America, the Tuskegee study raises the specter of discrimination in the choice of study populations that remains as worrisome today as it was in the 1930s.[5]

To overcome the apparent ethical blind spots of the scientific and medical communities, in the late 1970s the U.S. Department of Health, Education, and Welfare formed a National Commission for the Protection of Human Subjects of Biomedical and Behavioral Research. The commission, which was made up of lawyers, legislators, academic researchers, and physicians, convened to establish guidelines for research on human subjects. The fruit of this conference, *The Belmont Report: Ethical Principles and Guidelines for the Protection of Human Subjects of Research* (1978), is meant to serve as an "analytical framework that will guide the resolution of ethical problems arising from research involving human subjects." The *Belmont Report* is a foundational document in the history of institutional review practices: it does not make technical recommendations for how to evaluate the ethics of particular research projects, but rather enumerates three principles to guide ethical research with human subjects: respect for persons, beneficence, and justice. In the following pages I will demonstrate that the concrete examples in the *Belmont Report*, which takes biomedical and behavioral researchers as its audience, are not exhaustive of the challenges that arise with regard to field experiments. My aim is to interpret the principles of the report in light of experimental research, so that social scientists, in so far as they endorse these principles, will have an ethical framework on which to base experimental research.

3.1. Respect for Persons

According to the *Belmont Report*, respect for persons entails acknowledging that the subjects of research are autonomous individuals whose personal dignity and opinions must be considered and respected. This sometimes means protecting those whose autonomy is in some way diminished—by age, mental handicap, or other debilitating condition—and it generally requires that a participant's anonymity be protected. Moreover, a researcher must not obstruct a participant's ability to make a well-reasoned judgment about whether to participate in a given study, implying that she cannot withhold any information that may be relevant for the participant to give informed consent. In certain situations, including those where a participant is vulnerable, immature, or incapacitated, the report requires a researcher to take extra steps to ensure that the subject is protected.

Adhering to this principle is relatively straightforward: researchers must communicate the nature and level of risk associated with participation in the research and must procure a statement of consent that demonstrates the subject's awareness of the potential risks associated with participation and that confirms that the subject participates willingly. In all research, application of the respect for persons principle requires that the researcher have some idea of the risks associated with the treatment. I will speak more about the issue of risk in the next section, but for now suppose that the researcher is aware of the risks. For example, in biomedical trials a patient must be informed of potential side effects of a drug (that it could cause nausea, headaches, fever, and so on) and in behavioral studies the researcher must communicate essential facts about the research design—for example, that the subject may be exposed to loud noises, confined spaces, or some painful stimuli—before obtaining consent.

It is relatively clear how respect for persons translates into informed consent in biomedical and behavioral research, but in the case of field experiments its application is not straightforward. Many scholars, including Banerjee and Duflo (chapter 4 in this book) and Levitt and List (2009), point out that if participants are aware that they are participating in a field experiment, they may act differently and in such a way as to confound measurements and results that stem from the project. This phenomenon, which applies to all situations in which human behavior is measured, is widely known as the Hawthorne effect.[6] Though the problem is not unique to field experiments, it is particularly vexing to field experimenters, whose claim to methodological primacy rests on two promises: first, that there is internal validity to the research design, and, second, that opportunities for extrapolation to other contexts—external validity—are less compromised with field experiments than with other methods. The Hawthorne effect poses problems on both levels, as subjects' responses are due to other influences besides just the treatment, undermining internal validity. Second, if a subject acts differently when he knows he is being studied, then the study's findings will likely not apply to other nonexperimental contexts. Faced with these obstacles, many field experimenters argue for the use of "covert experimentation," in which people are unaware that they are participating in an experiment and are sometimes unaware that their behavior is being measured at all (Levitt and List 2009).

Here we are presented with a problem: if it is true that informed consent compromises both internal and external validity and thereby undermines the scientific integrity of social research, field experiments that necessitate forgoing procedures of informed consent fail to satisfy the first principle of respect for persons.[7] Humphreys and Weinstein (2009) speak of this dilemma as a trade-off between ethics and measurement, an ethical dilemma without a clear-cut solution. But this misstates the problem. An ethical dilemma arises when it is impossible to simultaneously meet the demands of two *ethical* principles, as, for example, when one is confronted with a situation in which lying to a friend is the only way to avoid insulting him. The ethical principles that conflict in this example are not to lie and also to be kind to others. The trade-off created by the Hawthorne effect between satisfying the principle of respect for persons by obtaining informed consent and generating unbiased measurements of causal effects does not have this character. It is more akin to the trade-off, in criminal justice, between respecting a suspect's Miranda rights and the prospects of securing evidence that will lead to conviction. In the latter trade-off, one can recognize that there may be some conceivable benefit to denying suspects their rights while still demanding that the principles embodied in the Miranda rights be satisfied; the problem here is not an ethical dilemma, but one of comporting with an ethical principle or not.

Given that the most important implication of the principle of respect for persons is that researchers gain informed consent from their subjects, field experiments that do not satisfy this demand fail to adhere to the principle and, as a result, are unethical under the principles of the *Belmont Report*. In the American criminal justice system, evidence gained through the use of improper procedures (for example, entrapment, denial of a lawyer, etc.) is inadmissible in court. One might argue that, by analogy, evidence procured in field experiments for which informed consent of subjects was not secured should not be admissible in peer-reviewed journals, the courts of scientific discussion.

There are two compelling counterarguments to the strong claim made above that all participants in field experiments must give informed consent. First, some researchers argue that given the everyday situations that are the site of behavioral studies, requiring informed consent would be not just impossible but in fact ridiculous.[8] What would life be like if supermarkets were forced to gain informed consent before they analyzed data on price changes and purchasing behavior? How could banks operate if they were forced to gain consent before they investigated responses to marketing letters? The tenor of these objections is that there are numerous situations in which behavior is already being manipulated and monitored and that to subject academic researchers to a standard different from that of private businesses is unfair. This objection has been confronted in work on ethical ethnography (Bosk and Vries 2004) and in the medical sciences (Gray 1978), where a similar resentment of academic research's comparatively stringent ethical principles has been expressed.[9]

But this logic should be rejected for two reasons: first, there is something fundamentally different about supermarket chains using experiments on nonconsenting shoppers to determine whether they are more likely to buy a product priced at $0.99 than $1.05 and a social scientist approaching an NGO or a village with an experiment that she seeks to implement. Upon entering a store, the shopper submits himself to the rules of the store, but the same is not necessarily true when an experimenter manipulates incentives in a real-world context (especially when she experiments on people outside of her own community, which is generally the case). Second, and more important, many research agendas are undergirded by a desire to promote positive changes in the world—higher levels of schooling for girls, less discrimination in the political sphere, human rights for the world's poorest—a motivation that would be compromised if the standards of the *Belmont Report* were neglected in favor of the standards of the business world.

In a second, related objection, some researchers contend that informed consent is unnecessary when the risks of a particular experiment are negligible. For example, it could be argued that there is absolutely no risk involved in nonpartisan get-out-the-vote experiments in which some people receive automated telephone calls reminding them to vote (the treatment) or to recycle (the control) (see the experiment in Gerber et al. 2009). In these risk-free scenarios experimenters argue that requiring informed consent would be an onerous bureaucratic hardship that hinders the advance of social scientific knowledge for no particular reason. But calculations of risk are independent of respect for individual autonomy, and the principle of respect for persons demands that people's judgment be respected regardless of the potential costs or benefits that the research exacts upon them. In other words, respecting a person's autonomy requires that participation in research be voluntary, and so, independent of the costs or benefits of the research, the researcher does not get to choose for the volunteer how much risk is tolerable.

Moreover, it should be noted that many people choose not to volunteer when asked to participate in a randomized experiment: were they asked for consent, some people would say no. Levitt and List write, "It is commonly known in the field of clinical drug trials that persuading patients to participate in randomized studies is much harder than persuading them to participate in non-randomized studies. . . . The same problem applies to social experiments, as evidenced by the difficulties that can be encountered when recruiting decentralized bureaucracies to administer the random treatment" (6). The authors identify this as the problem of randomization bias—in which the experimental pool is not representative of the population because some types choose not to participate. They advocate covert experimentation as a way to circumvent this type of bias. Advocating for covert experimentation does not seem like a tenable long-term solution to the problem of unwilling volunteers. Precisely because randomization bias indicates that people do in fact have preferences over their involvement in experimental social science, this means that no matter how great the potential gains to the research community, ethical research cannot put the prerogatives of the researcher over a person's right to volunteer or to decline to participate.

3.2. Beneficence

The second principle outlined in the *Belmont Report* is the principle of beneficence. Beneficence is an obligation that researchers have to secure the well-being of their subjects, which includes the obligation not to expose subjects to "more than minimal risk without immediate prospect of direct benefit" (*Belmont Report*: 6). In particular, the researcher must consider the nature and degree of risk to which the subject is exposed, the condition of the population that will be involved in the research, and the level of anticipated benefits for that population. In biomedical research, extensive pretesting (for example, on animals) is performed before a drug is approved for human testing,[10] and thus a researcher should have a good idea of what types of risk a given subject will face.

But the concept of risk may be more difficult to assess in social science field experiments than in biomedical or behavioral research. One reason is that social experiments take place in real-world settings, that is, within thick social, economic, and political contexts, the nuances of which often elude even a well-informed researcher. To give a concrete example, it is often argued that women who do not earn wages do not have bargaining power in the household equal to their wage-earning husbands, fathers and brothers. Targeted microcredit—small-principal group lending that is marketed to women in the developing world—has long been hailed as offering a path to women's empowerment by giving women access to capital of their own (e.g., Karlan et al. 2006).[11] At first glance, then, microcredit programs and the numerous field experiments structured around them seem unproblematically beneficent: women are subordinated because they have no capital; give them capital and right this social wrong.

But long-standing entitlements, patriarchy included, do not die swiftly. Programs that undermine age-old hierarchies in the family may provoke the violent behavior the program hoped to avoid (Schuler et al. 1998). Indeed, anthropological work from Bangladesh shows that, contrary to targeted microcredit programs' intentions, husbands are often the primary users of loans. More worrisome still, women who participate in microlending programs face increased risks of personal victimization after gaining this new financial access (Rahman 1999). The point to emphasize here is that while the risks of certain experimental and development initiatives might appear minimal, experiments conducted in complex social contexts involve risks that are unpredictable and even unknowable ex ante.[12]

Applying this logic to another context, consider a recent article by Paluck and Green (2009). The authors assert that social atrocities like the Rwandan genocide are facilitated by a political culture in which dissent is frowned upon and where authority is blindly followed. They argue that Rwandan society would be better off if more dissenting opinions were held and voiced. The authors carry out a field experiment in Rwanda to test whether radio soap operas that feature dynamic plots and dissenting voices inject this language into the discourse of those who listen to the program. The experimental results indicate that the group that received the dissent-imbued treatment was in fact more likely to voice opposing opinions and less likely to turn to authority figures to solve conflicts. The paper, which certainly strives to promote the widely held democratic value of contestation within Rwandan society, fails to consider the possibility that the experiment might carry some physical risk to the people who participate or invite violence in the community as the structure of its social fabric is rewoven.

But if extending microcredit to women can increase violence against them, it is not inconceivable that introducing the language of dissent in a postgenocidal society might carry similar risks. I should note that, to their distinct credit, Paluck and Green take care in appendix I (638–39) to discuss the "Procedural and Ethical" details of the experiment.[13] However, their discussion does not ask whether introducing the language of dissent brings any new risks to the community; their concerns were limited to the (important) issue of whether participants might experience psychological trauma when they speak of the genocide.[14] The issue to highlight is that no matter how well intentioned the researchers, which Paluck and Green certainly are, there are many contingencies in social environments. Understanding the risks involved in an intervention, in line with the *Belmont Report*'s principle of beneficence, is therefore not an easy task.

Besides unforeseen risks, a second concern raised by the principle of beneficence in a field experimental context is the uneven allocation of goods both within and between communities. In recent reviews of the emerging field experiments literature, both Banerjee and Duflo (chapter 4 in this book) and Humphreys and Weinstein (2009) acknowledge that many experiments necessitate doling out goodies to some and not to others. Both papers note that in many situations the researcher must confront and deal with bad feelings or jealousy among participants. According to Humphreys and Weinstein, jealousy is problematic because "differences in outcomes may be interpreted as evidence for a positive program effect on the treated community even if all that has occurred is an adverse effect on the control community" (2009: 375). In other words, jealousy is acknowledged as a potential problem for field experiments because it may alter behavior in the control group and confound precise measurement. But this rationale ignores the reasons that jealousy arises in the first place as well as its ethical implications: a randomized social intervention benefits some villages or villagers and not others. Even if this benefit is small, it is difficult to know ahead of time how it will be perceived or how long the changes in behavior it occasions will persist.

Banerjee and Duflo address this issue with the following advice: "Implementers may find that the easiest way to present [the project] to the community is to say that an expansion of the program is planned for the control areas in the future (especially when such is indeed the case, as in phased-in design)" (chapter 4 in this book, p. 101). Note first that the authors' suggestion that control villages should be told that the project will eventually be extended to them "especially" when it is true implies that in some cases it might make sense to mislead the villagers, suggesting that they will eventually receive some treatment even when the researchers know the program will never be extended. Banerjee and Duflo's work has been some of the most important in development economics over the last twenty years—theirs is both pathbreaking and compassionate scholarship that has affected development initiatives and undoubtedly done much good in the world. But their statement in the above quotation, besides being problematic in its own right, reveals a deeper issue: even when researchers are aware of the many levels on which social conflict can be introduced by experimental interventions, they treat it as a methodological rather than an ethical difficulty.

Moving forward, it is important that concerns about what is ethical not be solely interpreted as methodological problems. For this to happen, researchers will have to actually wrestle with the principle of beneficence. They need a fuller sense of the context and a more thoroughgoing commitment to understanding the risks of their research in these contexts. Banerjee and Duflo (chapter 4 in this book) claim that while scientifically interesting, measuring equilibrium effects can be extremely difficult. The principle of beneficence requires that we at least try.

Contrasted with biomedical and behavioral research, where community-wide equilibrium effects may be extremely rare, it is clear that field experiments pose particular challenges for understanding and communicating risk, especially when people who are not chosen as participants may be affected. If this is true, there can be little confidence that community-wide risks can be adequately accounted for in the design of field experiments. Perhaps by teaming up with ethnographers and social workers, field experimenters will be able to command a more thorough understanding of possible downstream effects of their interventions, that is, of the effects that an intervention might have on social processes aside from those that are part of the study.[15]

3.3. Justice

The last principle elaborated in the *Belmont Report* concerns justice: "Who ought to receive the benefits of research and who ought to bear its burdens?" The report acknowledges that there are competing ethical principles of resource distribution that could reasonably be called on when considering the benefits of research, but it emphasizes the following issues: first, the benefits of research should not accrue disproportionately to a class or race that does not itself participate in the research.[16]

And, second, "the selection of research subjects needs to be scrutinized in order to determine whether some classes (e.g., welfare patients, particular racial and ethnic minorities, or persons confined to institutions) are being systematically selected simply because of their easy availability, their compromised position, or their manipulability, rather than for reasons directly related to the problem being studied" (*Belmont Report*: 7).

As to which populations will benefit from field experimental research, there is good reason to believe that most experimental initiatives in developing countries are intended both to understand and to alleviate poverty. Indeed, results-based development initiatives are concerned primarily with how to allocate the tremendous amount of money that goes to international aid in a socially desirable and economically efficient way. Hence, many experiments are designed to evaluate the efficacy of a program for the people who are beneficiaries of the program. Some of this research has uncovered evidence that certain development practices are inefficacious. For example, Gugerty and Kremer (2008) find that development aid that is channeled to women's organizations in Kenya has the undesirable consequence of pushing less-educated, poorer women out of leadership positions. The authors argue that what seems good in theory (more money to community organizations) might be harmful in practice. In biomedical trials justice often entails ceasing the trial immediately if a drug is found to be harmful to participants, or making the drug available to all participants if the beneficial effects were found to be overwhelmingly clear. By analogy, the Gugerty and Kremer findings might, under the principle of justice, require that the funding be redirected toward areas that better serve the purpose of the initiative.

But though much of the field experimental work in the developing world has hitherto been associated with program evaluation, in other words, with measurement of treatment effects of public policy initiatives, most academic researchers would like to shift the trajectory toward initiatives that they propose themselves (Banerjee and Duflo, chapter 4 in this book; Humphreys and Weinstein 2009). As both Deaton (2009) and Heckman and Smith (1995) argue, academics cannot be concerned solely with "what" works from a policy standpoint, but also with "why" it works. They claim that academic research is not meant only to find out how to make some desired end come about through some available means, the goal of public policy evaluations, but rather to uncover the social and behavioral characteristics that undergird human interaction.

To the extent that field experimental research becomes detached from policy evaluation, complying with the principle of justice will require strong defenses that hypotheses being tested are specific to the population under study. Selection of subjects from either economically vulnerable groups (who may be more willing to participate because of the relative value of money or goods-in-kind offered by researchers) or politically vulnerable groups (who are less likely to challenge the authority and motives of a research scientist) will demand heightened scrutiny.[17] These concerns are particularly relevant for field experiments in developing countries, where subject populations are often both politically and economically vulnerable.

This is not an idle worry. In a frank admission, Banerjee and Duflo note that the particular conditions of people in developing countries make them good subjects for experimental research: "Limited government budgets and diverse actions by many small NGOs mean that villages or schools in most developing countries are used to the fact that some areas receive certain programs whereas others do not. . . . *When the control areas are given the explanation that the program has enough budget for a certain number of schools only, they typically agree that a lottery is a fair way to allocate those limited resources. They are often used to such arbitrariness and so randomization appears both transparent and legitimate*" (Banerjee and Duflo, chapter 4 in this book, 101; emphasis added).

The authors assert that because people in developing countries are used to "arbitrariness" in decision making, they will likely accept the randomization protocol without too much fuss. Said somewhat differently, the fact that life is unfair for the poor in the third world means subjects might not only agree to participate in a randomized experiment, but also will believe that randomization is a "fair" way to allocate resources.[18] Moreover, as a telling footnote reminds us, "It should also be noted that the lower cost of the programs and working with NGO partners greatly expand the feasible set of experiments in development, compared with what has been feasible in the United States" (Banerjee and Duflo, chapter 4 in this book, 113). By these lights, experimentation in the tropics is pursued not only because these populations tend not to be hostile toward researchers, but also because the costs of studying them are lower.[19] These sentiments clearly violate the spirit of the *Belmont Report*. To put it bluntly, taking advantage of populations' contextually induced vulnerability to random interventions and the reduced expenses that result from their relative poverty is simply and obviously unethical.

There are many instances in which a research question absolutely must be answered outside of the researcher's own community. For example, in a series of laboratory-like experiments in the field in fifteen small-scale communities around the world (hunter-gatherer groups, tribes, and so on), Henrich et al. (2001) study whether the assumptions of the neoclassical self-interested actor hold up in different social and economic contexts. A large body of research based on experiments with undergraduate students in the United States and around the world shows that the neoclassical self-interested actor may be the exception rather than the rule. In their study Henrich et al. (2001) hypothesize that these results will hold up across cultures and seek to test this in many different social contexts. Their research question thus drives the selection of their study populations, not the other way around. It is important to ask, then, in light of the justice principle elaborated in the *Belmont Report*, why certain projects must be carried out on populations far away from the researcher's home. In the very cities of American universities there are low take-up rates of social services, collective action failures of trash pickup, low savings, and other phenomena that might be of interest to scholars. A good justification, not just one of convenience or expense, should therefore be given for why a particular research question cannot be answered other than by experimenting on the economically and politically vulnerable populations of the developing world.[20]

Finally, the principle of justice serves to remind researchers that they are often in a powerful position relative to those they study. When an experimental intervention has some monetary or in-kind benefit associated with the treatment, social scientists should recall that uneven access to resources and the ability to decide who gets what and when are fundamental privileges of power. When social scientists enter into research relationships with governmental officials, NGO employees, and villagers the world over, they must consider the nature of their power in these contexts. Their power, which stems from their role as liaisons between cultures, also exists because research results influence international aid, public health initiatives, and foreign policy in nontrivial ways. This is true not only when academic researchers partner with organizations like USAID, the World Bank, and local governments; it is also true because their research, which is open to consumption by journalists and public intellectuals, can influence the views of the public at large.

A skeptical reader might argue that power differentials arise in all contexts in which a researcher studies vulnerable populations at home or abroad and that it is independent of the experimental research design. This is true: ethnographers who study tribes in the Brazilian rainforest, sociologists who study deviant behavior, and tenured laboratory experimenters working with undergraduate subjects might all be relatively advantaged vis-à-vis their research subjects. But field experiments are set apart because, as I argued in section 2, the object of the experiment is often not to observe people in their day-to-day lives but to intervene in a purposeful manner to affect social change. Moreover, many field experiments, especially those in which a researcher has partnered with an NGO or a development organization, are meant to actually change people's behavior in a direction that the organization and researcher deem more socially or economically desirable. This is a very different model from that followed by a participant observer—it is closer to social engineering than to social studies. Justice should therefore be a primary concern for experimenters who seek ethical interaction with their research populations.

4. Conclusion

Field experiments differ fundamentally from laboratory experiments or participant-observer field research in ways that compromise the ethical integrity of the method. The adage "No causation without manipulation" requires that experimenters alter something in a real-life setting in order to recover unbiased causal estimates of social relationships. The field experimental method also differs from biomedical research because, in the thick social contexts where they are carried out, community-level risks become a real concern. I have understood these differences as a call to reinterpret the principles of the *Belmont Report* with an eye to guiding ethical use of this method of social research. The principles—respect for human dignity, beneficence, and justice—should be adhered to in good faith by all field experimenters. Importantly, this is not to preserve the integrity of the document but rather because the principles are based on values that most contemporary researchers share.

Where ethical considerations might pose problems for experimenters, for example, if being observed influences behavior (the Hawthorne effect) or if knowledge of the randomization leads to few volunteers (randomization bias), experimenters must be more creative. Measurement in medical trials was compromised when physicians and patients were aware of treatment assignments. This problem is commonly addressed by double blinding, a practice that leaves physicians, nurses, and administrators in the dark about treatment assignments. Patients, for their part, consent to being in the trial, even if they are given a placebo rather than the treatment. To maintain high ethical standards, field experiments could also utilize placebo groups. This would allow for informed consent—volunteers agree to participate in the experiment—though they won't know what group they are in. Note that informed consent here does not require that participants know up-front what is being measured, as people can reasonably commit to not knowing the object of study while agreeing to participate in the study. Nevertheless, this commitment should be countered with commitments by the researcher: to bring the participants in on the study's purpose after the trial is over and to share research results after the report is finished. This common practice in anthropological work would be a welcome addition in the context of many research contexts.

Researchers also need to do a better job of understanding the potential downstream consequences—the community- and individual-level risks—associated with field experiments. This requires knowing a good deal about the people and groups that are being studied and may necessitate teaming with ethnographers or social workers to fully think through the ways in which perceptions of fairness and jealousy that are potentially induced by the experiment might pull at the social fabric in the community under study. Interestingly, where field experiments have been thought to offer a single methodological key to social scientific problems, the ethical challenges of the research may require working with scholars in other fields with other skill sets. It seems that mixed methods are here to stay.

Finally, in terms of justice, high standards must be set for a defense of the chosen subject population. The chosen population must be direct potential recipients of the research; thus, there have to be very clear reasons why the poor or the vulnerable in ones' own community or abroad are the subjects under study. That these groups are cheaper to study—either because money goes a long way in poor countries or because the gate-keepers are more lax about access to their citizens, subjects, or community members—is very far from the mark of ethical best practices.

In closing, I want to stress that the objective of this chapter is not to claim that more stringent regulations should be imposed by Institutional Review Boards across the country. Perhaps they should, but my concern lies elsewhere. I seek, rather, to convince us to be socially conscious in our role as experimenters. We need not think that the principles of the *Belmont Report* are barriers to scientific discoveries. Rather, adherence to its principles allows our values to be borne out within our research agendas. Scholars of development, governance, ethnic politics, and collective action should be particularly attuned to the problems that arise when some voices are given too little weight relative to others. Therefore, insisting on informed consent, full assessment of risk, and nonexploitative participant selection procedures are minimal steps toward ensuring that experimental social science lives up to its noblest aspirations.

Acknowledgments

This essay has benefited enormously from the guidance and encouragement of Elisabeth Wood, Nick Sambanis, Susan Stokes, Donald Green, and Matthew Kocher. I would also like to thank Peter Aronow, Blake Emerson, Navid Hassanpour, Malte Lierl, Rohit Naimpally, Erin Pineda, Joshua Simon, Alison Sovey Carnegie, and Rory Truex for their thoughtful comments on earlier versions of the chapter. Many of the counterarguments that appear here are the result of conversations with Dean Karlan, Donald Green, and Abhijit Banerjee, and several anonymous reviewers whose strong positions have, I hope, been given adequate audience here.

NOTES

1. I am not talking about the use of deception as a tactic within an experimental framework, whereby participants are misled as part of the experiment itself. The concern is rather with deception that is used before the participant has agreed to participate in the project. More on this below.

2. This leave-no-trace heuristic for ethnographic work is accompanied by a large body of post-fieldwork reflections on ethical issues (Whyte 1988; Barnes 1977: 34).

3. In his book, Milgram describes his inquiry as stemming from Hannah Arendt's work on the trial of Adolph Eichmann (1974: 175–78). His theoretical question asks how a seemingly ordinary person like Eichmann could carry out tasks that he knew led to the extermination of many of Europe's Jewish residents. The answer that Milgram's experiment provides is that ordinary people might do abhorrent things in the face of authority.

4. Patten also contends that the experiment is unethical because participants are encouraged to do something that that is "shockingly" immoral (1977: 350), a concern I would also raise in a discussion of recent work in political science, such as Lagunes et al. (2010).

5. Skloot (2010) reports on the tale of Henrietta Lacks, a black woman who died of cervical cancer in 1952. Her "immortal" cancer cells were the first ones scientists were ever able to grow in the lab, a process that contributed, among other things, to the polio vaccine (2010: 188). There are ethical and legal questions about the proper remuneration for the original owners of cells, but for our purposes the disturbing ethical question comes much later, in 1973, when the First International Workshop on Human Gene Mapping, held at Yale, decided to procure blood samples from the surviving children of Henrietta. A postdoctoral fellow carried out orders to get the blood samples from the Lacks children, with no instructions to inform the family of why the samples were needed (182). The unfortunate Lacks children, themselves having less than primary school education, thought they were talking to doctors in order to be tested for the cancer that killed their mothers. It is clear in Skloot's account that the family was deliberately misled and that the scientists that handled this case were not forthcoming with answers about their research and their need for the Lacks's involvement. Needless to say, the Lacks children were not treated with the dignity befitting human beings.

6. The Hawthorne effect was discovered in 1939 during a sociological study of the Western Electric Plant outside of Chicago. Barnes concludes that the discovery "was the first significant nail in the coffin of the natural science paradigm as used in social science, for it drew attention to the fact that the interaction between scientist and citizen is two-way, and that the process of inquiry itself has consequences for both parties" (Barnes 1977: 46).

7. Interestingly, there have been many discussions in the field of psychology as to whether it is ethical to deceive research participants that participate in laboratory experiments. Sometimes deception itself has been the object of inquiry, but often it is used so that participants do not alter their behavior based on a desire to help the researcher. In an interesting review of the deception question, Bonetti (1998) argues that deception should be part of the experimental economists' toolbox, but, more important, he also gives evidence that participants who are *not* deceived do not act much differently than those who are. This relates to my discussion because the experimenter's worry that informed consent will bias behavior may be unfounded. Thus

there is at least some evidence that forgoing informed consent may not be justified on measurement grounds.

8. I am indebted to Dean Karlan for raising this objection in conversation.

9. Gray notes that "one can still find an academic surgeon wistfully noting that the doctrine of informed consent does not apply to 'contractual arrangements in fields other than medicine; where caveat emptor remains the guide'" (Gray 1978: 40).

10. Some will argue that this preliminary testing on animals is itself unethical, but for present purposes we can table that very interesting issue.

11. Note that microlending programs have progressed *pari passu* with the new experimental development economics, and all the key ingredients are at play here: an initiative that has public benefit, science that satisfies the "facts-based" project of development, and, another undiscussed benefit, opportunity for profit, such as those made by the Grameen Bank, whose founder, Muhammad Yunus, won the Nobel Peace Prize in 2006.

12. An experimental intervention that had widespread benefits to participants and the community at large can be found in a now-famous paper by Miguel and Kremer (2004). The authors found that giving deworming drugs to children in some schools reduced the overall incidence of intestinal worms in the surrounding areas. In the parlance of economics, the deworming intervention was accompanied by a positive externality in that many who did not bear the cost of the treatment nevertheless gained from it. The benefit of the intervention, therefore, accrued both to subjects and to the community. But this may not always be the case.

13. Paluck and Green's appendix I also discusses their procedure for informed consent (verbal) and the details surrounding their use of covert observation, where the behavior of participants was recorded after the experiment was supposedly over. The authors write, "Widely adopted ethical standards for IRBs state that recording behaviors anonymously (without recording the names of people enacting the behavior) does not require informed consent or debriefing" (2009: 39). I should point out that IRBs are *legal* boards that are primarily designed to shield the researcher and the university from legal entanglements. Many do have designs to ethical considerations, but my discussion from above, which highlights the respect for human dignity and autonomy, would preclude deliberately deceiving people about when their behavior was being recorded, regardless of the anonymity of the data.

14. To this end the authors procured funding to serve as an "active control" of counseling in case such trauma surfaces.

15. One would typically use the term *general equilibrium effect* to describe the influence that a shock in one part of an economic system has on other elements of that system, but, as Banerjee and Duflo (chapter 4 in this book) point out, economists think of multiple markets when they conceive of a general equilibrium. Since the effects we are in interested with field experiments might not be in a separate market per se but in the changing social dynamics of a community, the authors prefer the term *equilibrium effects*. It would be even more precise to think of experiments as causing disequilibrium effects, in that experimental interventions are designed to take

relationships and structures that are, as it were, in some sort of equilibrium and upset them in order to see how people respond.

16. The principle of justice is therefore deliberately meant to discourage situations like the one in which rural men of color in Tuskegee, Alabama, are used as subjects in a study whose results might never be available to members of their communities (let alone to themselves).

17. In written comments to the author, Elizabeth Wood noted that the justice principle is sometimes interpreted to mean "that certain populations should not be excluded from experiments, and thus from the potential benefits (a critique that arose from gendered and racial bias in some medical experiments)." This is an interesting argument; it might be said that the "benefits" of research accrue to women and children, often the target populations of this research.

18. Another striking feature of the above quotation is that villagers are told that randomization is a "fair way" to allocate resources, when in fact resources are only allocated randomly so as to gain scientific leverage over the implemented program. At the most basic level, misrepresentation of the purposes of randomization as serving fundamental fairness rather than scientific measurement raises concerns within the principle of justice, which states that "equals ought to be treated equally" (*Belmont Report*: 6). In other words, participants should not be deliberately misled for reasons that are outside the research question.

19. The use of the word *tropics* here is an allusion to Deaton (2009), meant to highlight the bad taste that remains after confronting these types of arguments.

20. This is not to say that a similar problem does not arise when research is conducted on vulnerable populations in the United States. It does. I focus on developing countries because the locus of experimental work has shifted toward these areas, though there has been much discussion in the sociological literature already about this type of work in the United States.

6

INSTRUMENTS, RANDOMIZATION, AND LEARNING ABOUT DEVELOPMENT

Angus Deaton

1. Introduction

The effectiveness of development assistance is a topic of great public interest. Much of the public debate among noneconomists takes it for granted that, if the funds were made available, poverty would be eliminated (Pogge 2005; Singer 2004), and at least some economists agree (Sachs 2005, 2008). Others, most notably Easterly (2006, 2009), are deeply skeptical, a position that has been forcefully argued at least since Bauer (1971, 1981). Few academic economists or political scientists agree with Sachs's views, but there is a wide range of intermediate positions, well assembled by Easterly (2008). The debate runs the gamut from the macro (can foreign assistance raise growth rates and eliminate poverty?) to the micro (what sorts of projects are likely to be effective? should aid focus on electricity and roads or on the provision of schools and clinics or vaccination campaigns?). Here I shall be concerned with both the macro and micro kinds of assistance. I shall have very little to say about what actually works and what does not; but it is clear from the literature that we do not know. Instead, my main concern is with how we should go about finding out whether and how assistance works and with methods for gathering evidence and learning from it in a scientific way that has some hope of leading to the progressive accumulation of useful knowledge about development. I am not an econometrician, but I believe that econometric methodology needs to be assessed, not only by methodologists, but also by those who are concerned with the substance of the issue. Only they (we) are in a position to tell when something has gone wrong with the application of econometric methods, not because they are incorrect given their assumptions, but because their assumptions do not apply or because they are incorrectly conceived for the problem at hand. Or at least that is my excuse for meddling in these matters.

Any analysis of the extent to which foreign aid has increased economic growth in recipient countries immediately confronts the familiar problem of simultaneous causality; the effect of aid on growth, if any, will be disguised by effects running in the opposite direction, from poor economic performance to compensatory or humanitarian aid. It is not obvious how to disentangle these effects, and some have argued that the question is unanswerable and that econometric studies of it should be abandoned. Certainly, the econometric studies that use international evidence to examine aid effectiveness currently have low professional status. Yet it cannot be right to give up on the issue. There is no general or public understanding that nothing can be said, and to give up the econometric analysis is simply to abandon precise statements for loose and unconstrained histories of episodes selected to support the position of the speaker.

The analysis of aid effectiveness typically uses cross country growth regressions with the simultaneity between aid and growth dealt with using instrumental variable methods. I shall argue in the next section that there has been a good deal of misunderstanding in the literature about the use of instrumental variables. Econometric analysis has changed its focus over the years, away from the analysis of models derived from theory toward much looser specifications that are statistical representations of program evaluation. With this shift, instrumental variables have moved from being solutions to a well-defined problem of inference to being devices that induce quasi-randomization. Old and new understandings of instruments coexist, leading to errors, misunderstandings, and confusion as well as unfortunate and unnecessary rhetorical barriers between disciplines working on the same problems. These abuses of technique have contributed to a general skepticism about the ability of econometric analysis to answer these big questions.

A similar state of affairs exists in the microeconomic area, in the analysis of the effectiveness of individual programs and projects, such as the construction of infrastructure (dams, roads, water supply, electricity) and in the delivery of services (education, health, policing). There is frustration with aid organizations, particularly the World Bank, for allegedly failing to learn from its projects and to build up a systematic catalog of what works and what does not. In addition, some of the skepticism about macro econometrics extends to micro econometrics, so that there has been a movement away from such methods toward randomized controlled trials. According to Esther Duflo, one of the leaders of the new movement in development, "Creating a culture in which rigorous randomized evaluations are promoted, encouraged, and financed has the potential to revolutionize social policy during the 21st century, just as randomized trials revolutionized medicine during the 20th," this from a 2004 *Lancet* editorial headed "The World Bank is finally embracing science."

In section 4 of this chapter, I shall argue that *under ideal circumstances*, randomized evaluations of projects are useful for obtaining a convincing estimate of the average effect of a program or project. The price for this success is a focus that is too narrow and too local to tell us "what works" in development, to design policy, or to advance scientific knowledge about development processes. Project evaluations, whether using randomized controlled trials or nonexperimental methods, are unlikely to disclose the secrets of development nor, unless they are guided by theory that is itself open to revision, are they likely to be the basis for a cumulative research program that might lead to a better understanding of development. This argument applies *a fortiori* to instrumental variables strategies that are aimed at generating quasi-experiments; the value of econometric methods cannot and should not be assessed by how closely they approximate randomized controlled trials. Following Cartwright (2007a, b), I argue that evidence from randomized controlled trials can have no special priority. Randomization is not a gold standard because "there is no gold standard" (Cartwright 2007a). Randomized controlled trials cannot automatically trump other evidence, they do not occupy any special place in some hierarchy of evidence, nor does it make sense to refer to them as hard while other methods are soft. These rhetorical devices are just that; metaphor is not argument, nor does endless repetition make it so.

More positively, I shall argue that the analysis of projects needs to be refocused toward the investigation of potentially generalizable mechanisms that explain why and in what contexts projects can be expected to work. The best of the experimental work in development economics already does so because its practitioners are too talented to be bound by their own methodological prescriptions. Yet there would be much to be said for doing so more openly. I concur with Pawson and Tilley (1997), who argue that thirty years of project evaluation in sociology, education, and criminology were largely unsuccessful because they focused on *whether* projects worked instead of on *why* they worked. In economics, warnings along the same lines have been repeatedly given by James Heckman (see particularly Heckman 1992 and Heckman and Smith 1995), and much of what I have to say is a recapitulation of his arguments.

The chapter is organized as follows: section 2 lays out some econometric preliminaries concerning instrumental variables and the vexed question of exogeneity; section 3 is about aid and growth; section 4 is about randomized controlled trials; section 5 is about using empirical evidence and where we should go now.

2. Instruments, Identification, and the Meaning of Exogeneity

It is useful to begin with a simple and familiar econometric model that I can use to illustrate the differences between different flavors of econometric practice; this has nothing to do with economic development, but it is simple and easy to contrast with the development practice that I wish to discuss. In contrast to the models I will discuss later, I think of this as a model in the spirit of the Cowles Foundation. It is the simplest possible Keynesian macroeconomic model of national income determination taken from once-standard econometrics textbooks. There are two equations that together comprise a complete macroeconomic system. The first equation is a consumption function, in which aggregate consumption is a linear function of aggregate national income, while the second is the national income accounting identity that says that income is the sum of consumption and investment. I write the system in standard notation as

$$C = \alpha + \beta Y + u, \tag{1}$$

$$Y \equiv C + I. \tag{2}$$

According to (1), consumers choose the level of aggregate consumption with reference to their income, while in (2), investment is set by the "animal spirits" of entrepreneurs in some way that is outside of the model. No modern macroeconomist would take this model seriously, though the simple consumption function is an ancestor of more satisfactory and complete modern formulations; in particular, we can think of it (or at least its descendents) as being derived from a coherent model of intertemporal choice. Similarly, modern versions would postulate some theory for what determines investment I; here it is simply taken as given and assumed to be orthogonal to the consumption disturbance u.

In this model, consumption and income are simultaneously determined so that, in particular, a stochastic realization of u—consumers displaying animal spirits of their own—will affect not only C, but also Y through equation (2), so that there is a positive correlation between u and Y. As a result, ordinary least squares estimation of (1) will lead to upwardly biased and inconsistent estimates of the parameter β.

This simultaneity problem can be dealt with in a number of ways. One is to solve (1) and (2), to get the reduced form equations

$$C = \frac{\alpha}{1-\beta} + \frac{\beta}{1-\beta} I + \frac{u}{1-\beta}, \tag{3}$$

$$Y = \frac{\alpha}{1-\beta} + \frac{I}{1-\beta} + \frac{u}{1-\beta}. \tag{4}$$

Both of these equations can be consistently estimated by ordinary least squares (OLS), and it is easy to show that the same estimates of α and β will be obtained from either one. An alternative method of estimation is to focus on the consumption function (1) and to use our knowledge of (2) to note that investment can be used as an instrumental variable (IV) for income. In the IV regression, there is a "first stage" regression in which income is regressed on investment; this is identical to equation (4), which is part of the reduced form. In the second stage, consumption is regressed on the predicted value of income from (4). In this simple case, the IV estimate of β is identical to the estimate from the reduced form. This simple model may not be a very good model, but it *is* a model, if only a primitive one.

I now leap forward sixty years and consider an apparently similar setup, again using an absurdly simple specification. The World Bank (let us imagine) is interested in whether to advise the government of China to build more railway stations as part of its poverty reduction strategy. The bank economists write down an econometric model in which the poverty head count ratio in city c is taken to be a linear function of an indicator R of whether or not the city has a railway station,

$$P_c = \gamma + \theta R_c + v_c, \tag{5}$$

where θ (I hesitate to call it a parameter) indicates the effect—presumably negative—of infrastructure (here a railway station) on poverty. While we cannot expect to get useful estimates of θ from OLS estimation of (5)—railway stations may be built to serve more prosperous cities, they are rarely built in deserts where there are no people, or there may be "third factors" that influence both—this is seen as a "technical problem" for which there is a wide range of econometric treatments, including, of course, instrumental variables.

We no longer have the reduced form of the previous model to guide us, but if we can find an instrument Z that is correlated with whether a town has a railway station, but uncorrelated with v, we can do the same calculations and obtain a consistent estimate. For the record, I write this equation

$$R_c = \phi + \varphi Z_c + \eta_c. \tag{6}$$

Good candidates for Z might be indicators of whether the city has been designated by the government of China as belonging to a special infrastructure development area, or perhaps an earthquake that conveniently destroyed a selection of railway stations, or even the existence of river confluence near the city, since rivers were an early source of power and railways served the power-based industries. I am making fun, but not much. And these instruments all have the real merit that there is some mechanism linking them to whether or not the town has a railway station, something that is not automatically guaranteed by the instrument being correlated with R and uncorrelated with v (see, for example, Reiss and Wolak 2007: 4296–98).

My main argument is that the two econometric structures, in spite of their resemblance and the fact that IV techniques can be used for both, are in fact quite different. In particular, the IV procedures that work for the effect of national income on consumption are unlikely to give useful results for the effect of railway stations on poverty. To explain the differences, I begin with the language. In the original example, the reduced form is a fully specified system, since it is derived from a notionally complete model of the determination of income. Consumption and income are treated symmetrically and appear as such in the reduced form equations (3) and (4). In contemporary examples, such as the railways, there is no complete theoretical system and there is no symmetry. Instead, we have a "main" equation (5), which used to be the "structural" equation (1). We also have a "first-stage" equation, which is the regression of railway stations on the instrument. The now rarely considered regression of the variable of interest on the instrument, here of poverty on earthquakes or on river confluences, is nowadays referred to as *the* reduced form, although it was originally one equation of a multiple equation reduced form—equation (6) is also part of the reduced form—within which it had no special significance. These language shifts sometimes cause confusion, but they are not the most important differences between the two systems.

The crucial difference is that the relationship between railways and poverty is not a model at all, unlike the consumption model which embodied a(n admittedly crude) theory of income determination. While it is clearly *possible* that the construction of a railway station will reduce poverty, there are many possible mechanisms, some of which will work in one context and not in another. In consequence, θ is unlikely to be constant over different cities, nor can its variation be usefully thought of as random variation that is uncorrelated with anything else of interest. Instead, it is precisely the variation in θ that encapsulates the poverty reduction mechanisms that ought to be the main objects of our enquiry. Instead, the equation of interest—the so-called main equation (5)—is thought of as a representation of something more akin to an experiment or a biomedical trial, in which some cities get "treated" with a station, and some do not. The role of econometric analysis is not, as in the Cowles example, to estimate and investigate a casual model, but "to create an analogy, perhaps forced, between an observational study and an experiment" (Freedman 2006: 691).

One immediate task is to recognize and somehow deal with the variation in θ, which is typically referred to as the heterogeneity problem in the literature. The obvious way is to define a parameter of interest in a way that corresponds to something we want to know for policy evaluation—perhaps the average effect on poverty over some group of cities—and then devise an appropriate estimation strategy. However, this step is often skipped in practice, perhaps because of a mistaken belief that the main equation (5) is a structural equation in which θ is a constant, so that the analysis can go immediately to the choice of instrument Z, over which a great deal of imagination and ingenuity is often exercised. Such ingenuity is often needed because it is difficult simultaneously to satisfy both of the standard criteria required for an instrument, that it be correlated with R_c and uncorrelated with V_c. However, if heterogeneity is indeed present, even satisfying the standard criteria is not sufficient to prevent the probability limit of the IV estimator depending on the choice of instrument (Heckman 1997). Without explicit prior consideration of the effect of the instrument choice on the parameter being estimated, such a procedure is effectively the opposite of standard statistical practice, in which a parameter of interest is defined first, followed by an estimator that delivers that parameter. Instead, we have a procedure in which the choice of the instrument, which is guided by criteria designed for a situation in which there is no heterogeneity, is implicitly allowed to determine the parameter of interest. This goes beyond the old story of looking for an object where the light is strong enough to see; rather, we have at least some control over the light but choose to let it fall where it may and then proclaim that whatever it illuminates is what we were looking for all along.

Recent econometric analysis has given us a more precise characterization of what we can expect from such a method. In the railway example, where the instrument is the designation of a city as belonging to the "special infrastructure zone," the probability limit of the IV estimator is the average of poverty reduction effects over those cities that were induced to construct a railway station by being so designated. This average is known as the local average treatment effect (LATE), and its recovery by IV estimation requires a number of nontrivial conditions, including, for example, that no cities that would have constructed a railway station are perverse enough to be actually deterred from doing so by the positive designation; see Angrist and Imbens (1994), who established the LATE theorem. The LATE may or may not be a parameter of interest to the

World Bank or the Chinese government, and in general there is no reason to suppose that it will be. For example, the parameter estimated will typically *not* be the average poverty reduction effect over the designated cities, nor will it be the average effect over all cities.

I find it hard to make any sense of the LATE. We are unlikely to learn much about the processes at work if we refuse to say *anything* about what determines θ; heterogeneity is not a technical problem calling for an econometric solution but a reflection of the fact that we have not started on our proper business, which is trying to understand what is going on. If we are as skeptical of the ability of economic theory to deliver useful models as are many applied economists today, the ability to avoid modeling can be seen as an advantage, though it should not be a surprise when such an approach delivers answers that are hard to interpret. Note that my complaint is not with the local nature of the LATE; that property is shared by many estimation strategies, and I will discuss later how we might overcome it. The issue here is rather the average and the lack of an ex ante characterization of the set over which the averaging is done. Angrist and Pischke (2010) have recently claimed that the explosion of instrumental variables methods, including LATE estimation, has led to greater "credibility" in applied econometrics. I am not entirely certain what *credibility* means, but it is surely undermined if the parameter being estimated is not what we want to know. While in many cases what is estimated may be close to, or may contain information about, the parameter of interest, that this is actually so requires demonstration and is not true in general; see Heckman and Urzua (2010), who analyze cases where the LATE is an uninteresting and potentially misleading assemblage of parts of the underlying structure.

There is a related issue that bedevils a good deal of contemporary applied work, which is the understanding of *exogeneity*, a word I have so far avoided. Suppose, for the moment, that the effect of railway stations on poverty is the same in all cities, and we are looking for an instrument which is required to be exogenous in order to consistently estimate θ. According to Merriam-Webster's dictionary, *exogenous* means "caused by factors or an agent from outside the organism or system," and this common usage is often employed in applied work. However, the consistency of IV estimation requires that the instrument be orthogonal to the error term v in the equation of interest, which is not implied by the Merriam-Webster definition (see Leamer 1985: 260). Wooldridge (2002: 50) warns his readers that "you should not rely too much on the meaning of 'endogenous' from other branches of economics" and goes on to note that "the usage in econometrics, while related to traditional definitions, is used broadly to describe any situation where an explanatory variable is correlated with the disturbance." Heckman (2000) suggests using the term *external* (which he traces back to Wright and Frisch in the 1930s) for the Merriam-Webster definition, for variables whose values are not set or caused by the variables in the model and keeping *exogenous* for the orthogonality condition that is required for consistent estimation in this instrumental variable context. The terms are hardly standard, but I adopt them here because I need to make the distinction. The main issue, however, is not the terminology, but that the two concepts be kept distinct, so that we can see when the argument being *offered* is a justification for externality when what is *required* is a justification for exogeneity. An instrument that is external but not exogenous will not yield consistent estimates of the parameter of interest, even when the parameter of interest is a constant.

An alternative approach is to keep the Merriam-Webster (or "other branches of economics") definition for *exogenous* and to require that, in addition to being exogenous, an instrument satisfy the "exclusion restrictions" of being uncorrelated with the disturbance. I have no objection to this usage, though the need to defend these additional restrictions is not always appreciated in practice. Yet exogeneity in this sense has no consequences for the consistency of econometric estimators, and so is effectively meaningless.

Failure to separate externality and exogeneity—or to build a case for the validity of the exclusion restrictions—has caused and continues to cause endless confusion in the applied development (and other) literatures. Natural or geographic variables—distance from the equator (as an instrument for per capita GDP in explaining religiosity) (McCleary and Barro 2006), rivers (as an instrument for the number of school districts in explaining educational outcomes) (Hoxby 2000), land gradient (as an instrument for dam construction in explaining poverty) (Duflo and Pande, 2007), or rainfall (as an instrument for economic growth in explaining civil war) (Miguel, Satyanath, and Sergenti 2004), and the examples could be multiplied ad infinitum—are not affected by the variables being explained and are clearly external. So are historical variables—the mortality of colonial settlers is not influenced by current institutional arrangements in ex-colonial countries (Acemoglu, Johnson, and Robinson 2001), nor does the country's growth rate today influence the identity of their past colonizers (Barro 1998). Whether any of these instruments is exogenous (or satisfies the exclusion restrictions) depends on the specification of the equation of interest and is not guaranteed by its externality. And because exogeneity is an identifying assumption that must be made prior to analysis of the data, empirical tests cannot settle the question. This does not prevent many attempts in the literature, often by misinterpreting a satisfactory *overidentification* test as evidence for valid identification. Such tests can tell us whether estimates change when we select different subsets from a set of possible instruments. While the test is clearly useful and informative, acceptance is consistent with all of the instruments being invalid, while failure is consistent with a subset being correct. Passing an overidentification test does not validate instrumentation.

In my running example, earthquakes and rivers are external to the system and are caused neither by poverty nor by the construction of railway stations, and the designation as an infrastructure zone may also be determined by factors independent of poverty or railways. But even earthquakes (or rivers) are not exogenous if they have an effect on poverty other than through their destruction (or encouragement) of railway stations, as will almost always be the case. The absence of simultaneity does not guarantee exogeneity; exogeneity requires the absence of simultaneity but is not implied by it. Even random numbers—the ultimate external variables—may be endogenous, at least in the presence of heterogeneous effects, if agents choose to accept or reject their assignment in a way that is correlated with the heterogeneity. Again, the example comes from Heckman's (1997) discussion of Angrist's (1990) famous use of draft lottery numbers as an instrumental variable in his analysis of the subsequent earnings of Vietnam veterans.

I can illustrate Heckman's argument using the Chinese railways example with the zone designation as instrument. Rewrite the equation of interest, (5), as

$$P_c = \gamma + \bar{\theta} R_c + w_c = \gamma + \bar{\theta} R_c + \{v_c + (\theta - \bar{\theta})R_c\}, \tag{7}$$

where W_c is defined by the term in curly brackets, and $\bar{\theta}$ is the mean of θ over the cities that get the station so that the compound error term w has mean zero. Suppose the designation as an infrastructure zone is D_c, which takes values 1 or 0, and that the Chinese bureaucracy, persuaded by young development economists, decides to randomize and designates cities by flipping a *yuan*. For consistent estimation of $\bar{\theta}$, we want the covariance of the instrument with the error to be zero. The covariance is

$$E(D_c w_c) = E[(\theta - \bar{\theta})RD] = E[(\theta - \bar{\theta}) \mid D = 1, R = 1]P(D = 1, R = 1), \quad (8)$$

which will be zero if either (a) the average effect of building a railway station on poverty among the cities induced to build one by the designation is the same as the average effect among those who would have built one anyway, or (b) no city not designated builds a railway station. If (b) is not guaranteed by fiat, we cannot suppose that it will otherwise hold, and we might reasonably hope that among the cities who build railway stations, those induced to do so by the designation are those where there is the largest effect on poverty, which violates (a). In the example of the Vietnam veterans, the instrument (the draft lottery number) fails to be exogenous because the error term in the earnings equation depends on each individual's rate of return to schooling, and whether or not each potential draftee accepted their assignment—their veteran's status—depends on that rate of return. This failure of exogeneity is referred to by Blundell and Costa Dias (2009) as selection on idiosyncratic gain, and it adds to any bias caused by any failure of the instrument to be orthogonal to V_c, ruled out here by the randomness of the instrument.

The general lesson is once again the ultimate futility of trying to avoid thinking about how and why things work; if we do not do so, we are left with undifferentiated heterogeneity that is likely to prevent consistent estimation of any parameter of interest. One appropriate response is to specify exactly how cities respond to their designation, an approach that leads to Heckman's local instrumental variable methods (Heckman and Vytlacil 1999, 2007; Heckman, Urzua, and Vytlacil 2006). In a similar vein, Card (1999) reviews estimates of the rate of return to schooling and explores how the choice of instruments leads to estimates that are averages over different subgroups of the population, so that by thinking about the implicit selection, evidence from different studies can be usefully summarized and compared. Similar questions are pursued in van den Berg (2008).

3. Instruments of Development

The question of whether aid has helped economies grow faster is typically asked within the framework of standard growth regressions. These regressions use data for many countries over a period of years, usually from the Penn World Table, the current version of which provides data on real per capita GDP and its components in purchasing power dollars for more than 150 countries as far back as 1950. The model to be estimated has the rate of growth of per capita GDP as the dependent variable, while the explanatory variables include the lagged value of GDP per capita, the share of investment in GDP, and measures of the educational level of the population; see, for example, Barro and Sala-i-Martin (1995, chapter 12) for an overview. Other variables are often added, and my main concern here is with one of these, external assistance (aid) as a fraction of GDP. A typical specification can be written

$$\Delta \ln \Upsilon_{ct+1} = \beta_0 + \beta_1 \ln \Upsilon_{ct} + \beta_2 \frac{I_{ct}}{\Upsilon_{ct}} + \beta_3 H_{ct} + \beta_4 Z_{ct} + \theta A_{ct} + u_{ct}, \qquad (9)$$

where Υ is per capita GDP, I is investment, H is a measure of human capital or education, and A is the variable of interest, aid as a share of GDP. Z stands for whatever other variables are included. The index c is for country and t for time. Growth is rarely measured on a year-to-year basis—the data in the Penn World Table are not suitable for annual analysis—so that growth may be measured over ten-, twenty-, or forty-year intervals. With around forty years of data, there are four, two, or one observation for each country.

An immediate question is whether the growth equation (9) is a model-based Cowles-type equation, as in my national income example, or whether it is more akin to the atheoretical analysis in my invented Chinese railway example. There are elements of both here. If we ignore the Z and A variables in (9), the model can be thought of as a Solow growth model, extended to add human capital to physical capital; see again Barro and Sala-i-Martin, who derive their empirical specifications from the theory, and also Mankiw, Romer, and Weil (1992), who extended the Solow model to include education. However, the addition of the other variables, including aid, is typically less well justified. In some cases, for example, under the assumption that all aid is invested, it is possible to calculate what effect we might expect aid to have (Rajan and Subramanian 2008). If we follow this route, (9) would not be useful—because aid is already included—and we should instead investigate *whether* aid is indeed invested and then infer the effectiveness of aid from the effectiveness of investment. Even so, it presumably matters what kind of investment is promoted by aid, and aid for roads, for dams, for vaccination programs, or for humanitarian purposes after an earthquake are likely to have different effects on subsequent growth. More broadly, one of the main issues of contention in the debate is what aid actually does. Just to list a few of the possibilities, does aid increase investment, does aid crowd out domestic investment, is aid stolen, does aid create rent-seeking, or does aid undermine the institutions that are required for growth? Once all of these possibilities are admitted, it is clear that the analysis of (9) is not a Cowles model at all but is seen as analogous to a biomedical experiment in which different countries are "dosed" with different amounts of aid, and we are trying to measure the average response. As in the Chinese railways case, a regression such as (9) will not give us what we want because the doses of aid are not randomly administered to different countries, so our first task is to find an instrumental variable that will generate quasi-randomness.

The most obvious problem with a regression of aid on growth is the simultaneous feedback from growth to aid that is generated by humanitarian responses to economic collapse or to natural or man-made disasters that engender economic collapse. More generally, aid flows from rich countries to poor countries, and poor countries, almost by definition, are those with poor records of economic growth. This feedback, from low growth to high aid, will obscure, nullify, or reverse any positive effects of aid. Most of the literature attempts to eliminate this feedback by using one or more instrumental variables and, although they would not express it in these terms, the aim of the instrumentation is to restore a situation in which the pure effect of aid on growth can be observed as if in a randomized situation. How close we get to this ideal depends on the choice of instrument.

Although there is some variation across studies, there is a standard set of instruments, originally proposed by Boone (1996), which include the log of population size and various country dummies, for example, a dummy for Egypt or for francophone West Africa. One or both of these instruments are used in almost all the papers in a large subsequent literature, including Burnside and Dollar (2000), Hansen and Tarp (2000, 2001), Dalgaard and Hansen (2001), Guillamont and Chauvet (2001), Lensink and White (2001), Easterly, Levine, and Roodman (2003), Dalgaard, Hansen, and Tarp (2004), Clemens, Radelet, and Bhavani (2004), Rajan and Subramanian (2008), and Roodman (2008). The rationale for population size is that larger countries get less aid per capita because the aid agencies allocate aid on a country basis, with less than full allowance for population size. The rationale for what I shall refer to as the "Egypt instrument" is that Egypt gets a great deal of American aid as part of the Camp David accords in which it agreed to a partial rapprochement with Israel. The same argument applies to the francophone countries, which receive additional aid from France because of their French colonial legacy. By comparing these countries with countries not so favored or by comparing populous with less populous countries, we can observe a kind of variation in the share of aid in GDP that is unaffected by the negative feedback from poor growth to compensatory aid. In effect, we are using the variation across populations of different sizes as a natural experiment to reveal the effects of aid.

If we examine the effects of aid on growth without any allowance for reverse causality, for example, by estimating equation (9) by ordinary least squares, the estimated effect is typically negative. For example, Rajan and Subramanian (2008), in one of the most careful recent studies, find that an increase in aid by 1 percent of GDP comes with a reduction in the growth rate of one-tenth of a percentage point a year. Easterly (2006) provides many other (sometimes spectacular) examples of negative associations between aid and growth. When instrumental variables are used to eliminate the reverse causality, Rajan and Subramanian find a weak or zero effect of aid and contrast that finding with the robust positive effects of investment on growth in specifications like (9). I should note that although Rajan and Subramanian's study is an excellent one, it is certainly not without its problems, and, as the authors note, there are many difficult econometric problems over and above the choice of instruments, including how to estimate dynamic models with country fixed effects on limited data, the choice of countries and sample period, the type of aid that needs to be considered, and so on. Indeed, it is those other issues that are the focus of most of the literature cited above. The substance of this debate is far from over.

My main concern here is with the use of the instruments, what they tell us, and what they might tell us. The first point is that neither the "Egypt" (or colonial heritage) nor the population instrument is plausibly exogenous; both are external—Camp David is not part of the model, nor was it caused by Egypt's economic growth, and similarly for population size—but exogeneity would require that neither "Egypt" nor population size have any influence on economic growth except through the effects on aid flows, which makes no sense at all. We also need to recognize the heterogeneity in the aid responses and try to think about how the different instruments are implicitly choosing different averages, involving different weightings or subgroups of countries. Or we could stop right here, conclude that there are no valid instruments and that the aid to growth question is not answerable in this way. I shall argue otherwise, but I should also note that similar challenges over the validity of instruments have become routine in applied econometrics, leading to widespread skepticism by some, while others press on undaunted in an ever more creative search for exogeneity.

Yet consideration of the instruments is not without value, especially if we move away from instrumental variable estimation, with the use of instruments seen as technical, not substantive, and think about the reduced form which contains substantive information about the relationship between growth and the instruments. In the case of population size we find that, conditional on the other variables, it is unrelated to growth, which is one of the reasons the IV estimates of the effects of aid are small or zero. This (partial) regression coefficient is a much simpler object than is the instrumental variable estimate; under standard assumptions, it tells us how much faster large countries grow than small countries, once the standard effects of the augmented Solow model have been taken into account. Does this tell us anything about the effectiveness of aid? Not directly, though it is surely useful to know that, while larger countries receive less per capita aid in relation to per capita income, they grow just as fast as countries that have received more, once we take into account the amount they invest, their levels of education, and their starting level of GDP. But we would hardly conclude from this fact alone that aid does not increase growth. Perhaps aid works less well in small countries, or perhaps there is an offsetting positive effect of population size on economic growth. Both are possible, and both are worth further investigation. More generally, such arguments are susceptible to fruitful discussions, not only among economists but also with other social scientists and historians who study these questions, something that is typically difficult with instrumental variable methods. Economists' claims to methodological superiority based on instrumental variables ring particularly hollow when it is economists themselves who are so often misled. My argument is that for both economists and noneconomists, the direct consideration of the reduced form is likely to generate productive lines of enquiry.

The case of the "Egypt" instrument is somewhat different. Once again the reduced form is useful (Egypt doesn't grow particularly fast in spite of all the aid it gets in consequence of Camp David), though mostly for making it immediately clear that the comparison of Egypt versus non-Egypt or francophone versus non-francophone is not a useful way of assessing the effectiveness of aid on growth. There is no reason to suppose that "being Egypt" has no effect on its growth other than through aid from the United States. Yet almost every paper in this literature unquestioningly uses the Egypt dummy as an instrument. Similar instruments based on colonial heritage face exactly the same problem; colonial heritage certainly affects aid, and colonial heritage is not influenced by current growth performance, but different colonists behaved differently and left different legacies of institutions and infrastructure, all of which have their own persistent effect on growth today.

The use of population size, an Egypt dummy, or colonial heritage variables as instruments in the analysis of aid effectiveness cannot be justified. These instruments are external, not exogenous, or if we use the Webster definition of exogeneity, they clearly fail the exclusion restrictions. Yet they continue in almost universal use in the aid-effectiveness literature and are endorsed for this purpose by the leading exponents of IV methods, Angrist and Pischke (2010).

I conclude this section with an example that helps bridge the gap between analyses of the macro and analyses of the micro effects of aid. Many microeconomists agree that instrumentation in cross-country regressions is unlikely to be useful, while claiming that microeconomic analysis is capable of doing better. We may not be able to answer ill-posed questions about the macroeconomic effects of foreign assistance, but we can surely do better on specific projects and programs. Banerjee and He (2008) have provided a list of the sort of studies that they like and that they believe should be replicated more widely. One of these, also endorsed by Duflo (2004), is a famous paper by Angrist and Lavy (1999) on whether schoolchildren do better in smaller classes, a position frequently endorsed by parents and by teachers' unions but not always supported by empirical work. The question is an important one for development assistance because smaller class sizes cost more and are a potential use for foreign aid. Angrist and Lavy's paper uses a natural experiment, not a real one, and relies on IV estimation, so it provides a bridge between the relatively weak natural experiments in this section and the actual randomized controlled trials in the next.

Angrist and Lavy's study is about the allocation of children enrolled in a school into classes. Many countries set their class sizes to conform to some version of Maimonides' rule, which sets a maximum class size, beyond which additional teachers must be found. In Israel the maximum class size is set at 40. If there are fewer than 40 children enrolled, they will all be in the same class. If there are 41, there will be two classes, one of 20, and one of 21. If there are 81 or more children, the first two classes will be full, and more must be set up. Angrist and Lavy's figure 1 plots actual class size and Maimonides' rule class size against the number of children enrolled; this graph starts off running along the 45-degree line and then falls discontinuously to 20 when enrollment is 40, increasing with slope of 0.5 to 80, falling to 27.7 (80 divided by 3) at 80, rising again with a slope of 0.25, and so on. They show that actual class sizes, while not exactly conforming to the rule, are strongly influenced by it and exhibit the same sawtooth pattern. They then plot test scores against enrollment and show that they display the opposite pattern, rising at each of the discontinuities where class size abruptly falls. This is a natural experiment, with Maimonides' rule inducing quasi-experimental variation and generating a predicted class size for each level of enrollment which serves as an instrumental variable in a regression of test scores on class size. These IV estimates, unlike the OLS estimates, show that children in smaller classes do better.

Angrist and Lavy's paper, the creativity of its method, and the clarity of its result have set the standard for microempirical work since it was published, and it has had a far-reaching effect on subsequent empirical work in labor and development economics. Yet there is a problem, one that has become apparent over time. Note first the heterogeneity; it is improbable that the effect of lower class size is the same for all children so that, under the assumptions of the LATE theorem, the IV estimate recovers a weighted average of the effects for those children who are shifted by Maimonides' rule from a larger to a smaller class. Those children might not be the same as other children, which makes it hard to know how useful the numbers might be in other contexts, for example, when all children are put in smaller class sizes. The underlying reasons for this heterogeneity are not addressed in this quasi-experimental approach. To be sure of what is happening here, we need to know more about how different children finish up in different classes, which raises the possibility that the variation across the discontinuities may not be orthogonal to other factors that affect test scores.

A paper by Urquiola and Verhoogen (2009) explores how it is that children are allocated to different class sizes in a related, but different, situation in Chile, where a version of Maimonides' rule is in place. Urquiola and Verhoogen note that parents care a great deal about whether their children are in the 40-child class or the 20-child class, and for the private schools they study, they construct a model in which there is sorting across the boundary, so that the children in the smaller classes have richer, more educated parents than the children in the larger classes. Their data match such a model, so that at least some of the differences in test scores across class size come from differences in the children that would be present whatever the class size. This paper is an elegant example of why it is so dangerous to make inferences from natural experiments without understanding the mechanisms at work. It also strongly suggests that the question of the effects of class size on student performance is not well defined if there is no description of the environment in which class size is being changed (see also Sims 2010).

Another good example comes to me in private correspondence from Branko Milanovic, who as a child in Belgrade attended a school in which only half of the teachers could teach in English and who was randomly assigned to a class taught in Russian. He remembers losing friends whose parents (correctly) perceived the superior value of an English education and were insufficiently dedicated socialists to accept their assignment. The two language groups of children remaining in the school, although "randomly" assigned, are far from identical, and IV estimates using the randomization could wrongly conclude that English-medium education is inferior.

More generally, these are examples in which an instrument induces actual or quasi-random assignment, in this case of children into different classes, but in which the assignment can be undone, at least partially, by the actions of the subjects. If children (or their parents) care about whether they are in small or large classes or in Russian or English classes, some will take evasive action—by protesting to authorities, finding a different school, or even moving—and these actions will generally differ by rich and poor children, by children with more or less educated parents, or by any factor that affects the cost to the child of being in a larger class. The behavioral response to the quasi-randomization (or indeed, randomization) means that the groups being compared are not identical to start with; see also McCrary (2008) and Lee and Lemieux (2010) for further discussion and for methods of detection when this is happening.

In preparation for the next section, I note that the problem here is not the fact that we have a quasi-experiment rather than a real experiment, so that there was no actual randomization. If children had been randomized into class size, as in the Belgrade example, the problems would have been the same, unless there had been some mechanism for forcing the children (and their parents) to accept the assignment.

4. Randomization in the Tropics

Skepticism about econometrics, doubts about the usefulness of structural models in economics, and the endless wrangling over identification and instrumental variables have led to a search for alternative ways of learning about development. There has also been frustration with the World Bank's apparent failure to learn from its own projects and with its inability to provide a convincing argument that its past activities have enhanced economic growth and poverty reduction. Past development practice is seen as a succession of fads, with one supposed magic bullet replacing another—from planning to infrastructure to human capital to structural adjustment to health and social capital to the environment and back to infrastructure—a process that seems not to be guided by progressive learning. For many economists, and particularly for the group at the Poverty Action Lab at MIT, the solution has been to move toward randomized controlled trials (RCTs) of projects, programs, and policies. RCTs are seen as generating gold standard evidence that is superior to econometric evidence and immune to the methodological criticisms that are typically directed at econometric analyses. Another aim of the program is to persuade the World Bank to replace its current evaluation methods with RCTs; Duflo (2004) argues that randomized trials of projects would generate knowledge that could be used elsewhere, an international public good. Banerjee (2007, chapter 1) accuses the World Bank of "lazy thinking," of a "resistance to knowledge," and notes that its recommendations for poverty reduction and empowerment show a striking "lack of distinction made between strategies founded on the hard evidence provided by randomized trials or natural experiments and the rest." In all this there is a close parallel with the evidence-based movement in medicine that preceded it, and the successes of RCTs in medicine are frequently cited. Yet the parallels are almost entirely rhetorical, and there is little or no reference to the dissenting literature, as surveyed, for example, in Worrall (2007a), who documents the rise and fall in medicine of the rhetoric used by Banerjee. Nor is there any recognition of the many problems of medical RCTs, some of which I shall discuss as I go.

The movement in favor of RCTs is currently very successful. The World Bank is now conducting substantial numbers of randomized trials, and the methodology is sometimes explicitly requested by governments, who supply the World Bank with funds for this purpose (see World Bank 2008a for details of the Spanish Trust Fund for Impact Evaluation). There is a new International Initiative for Impact Evaluation which "seeks to improve the lives of poor people in low- and middle-income countries by providing, and summarizing, evidence of what works, when, why and for how much" (International Initiative for Impact Evaluation 2008), although not exclusively by randomized controlled trials. The Poverty Action Lab lists dozens of completed and ongoing projects in a large number of countries, many of which are project evaluations. Many development economists would join many physicians in subscribing to the jingoist view proclaimed by the editors of the *British Medical Journal* (quoted by Worrall 2007a), which noted that "Britain has given the world Shakespeare, Newtonian physics, the theory of evolution, parliamentary democracy—and the randomized trial."

4.1. The Ideal RCT

Under ideal conditions and when correctly executed, an RCT can estimate certain quantities of interest with minimal assumptions, thus absolving RCTs of one complaint against econometric methods, namely, that they rest on often implausible economic models. It is useful to lay out briefly the (standard) framework for these results, originally due to Jerzy Neyman in the 1920s, currently often referred to as the Holland-Rubin framework or the Rubin causal model (see Freedman 2006 for a discussion of the history). According to this, each member of the population under study, labeled i, has two possible values associated with it, Y_{i0} and Y_{i1}, which are the outcomes that i would display if it did not get the treatment, $T_i = 0$, and if it did get the treatment, $T_i = 1$, Since each i is either in the treatment group or in the control group, we observe one of Y_{i0} and Y_{i1}, but not both. We would like to know something about the distribution over i of the effects of the treatment, $Y_{i1} - Y_{i0}$, in particular its mean $Y_1 - Y_0$. In a sense, the most surprising thing about this setup is that we can say anything at all without further assumptions or without any modeling. But that is the magic that is wrought by the randomization.

What we *can* observe in the data is the difference between the average outcome in the treatments and the average outcome in the controls, or $E(Y_i | T_i = 1) - E(Y_i | T_i = 0)$. This difference can be broken up into two terms

$$E(Y_{i1} \mid T_i = 1) - E(Y_{i0} \mid T_i = 0) = [E(Y_{i1} \mid T_i = 1) - E(Y_{i0} \mid T_i = 1)] \\ + [E(Y_{i0} \mid T_i = 1) - E(Y_{i0} \mid T_i = 0)]. \quad (10)$$

Note that on the right-hand side the second term in the first square bracket cancels out with the first term in the second square bracket. But the term in the second square bracket is zero by randomization; the non-treatment outcomes, like any other characteristic, are identical in expectation in the control and treatment groups. We can therefore write (10)

$$E(Y_{i1} \mid T_i = 1) - E(Y_{i0} \mid T_i = 0) = [E(Y_{i1} \mid T_i = 1) - E(Y_{i0} \mid T_i = 1)], \quad (11)$$

so that the difference in the two observable outcomes is the difference between the average treated outcome and the average untreated outcome in the treatment group. The last term on the right-hand side would be unobservable in the absence of randomization.

We are not quite done. What we would like is the average of the difference rather than the difference of averages that is currently on the right-hand side of (11). But the expectation is a linear operator, so that the difference of the averages is identical to the average of the differences, so that we reach, finally

$$E(Y_{i1} \mid T_i = 1) - E(Y_{i0} \mid T_i = 0) = E(Y_{i1} - Y_{i0} \mid T_i = 1). \quad (12)$$

The difference in means between the treatments and controls is an estimate of the average treatment effect among the treated, which, since the treatment and controls differ only by randomization, is an estimate of the average treatment effect for all. This standard but remarkable result depends both on randomization and on the linearity of expectations.

One immediate consequence of this derivation is a fact that is often quoted by critics of RCTs but often ignored by practitioners, at least in economics: RCTs are informative about the *mean* of the treatment effects, $Y_{i1} - Y_{i0}$ but do not identify other features of the distribution. For example, the median of the difference is not the difference in medians, so an RCT is not, by itself, informative about the median treatment effect, something that could be of as much interest to policymakers as the mean treatment effect. It might also be useful to know the fraction of the population for which the treatment effect is positive, which once again is not identified from a trial. Put differently, the trial might reveal an average positive effect although nearly all of the population is hurt, with a few receiving very large benefits, a situation that cannot be revealed by the RCT, although it might be disastrous if implemented. Indeed, Kanbur (2001) has argued that much of the disagreement about development policy is driven by differences of this kind.

Given the minimal assumptions that go into an RCT, it is not surprising that it cannot tell us everything we would like to know. Heckman and Smith (1995) discuss these issues at greater length and also note that in some circumstances more can be learned. Essentially, the RCT gives us two marginal distributions, from which we would like to infer a joint distribution; this is impossible, but the marginal distributions limit the joint distribution in ways that can be useful. For example, Manski (1996) notes that a planner who is maximizing the expected value of a social welfare function needs only the two marginal distributions to check the usefulness of the treatment. Beyond that, if the probability distribution of outcomes among the treated stochastically dominates the distribution among the controls, we know that appropriately defined classes of social welfare functions will show an improvement without having to know what the social welfare function is. Not all relevant cases are covered by these examples; even if a drug saves lives on average, we need to know whether it is uniformly beneficial, or kills some and saves more. To answer such questions, we will have to make assumptions beyond those required for an RCT; as usual, some questions can be answered with fewer assumptions than others.

In practice, researchers who conduct RCTs often do present results on statistics other than the mean. For example, the results can be used to run a regression of the form

$$Y_i = \beta_0 + \beta_1 T_i + \sum_j \theta_j X_{ij} + \sum_j \phi_j X_{ij} \times T_i + u_i, \tag{13}$$

where T is a binary variable that indicates treatment status, and the X's are various characteristics measured at baseline that are included in the regression both on their own (main effects) and as interactions with treatment status (see de Mel, McKenzie, and Woodruff 2008 for an example of a field experiment with microenterprises in Sri Lanka). The estimated treatment effect now varies across the population, so it is possible, for example, to estimate whether the average treatment effect is positive or negative for various subgroups of interest. These estimates depend on more assumptions than the trial itself, in particular on the validity of running a regression like (13), on which I shall have more to say below. One immediate charge against such a procedure is data mining. A sufficiently determined examination of any trial will eventually reveal some subgroup for which the treatment yielded a significant effect of some sort, and there is no general way of adjusting standard errors to protect against the possibility. A classic example from medicine comes from the ISIS-2 trial of the use of aspirin after heart attacks, Peto, Collins, and Gray (1995). A randomized trial established a beneficial effect with a significance level of better than 10^{-6}, yet ex post analysis of the data showed that there was no significant effect for trial subjects whose astrological signs were Libra or Gemini. In drug trials the FDA rules require that analytical plans be submitted prior to trials, and drugs cannot be approved based on ex post data analysis. As noted by Sampson (2008), one analysis of the recent Moving to Opportunity (MTO) experiment has an appendix listing tests of many thousands of outcomes (Sanbonmatsu, Kling, Duncan, and Brooks-Gunn 2006).

I am not arguing against post-trial subgroup analysis, only that, as is enshrined in the FDA rules, any special epistemic status (as in gold standard, hard, or rigorous evidence) possessed by RCTs does not extend to ex post subgroup analysis if only because there is no guarantee that a new RCT on postexperimentally defined subgroups will yield the same result. Such analyses do not share any special evidential status that might arguably be accorded to RCTs and must be assessed in exactly the same way as we would assess any nonexperimental or econometric study. These issues are wonderfully exposed by the subgroup analysis of drug effectiveness by Horwitz et al. (1996), criticized by Altmann (1998), who refers to such studies as "a false trail," by Senn and Harrell (1997), who call them "wisdom after the event," and by Davey Smith and Egger (1998), who call them "incommunicable knowledge," drawing the response by Horwitz et al. (1997) that their critics have reached "the tunnel at the end of the light." While it is clearly absurd to discard data because we do not know how to analyze them with sufficient purity, and while many important findings have come from post-trial analysis of experimental data, both in medicine and in economics, for example, of the negative income tax experiments of the 1960s, the concern about data-mining remains is real enough. In large-scale, expensive, trials, a zero or very small result is unlikely to be welcomed, and there is likely to be considerable pressure to search for some subpopulation or some outcome that shows a more palatable result, if only to help justify the cost of the trial.

The mean treatment effect from an RCT may be of limited value to a physician or a policymaker contemplating specific patients or policies. A new drug might do better than a placebo in an RCT, yet a physician might be entirely correct in not prescribing it for a patient whose characteristics, according to the physician's theory of the disease, might lead her to suppose the drug would be harmful. Similarly, if we are convinced that dams in India do not reduce poverty on average, as in Duflo and Pande's (2007) IV study, there is no implication about any specific dam, even one of the dams included in the study, yet it is always a specific dam that a policymaker has to approve. Their evidence certainly puts a higher burden of proof on those proposing a new dam, as would be the case for a physician prescribing in the face of an RCT, though the force of the evidence depends on the size of the mean effect and the extent of the heterogeneity in the responses. As was the case with the material discussed in sections 2 and 3 above, heterogeneity poses problems for the analysis of RCTs, just as it posed problems for nonexperimental methods that sought to approximate randomization. For this reason, in his *Planning of Experiments*, Cox (1958: 15) begins his book with the *assumption* that the treatment effects are identical for all subjects. He notes that the RCT will still estimate the mean treatment effect with heterogeneity but argues that such estimates are "quite misleading," citing the example of two internally homogeneous subgroups with distinct average treatment effects, so that the RCT delivers an estimate that applies to no one. Cox's recommendation makes a good deal of sense when the experiment is being applied to the parameter of a well-specified model, but it could not be further away from most current practice in either medicine or economics.

One of the reasons subgroup analysis is so hard to resist is that researchers, however much they may wish to escape the straitjacket of theory, inevitably have some mechanism in mind, and some of those mechanisms can be "tested" on the data from the trial. Such testing, of course, does not satisfy the strict evidential standards that the RCT has been set up to satisfy, and if the investigation is constrained to satisfy those standards, no ex post speculation is permitted. Without a prior theory and within its own evidentiary standards, an RCT targeted at "finding out what works" is not informative about mechanisms, if only because there are always multiple mechanisms at work. For example, when two independent but identical RCTs in two cities in India find that children's scores improved less in Mumbai than in Vadodora, the authors state "this is likely related to the fact that over 80% of the children in Mumbai had already mastered the basic language skills the program was covering" (Duflo, Kremer, and Glennerster 2008b). It is not clear how "likely" is established here, and there is certainly no evidence that conforms to the gold standard that is seen as one of the central justifications for the RCTs. For the same reason, repeated *successful* replications of a "what works" experiment, i.e., one that is unrelated to some underlying or guiding mechanism, is both unlikely and unlikely to be persuasive. Learning about theory, or mechanisms, requires that the investigation be targeted towards that theory, towards *why* something works, not *whether* it works. Projects can rarely be replicated, though the mechanisms underlying success or failure will often be replicable and transportable. This means that if the World Bank had indeed randomized all of its past projects, it is unlikely that the cumulated evidence would contain the key to economic development.

Cartwright (2007a) summarizes the benefits of RCTs relative to other forms of evidence. In the ideal case, "if the assumptions of the test are met, a positive result *implies* the appropriate causal conclusion" that the intervention "worked" and caused a positive outcome. She adds, "The benefit that the conclusions follow deductively in the ideal case comes with great cost: narrowness of scope" (11).

4.2. Tropical RCTs in Practice

How well do actual RCTs approximate the ideal? Are the assumptions generally met in practice? Is the narrowness of scope a price that brings real benefits, or is the superiority of RCTs largely rhetorical? RCTs allow the investigator to induce variation that might not arise nonexperimentally, and this variation can reveal responses that could never have been found otherwise. Are these responses the relevant ones? As always, there is no substitute for examining each study in detail, and there is certainly nothing in the RCT methodology itself that grants immunity from problems of implementation. Yet there are some general points that are worth discussion.

The first is the seemingly obvious practical matter of how to compute the results of a trial. In theory this is straightforward: we simply compare the mean outcome in the experimental group with the mean outcome in the control group, and the difference is the causal effect of the intervention. This simplicity, compared with the often baroque complexity of econometric estimators, is seen as one of the great advantages of RCTs, both in generating convincing results and in explaining those results to policymakers and the lay public. Yet any difference is not useful without a standard error, and the calculation of the standard error is rarely quite so straightforward. As Fisher (1960 [1935]) emphasized from the very beginning in his famous discussion of the tea lady, randomization plays two separate roles. The first is to guarantee that the probability law governing the selection of the control group is the same as the probability law governing the selection of the experimental group. The second is to provide a probability law that enables us to judge whether a difference between the two groups is significant. In his tea lady example, Fisher uses combinatoric analysis to calculate the exact probabilities of each possible outcome, but in practice this is rarely done.

Duflo, Kremer, and Glennerster (2008b: 3921) (hereafter DKG) explicitly recommend what seems to have become the standard method in the development literature, which is to run a restricted version of the regression (13), including only the constant and the treatment dummy,

$$Y_i = \beta_0 + \beta_1 T_i + u_i. \tag{14}$$

As is easily shown, the OLS estimate of β_1 is simply the difference between the mean of the Y_i in the experimental and control groups, which is exactly what we want. However, the *standard error* of β_1 from the OLS regression is not generally correct. One problem is that the variance among the experimentals may be different from the variance among the controls, and to assume that the experiment *does not* affect the variance is very much against the minimalist spirit of RCTs. If the regression (14) is run with the standard heteroskedasticity correction to the standard error, the result will be the same as the formula for the standard error of the difference between two means, but not otherwise except in the special case where there are equal numbers of experimental and controls, in which case it turns out that the correction makes no difference and the OLS standard error is correct. It is not clear in the experimental development literature whether the correction is routinely done in practice, and the handbook review by DKG makes no mention of it, although it provides a thoroughly useful review of many other aspects of standard errors.

Even with the correction for unequal variances, we are not quite done. The general problem of testing the significance of the differences between the means of two normal populations with different variances is known as the Fisher-Behrens problem. The test statistic computed by dividing the difference in means by its estimated standard error does not have the t-distribution when the variances are different in treatments and controls, and the significance of the estimated difference in means is likely to be overstated if no correction is made. If there are equal numbers of treatments and controls, the statistic will be approximately distributed as Student's t, but with degrees of freedom that can be as little as half the nominal degrees of freedom when one of the two variances is zero. In general, there is also no reason to suppose that the heterogeneity in the treatment effects is normal, which will further complicate inference in small samples.

Another standard practice, recommended by DKG and common in medical RCTs, according to Freedman (2008), is to run the regression (14) with additional controls taken from the baseline data, or equivalently (13) with the X_i but without the interactions,

$$Y_i = \beta_0 + \beta_1 T_i + \sum_j \theta_j X_{ij} + u_i. \tag{15}$$

The standard argument is that if the randomization is done correctly the X_i will be orthogonal to the treatment variable T_i so that their inclusion does not affect the estimate of β_1, which is the parameter of interest. However, by absorbing variance, as compared with (14), they will increase the precision of the estimate—this is not necessarily the case but will often be true. DKG give an example: "Controlling for baseline test scores in evaluations of educational interventions greatly improves the precision of the estimates, which reduces the cost of these evaluations when a baseline test can be conducted" (3924).

There are two problems with this procedure. The first, which is noted by DKG, is that, as with post-trial subgroup analysis, there is a risk of data mining—trying different control variables until the experiment works—unless the control variables are specified in advance. Again, it is hard to tell whether or how often this dictum is observed. The second problem is analyzed by Freedman (2008), who notes that (15) is not a standard regression because of the heterogeneity of the responses. Write α_1 for the (hypothetical) treatment response of unit i, so that, in line with the discussion in the previous subsection, $\alpha_1 = \Upsilon_{i1} - \Upsilon_{i0}$, and we can write the identity

$$\Upsilon_i = \Upsilon_{i0} + \alpha_i T_i = \bar{\Upsilon}_0 + \alpha_i T_i + (\Upsilon_{i0} - \bar{\Upsilon}_0), \tag{16}$$

which looks like the regression (15) with the X's and the error term capturing the variation in Υ_{i0}. The only difference is that the coefficient on the treatment term has an i suffix because of the heterogeneity. If we define $\alpha = E(\alpha_i \mid T_i = 1)$, the average treatment effect among the treated, as the parameter of interest, as in section 4.1, we can rewrite (16) as

$$\Upsilon_i = \bar{\Upsilon}_0 + \alpha T_i + (\Upsilon_{i0} - \bar{\Upsilon}_0) + (\alpha_i - \alpha)T_i. \tag{17}$$

Finally, and to illustrate, suppose that we model the variation in Υ_{i0} as a linear function of an observable scalar X_{i0} and a residual η_i, we have

$$\Upsilon_i = \beta_0 + \alpha T_i + \theta(X_i - \bar{X}) + [\eta_i + (\alpha_i - \alpha)T_i], \tag{18}$$

with $\beta_0 = T_0$, which is in the regression form (15) but allows us to see the links with the experimental quantities.

Equation (18) is analyzed in some detail by Freedman (2008). It is easily shown that T_i is orthogonal to the compound error, but that this is not true of $X_i - \bar{X}$. However, the two right-hand side variables are uncorrelated because of the randomization, so the OLS estimate of $\beta_1 = \alpha$ is consistent. This is not true of θ, though this may not be a problem if the aim is simply to reduce the sampling variance. A more serious issue is that the dependency between T_i and the compound error term means that the OLS estimate of the average treatment effect α is biased, and in small samples this bias—which comes from the heterogeneity—may be substantial. Freedman notes that the leading term in the bias of the estimate of the OLS estimate of α is φ/n where n is the sample size and

$$\varphi = -\lim \frac{1}{n} \sum_{i=1}^{n} (\alpha_i - \alpha) Z_i^2 \tag{19}$$

where Z_i is the standardized (z-score) version of X_i. Equation (19) shows that the bias comes from the heterogeneity or, more specifically, from a covariance between the heterogeneity in the treatment effects and the

squares of the included covariates. With the sample sizes typically encountered in these experiments, which are often expensive to conduct,
the bias can be substantial. One possible strategy here would be to compare the estimates of α with and without covariates; even ignoring pre-
test bias, it is not clear how to make such a comparison without a good
estimate of the standard error. Alternatively, as noted by Imbens (2009)
in his commentary on this paper, it is possible to remove bias using a
"saturated" regression model, for example, by estimating (15) when the
covariates are discrete and there is a complete set of interactions. This is
equivalent to stratifying on each combination of values of the covariates,
which diminishes any effect on reducing the standard errors and, unless
the stratification is done ex ante, raises the usual concerns about data
mining.

Of these and related issues in medical trials, Freedman writes, "Practitioners will doubtless be heard to object that they know all this perfectly
well. Perhaps, but then why do they so often fit models without discussing assumptions?"

All of the issues so far can be dealt with, either by appropriately calculating standard errors or by refraining from the use of covariates, though
this might involve drawing larger and more expensive samples. However,
there are other practical problems that are harder to fix. One of these is
that subjects may fail to accept assignment, so that people who are assigned to the experimental group may refuse, and controls may find a
way of getting the treatment, and either may drop out of the experiment
altogether. The classic remedy of double blinding, so that neither the
subject nor the experimenter knows which subject is in which group, is
rarely feasible in social experiments—children know their class size—and
is often not feasible in medical trials (subjects may decipher the randomization, for example, by asking a laboratory to check that their medicine is
not a placebo). Heckman (1992) notes that, in contrast to people, "plots
of ground do not respond to anticipated treatments of fertilizer, nor can
they excuse themselves from being treated." This makes the important
point, further developed by Heckman in later work, that the deviations
from assignment are almost certainly purposeful, at least in part. The
people who struggle to escape their assignment will do so more vigor-
ously the higher the stakes are, so that the deviations from assignment

cannot be treated as random measurement error but will compromise the results in fundamental ways.

Once again, there is a widely used technical fix, which is to run regressions like (15) or (18), with *actual* treatment status in place of the *assigned* treatment status T_i. This replacement will destroy the orthogonality between treatment and the error term, so that OLS estimation will no longer yield a consistent estimate of the average treatment effect among the treated. However, the assigned treatment status, which is known to the experimenter, is orthogonal to the error term and is correlated with the actual treatment status and thus can serve as an instrumental variable for the latter. But now we are back to the discussion of instrumental variables in section 2, and we are doing econometrics, not an ideal RCT. Under the assumption of no "defiers"—people who do the opposite of their assignment just because of the assignment (and it is not clear "just why are there no defiers" [Freedman 2006])—the instrumental variable converges to the LATE. As before, it is unclear whether this is what we want, and there is no way to find out without modeling the behavior that is responsible for the heterogeneity of the response to assignment, as in the local instrumental variable approach developed by Heckman and his coauthors (Heckman and Vytlacil 1999, 2007). Alternatively, as recommended by Freedman (2004: 4; 2006), it is always informative to make a simple unadjusted comparison of the average outcomes between treatments and controls according to the original assignment. This may also be enough if what we are concerned with is whether the treatment works or not rather than with the size of the effect. In terms of instrumental variables, this is a recommendation to look at the reduced form and again harks back to similar arguments in section 2 on aid effectiveness.

One common problem is that the people who agree to participate in the experiment (as either experimental or controls) are not themselves randomly drawn from the general population so that, even if the experiment itself is perfectly executed, the results are not transferrable from the experimental to the parent population and will not a reliable guide to policy in the that population. In effect, the selection or omitted variable bias that is a potential problem in nonexperimental studies comes back in a different form, and without an analysis of the two biases it is impossible to conclude which estimate is better; a biased nonexperimental analysis might do better than an RCT if enrollment into the trial is nonrepresentative. In drug trials, ethical protocols typically require the principle of "equipoise," that is, that the physician or at least physicians in general believe that the patient has an equal chance of improvement with the experimental and control drug. Yet risk-averse patients will not accept such a gamble, so that there is selection into treatment, and the requirements of ethics and of representativity come into direct conflict. While this argument does not apply to all trials, there are many ways in which the experimental (experimentals plus controls) and parent populations can differ.

There are also operational problems that afflict every actual experiment; these can be mitigated by careful planning—in RCTs, compared with econometric analysis, most of the work is done before data collection, not after—but not always eliminated.

In this context, I turn to the flagship study of the new movement in development economics, Miguel and Kremer's (2004) study of intestinal worms in Kenya. This paper is repeatedly cited in DKG's manual, and it is one of the exemplary studies cited by Duflo (2004) and by Banerjee and He (2008). It was written by two senior authors at leading research universities and published in the most prestigious technical journal in economics. It has also received a great deal of positive attention in the popular press (see, for example, Leonhardt 2008) and has been influential in policy (see Poverty Action Lab 2007). In this study, a group of "seventy-five rural primary schools were phased into treatment in a randomized order," with the finding "that the program reduced school absenteeism by at least one quarter, with particularly large participation gains among the youngest children, making deworming a highly effective way to boost school participation among young children" (Miguel and Kremer 2004: 159). The point of the RCT is less to show that deworming medicines are effective than to show that school-based treatment is more effective than individual treatment because children infect one another. As befits a paper that aims to change method, there is emphasis on the virtues of randomization, and the word *random* and its derivatives appear some sixty times in the paper. However, the supposed randomization in the study is actually an assignment of schools to three groups by their order in the alphabet, as in Albert Infant School to group 1, Alfred Elementary to group 2,

Bell's Academy to group 3, Christopher School to group 1 again, Dean's Infants to group 2, and so on. Alphabetization, not randomization, was also used in the experiment on flip charts in schools by Glewwe, Kremer, Moulin, and Zitzewitz (2004); this paper, like "Worms," is much cited as evidence in favor of the virtues of randomization.

Alphabetization may be a reasonable solution when randomization is impossible, but we are then in the world of quasi-experiments or natural experiments, not randomized ones. In the latter the balance of observable and unobservable factors in treatments and controls is guaranteed by design, at least in expectation; in the former it has to be argued for each case, and the need for such argument is one of the main claims for the superiority of the randomized approach. As is true of all forms of quasi-randomization, alphabetization does not guarantee orthogonality with potential confounders, however plausible it may be in the Kenyan case. Resources are often allocated alphabetically because that is how many lists are presented (see, for example, Jurajda and Münich 2009) for documentation of students being admitted into selective schools (partly) based on their position in the alphabet. If this were the case in Kenya, schools higher in the alphabet would be systematically different, and this difference would be inherited in an attenuated form by the three groups. Indeed, this sort of contamination is described by Cox (1958: 74–75), who explicitly warns against such designs. It is also possible that, in this case, the alphabetization causes no confounding with factors known or unknown. If so, there is still an issue with the calculation of standard errors. Without a probability law, we have no way of discovering whether the difference between treatments and controls could have arisen by chance. We might think of modeling the situation here by imagining that the assignment was equivalent to taking a random starting value and assigning every third school to treatment. If so, the fact that there are only three possible assignments of schools would have to be taken into account in calculating the standard errors, and nothing of this kind is reported. As it is, it is impossible to tell whether the experimental differences in these studies are or are not due to chance.

In this subsection I have dwelt on practice not to critique particular studies or particular results; indeed, it seems entirely plausible that deworming is a good idea and that the costs are low relative to other interventions. My main point here is different, namely, that conducting good RCTs is exacting and often expensive, so that problems that need to be dealt with by various econometric or statistical fixes often arise. There is nothing wrong with such fixes in principle—though they often compromise the substance, as in the instrumental variable estimation to correct for failure of assignment—but their application takes us out of the world of ideal RCTs and back into the world of everyday econometrics and statistics. So that RCTs, although frequently useful, carry no special exemption from the routine statistical and substantive scrutiny that should be routinely applied to any empirical investigation.

Although it is well beyond my scope in this chapter, I note that RCTs in medicine—the gold standard to which development RCTs often compare themselves—also encounter practical difficulties, and their primacy is not without challenge. In particular, ethical (human subjects) questions surrounding RCTs in medicine have become severe enough to seriously limit what can be undertaken, and there is still no general agreement on a satisfactory ethical basis for RCTs. Selection into medical trials is not random from the population; in particular, patients are typically excluded if they suffer from conditions other than those targeted in the trial, so that researchers can examine effects without contamination from comorbidities. Yet many actual patients do have comorbidities—this is particularly true among the elderly—so drugs are frequently prescribed to those who were not represented in the original trials (Groopman 2009). In RCTs of some medical procedures, the hospitals chosen to participate are carefully selected, and favorable trial results may not be obtainable elsewhere. See Wennberg et al. (1998) for an example in which actual mortality is many times higher than in the trials, sufficiently so as to reverse the desirability of the adoption of the procedure. There is also a concern that those who sponsor trials, those who analyze them sometimes, and those who set evidence-based guidelines using them sometimes have financial stakes in the outcome, which can cast doubts on the results. This is currently not a problem in economics but would surely become one if, as the advocates argue, successful RCTs became a precondition for the rollout of projects. Beyond that, Concato et al. (2000) argue that, in practice, RCTs do not provide useful information beyond what can be learned from well-designed and carefully interpreted observational studies.

5. Where Should We Go from Here?

Cartwright (2007b) maintains a useful distinction between "hunting" causes and "using" them, and this section is about the use of RCTs for policy. Here I address the issue of generalizability or external validity—as opposed to internal validity, as discussed in the previous section—grounds on which development RCTs are sometimes criticized (see, for example, Rodrik 2009). We need to know when we can use local results, whether from instrumental variables, from RCTs, or from non-experimental analyses, in contexts other than those in which they were obtained.

There are certainly cases in both medicine and economics in which an RCT has had a major effect on the way people think beyond the original local context of the trial. In the recent development literature, my favorite is Chattopadhyay and Duflo's (2004) study of female leaders in India. The government of India randomly selected some *panchayats*, or village councils, and forced them to have female leaders, and the paper explores the differences in outcomes between such villages and others with male leaders. There is a theory (of sorts) underlying these experiments; the development community had briefly adopted the view that a key issue in development was the empowerment of women (or perhaps just giving them voice), and that if this was done, more children would be educated, more money would be spent on food and on health, and so on. Women are altruistic, and men are selfish. Chattopadhyay and Duflo's analysis of the Indian government's experiments shows that this is most likely wrong; I say "most likely" because, as in all experiments, the mechanisms are unclear. It is possible, for example, that women do indeed want the socially desirable outcomes but are unable to obtain them in a male-dominated society, even when women are nominally in power. Even so, this study reversed previously held general beliefs. There are also many examples in medicine where knowledge of the mean treatment effect among the treated from a trial, even with some allowance for practical problems, has reversed previously held beliefs (see Davey Smith and Egger 1998; Davey Smith and Ibrahim 2002, who note, "Observational studies propose, RCTs dispose").

Yet I also believe that RCTs of "what works," even when done without error or contamination, are unlikely to be helpful for policy or to move beyond the local unless they tell us something about why the program worked, something to which they are often neither targeted nor well suited. Some of the issues are familiar and widely discussed in the literature. Actual policy is always likely to be different from the experiment, for example, because there are general equilibrium effects that operate on a large scale that are absent in a pilot or because the outcomes are different when everyone is covered by the treatment rather than just a selected group of experimental subjects who are not representative of the population to be covered by the policy. Small development projects that help a few villagers or a few villages may not attract the attention of corrupt public officials because it is not worth their while to undermine or exploit them, yet they would do so as soon as any attempt were made to scale up. The scientists who run the experiments are likely to do so more carefully and conscientiously than would the bureaucrats in charge of a full-scale operation. In consequence, there is no guarantee that the policy tested by the RCT will have the same effects as in the trial, even on the subjects included in the trial or in the population from which the trialists were selected. For an RCT to produce useful knowledge beyond its local context, it must illustrate some general tendency, some effect that is the result of a mechanism that is likely to apply more broadly.

It is sometimes argued that skepticism about generalizability is simply "a version of David Hume's famous demonstration of the lack of a rational basis for induction" (Banerjee 2005). But what is going on here is often a good deal more mundane. Worrall (2007a: 995) responds to the same argument with the following: "One example is the drug benoxaprophen (trade name: Opren), a nonsteroidal inflammatory treatment for arthritis and musculo-skeletal pain. This passed RCTs (explicitly restricted to 18 to 65 year olds) with flying colors. It is however a fact that musculo-skeletal pain predominately afflicts the elderly. It turned out, when the (on average older) 'target population' were given Opren, there were a significant number of deaths from hepato-renal failure and the drug was withdrawn." In the same way, an educational protocol that was successful when randomized across villages in India holds many things constant that would not be constant if the program were transported to Guatemala or Vietnam, even as an RCT, let alone when enacted into policy (Cartwright 2010). These examples demonstrate either a failure to control for relevant factors or nonrandom participation in the trial, not the general impossibility of induction. RCTs, like nonexperimental results, cannot automatically be extrapolated outside the context in which they were obtained.

Perhaps the most famous randomization in development economics is Progresa (now Oportunidades) in Mexico, a conditional cash transfer scheme in which welfare benefits to parents were paid conditional on their children attending schools and clinics. Angrist and Pischke (2010) approvingly quote Paul Gertler's statement that "Progresa is why now thirty countries worldwide have conditional cash transfer programs," and there is no doubt that the spread of Progresa depended on the fact that its successes were supported by a randomized evaluation. Yet it is unclear that this wholesale imitation is a good thing. Santiago Levy (2006), the architect of Progresa, notes that the Mexican scheme cannot simply be exported to other countries if, for example, those countries have a pre-existing antipoverty program with which conditional cash transfers might not fit, or if they do not have the capacity to meet the additional demand for education or healthcare, or if the political support is absent. Incentivizing parents to take their children to clinics will not improve child health if there are no clinics to serve them, a detail that can easily be overlooked in the enthusiasm for the credibility of the Mexican evaluation.

Pawson and Tilley (1997) argue that it is the combination of mechanism and context that generates outcomes and that without understanding that combination, scientific progress is unlikely. Nor can we safely go from experiments to policy. In economics, the language would refer to theory, building models, and tailoring them to local conditions. Policy requires a causal model; without it, we cannot understand the welfare consequences of a policy, even a policy where causality is established and that is proven to work on its own terms. Banerjee (2007) describes an RCT by Duflo, Hanna, and Ryan (2007) as "a new economics being born." This experiment used cameras to monitor and prevent teacher absenteeism in villages in the Indian state of Rajasthan. Curiously, Pawson and Tilley (1997: 78–82) use the example of cameras (to deter crime in car parks) as one of their running examples. They note that cameras do not, in and of themselves, prevent crime because they do not make it impossible to break into a car. Instead, they depend on triggering a series of behavioral changes. Some of those changes show positive experimental outcomes—crime is down in the car parks with cameras—but are undesirable, for example, because crime is shifted to other car parks or because the cameras change the mix of patrons of the car park. There are also cases in which the experiment fails but has beneficial effects. It would not be difficult to construct similar arguments for the cameras in the Indian schools, and welfare conclusions cannot be supported unless we understand the behavior of teachers, pupils, and their parents. Duflo, Hanna, and Ryan (2008) understand this and use their experimental results to construct a model of teacher behavior. Other papers that use structural models to interpret experimental results include Todd and Wolpin (2006) and Attanasio, Meghir, and Santiago (2005); these and the other studies reviewed in Todd and Wolpin (2010) are surely a good avenue for future explanation.

Cartwright (2007a) draws a contrast between the rigor applied to establish internal validity—to establish the gold standard status of RCTs—and the much looser arguments used to defend the transplantation of the experimental results to policy. For example, running RCTs to find out whether a project works is often defended on the grounds that the experimental project is like the policy that it might support. But the "like" is typically argued by an appeal to similar circumstances or a similar environment, arguments that depend entirely on observable variables. Yet controlling for observables is the key to the matching estimators that are one of the main competitors of RCTs and that are typically rejected by the advocates of RCTs on the grounds that RCTs control, not only for things we can observe but for things we cannot. As Cartwright notes, the validity of evidence-based policy depends on the *weakest* link in the chain of argument and evidence, so that by the time we seek to use the experimental results, the advantage of RCTs over matching or other econometric methods has evaporated. In the end, there is no substitute for careful evaluation of the chain of evidence and reasoning by people who have the experience and expertise in the field. The demand that experiments be theory-driven is no guarantee of success, though the lack of it is close to a guarantee of failure.

It is certainly not always obvious how to combine theory with experiments. Indeed, much of the interest in RCTs—and in instrumental variables and other econometric techniques that mimic random allocation—comes from a deep skepticism of economic theory and impatience with its ability to deliver structures that seem at all helpful in interpreting reality. Applied and theoretical economists seem to be further apart now than at any period in the last quarter century. Yet failure to reintegrate is hardly an option because without it there is no chance of long-term scientific progress or of maintaining and extending the results of experimentation. RCTs that are not theoretically guided are unlikely to have more than local validity, a warning that applies equally to nonexperimental work. In Deaton (2010a), where I develop these arguments further, I discuss a number of examples of nonexperimental work in economic development where theories are developed to the point where they are capable of being tested on nonexperimental data, with the results used to refute, refine, or further develop the theory. Randomized experiments, which allow the researcher to induce controlled variance, should be a powerful tool in such programs and make it possible to construct tests of theory that might otherwise be difficult or impossible. The difference is not in the methods, experimental and nonexperimental, but in what is being investigated, projects on the one hand and mechanisms on the other.

One area in which this is already happening is in behavioral economics and the merging of economics and psychology, whose own experimental tradition is clearly focused on behavioral regularities. The experiments reviewed in Levitt and List (2009), often involving both economists and psychologists, cover such issues as loss aversion, procrastination, hyperbolic discounting, and the availability heuristic, all of which are examples of behavioral mechanisms that promise applicability beyond the specific experiments. There also appears to be a good deal of convergence between this line of work, inspired by earlier experimental traditions in economic theory and in psychology, and the most recent work in development. Instead of using experiments to evaluate projects, looking for which projects work, development work designs its experiments to test predictions of theories that are generalizable to other situations. Without any attempt to be comprehensive, some examples are Karlan and Zinman (2008), who are concerned with the price elasticity of the demand for credit; Bertrand et al. (2010), who take predictions about the importance of context from the psychology laboratory to the study of advertising for small loans in South Africa; Duflo, Kremer, and Robinson (2009), who construct and test a behavioral model of procrastination for the use of fertilizers by small farmers in Kenya; and Giné, Karlan, and Zinman (2010), who use an experiment in the Philippines to test the efficacy of a smoking-cessation product designed around behavioral theory. In all of this work, the project, when it exists at all, is an embodiment of the theory that is being tested and refined, not the object of evaluation in its own right, and the field experiments are a bridge between the laboratory and the analysis of "natural" data (List 2006). The collection of purpose-designed data and the use of randomization often make it easier to design an acid test that can be more difficult to construct without them. If we are lucky, this work will provide the sort of behavioral realism that has been lacking in much of economics while at the same time identifying and allowing us to retain the substantial parts of existing economic theory that are genuinely useful.

In this context, it is worth looking back to the previous phase of experimentation in economics that started with the New Jersey income tax experiments. A rationale for these experiments is laid out in Orcutt and Orcutt (1968), in which the vision is a formal model of labor supply with the experiments used to estimate its parameters. By the early 1990s, however, experimentation had moved on to a what works basis, and Manski and Garfinkel (1992), surveying the experience, write, "There is, at present, no basis for the popular belief that extrapolation from social experiments is less problematic than extrapolation from observational data. As we see it, the recent embrace of reduced-form social experimentation to the exclusion of structural evaluation based on observational data is not warranted." Their statement still holds good, and it would be worth our while trying to return to something like Orcutt and Orcutt's vision in experimental work as well as to reestablishing the relevance and importance of theory-driven nonexperimental work. The more recent Moving to Opportunity (MTO) is another example of an experiment that was more successful as a black-box test of what works, in this case giving housing vouchers to a small segment of the most disadvantaged population, than it was in illuminating general long-standing questions about the importance of neighborhoods (Sampson 2008). Sampson concludes his review of the MTO experiment with "a plea for the old-fashioned but time-proven benefits of theoretically motivated descriptive research and synthetic analytical efforts."

Finally, I want to return to the issue of heterogeneity, a running theme in this chapter. Heterogeneity of responses first appeared in section 2 as a technical problem for instrumental variable estimation, dealt with in the literature by local average treatment estimators. RCTs provide a method for estimating quantities of interest in the presence of heterogeneity and can therefore be seen as another technical solution for the heterogeneity problem. They allow estimation of mean responses under extraordinarily weak conditions. But as soon as we deviate from ideal conditions and try to correct the randomization for inevitable practical difficulties, heterogeneity again rears its head, biasing estimates and making it difficult to interpret what we get. In the end, the technical fixes fail and compromise our attempts to learn from the data. What this should tell us is that the heterogeneity problem is not a technical problem but a symptom of something deeper, which is the failure to specify causal models of the processes we are examining. Technique is never a substitute for the business of doing economics.

Perhaps the most successful example of learning about economic development is the Industrial Revolution in Britain, described by Mokyr (2009). Much of the learning was indeed accomplished by trial and error—RCTs had yet to be invented—though the practical and often uneducated people who did the experimentation were constantly in contact with leading scientists, often through hundreds of local societies dedicated to the production of useful knowledge and its application to the benefit of mankind (see also Porter 2000). Mokyr sees the Enlightenment as a necessary precondition for the revolution and of the escape from poverty and disease. Yet the application and development of scientific ideas were uneven, and progress was faster where there was less heterogeneity, for example, in chemical and mechanical processes, which tended to work in much the same way everywhere, than where heterogeneity was important, as in agriculture, where soils and farms differed by the mile (Mokyr 2009: 192). Even so, as with sanitation, progress was often made without a correct understanding of mechanisms and with limited or no experimentation; Murnane and Nelson (2007) argue that the same is frequently true in modern medicine. In the end, many problems were simply too hard to be solved without theoretical guidance, which in areas such as soil chemistry and the germ theory of disease lay many decades in the future. It took scientific understanding to overcome the heterogeneity of experience, which ultimately defeats trial and error. As was the case then, so it is now, and I believe we are unlikely to banish poverty in the modern world by trials alone unless they are guided by and contribute to theoretical understanding.

Acknowledgments

This is a lightly revised, updated version of "Instruments of development: randomization in the tropics and the search for the elusive keys to economic development," originally given as the Keynes Lecture, British Academy, October 9, 2008, and published in the Proceedings. I am grateful to the British Academy for permission to reprint the unchanged material. This article also appeared in the *Journal of Economic Literature*, June 2010 (48): 424–55, which has also graciously granted permission to reprint. I have clarified some points in response to Imbens (2009) but have not changed anything of substance and stand by my original arguments. For helpful discussions and comments on earlier versions, I am grateful to Abhijit Banerjee, Tim Besley, Richard Blundell, Ron Brookmayer, David Card, Anne Case, Hank Farber, Bill Easterly, Erwin Diewert, Jean Drèze, Esther Duflo, Ernst Fehr, Don Green, Jim Heckman, Ori Heffetz, Karla Hoff, Bo Honoré, Štěpán Jurajda, Dean Karlan, Aart Kraay, Michael Kremer, David Lee, Steve Levitt, Winston Lin, John List, David McKenzie, Margaret McMillan, Costas Meghir, Branko Milanovic, Chris Paxson, Franco Peracchi, Dani Rodrik, Sam Schulhofer-Wohl, Jonathan Skinner, Jesse Rothstein, Rob Sampson, Burt Singer, Finn Tarp, Alessandro Tarozzi, Chris Udry, Gerard van den Berg, Eric Verhoogen, Susan Watkins, Frank Wolak, and John Worrall. I acknowledge a particular intellectual debt to Nancy Cartwright, who has discussed these issues patiently with me for several years, whose own work on causality has greatly influenced me, and who pointed me toward other important work; to Jim Heckman, who has long thought deeply about these issues, and many of whose views are recounted here; and to the late David Freedman, who consistently and effectively fought against the (mis)use of technique as a substitute for substance and thought. None of which removes the need for the usual disclaimer, that the views expressed here are entirely my own. I acknowledge financial support from NIA through grant P01 AG05842–14 to the National Bureau of Economic Research.

7

EXPERIMENTAL REASONING IN SOCIAL SCIENCE

Andrew Gelman

As a statistician I was trained to think of randomized experimentation as representing the gold standard of knowledge in the social sciences, and, despite having seen occasional arguments to the contrary, I still hold that view, expressed pithily by Box, Hunter, and Hunter (1978): "To find out what happens when you change something, it is necessary to change it."[1]

At the same time, in my capacity as a social scientist I've published many applied research papers, almost none of which have used experimental data.[2] In this chapter I'll address the following questions:

1. Why do I agree with the consensus characterization of randomized experimentation as a gold standard?
2. Given point 1 above, why does almost all my research use observational data?

In confronting these issues, we must consider some general problems in the strategy of social science research. We also take from the psychology methods literature a more nuanced perspective that considers several different aspects of research design and goes beyond the simple division into randomized experiments, observational studies, and formal theory.

My practical advice is that we should be doing more field experiments but that simple comparisons and regressions are and should be here to stay. We can always interpret such analyses descriptively, and description is an important part of social science, both in its own right and in providing foundations upon which to build formal models. Observational studies can also be interpreted causally when attached to assumptions which can be attacked or defended on their own terms (Dehejia and Wahba 1999; Dehejia 2005a).

Beyond this, the best statistical methods for experiments and observational studies are not so different. There are historical and even statistical reasons why experimentalists have focused on simple differences whereas observational researchers use regression, matching, multilevel models, and other complex tools. But, as Susan Stokes points out in chapter 2 of this book, interactions are crucial in understanding social science research. Once you start looking at interactions, you're led inexorably to regression-type models and complex data summaries.

There is an analogous issue in survey research. Real-world surveys have complicated patterns of nonavailability and nonresponse and are typically adjusted using poststratification on demographic variables such as age, sex, ethnicity, education, and region of the country (see, for example, Voss, Gelman, and King 1995). These adjustments can be performed via multilevel regression and poststratification (Gelman and Little 1997), in which a statistical model such as logistic regression is fit, conditional on all variables used in the nonresponse adjustment, and then the estimates from this model are averaged over the general population—poststratified—using census information or other estimates of the distribution of the demographic variables.

If you had a simple random sample of Americans, say, you wouldn't need to do poststratification if your only goal is to estimate the national average. But why stop at that? Once you realize you can estimate public opinion by state and by subgroup within each state (Lax and Phillips 2009), you'll want to fit the full model even if your data happened to come from a random sample. The statistical adjustment tools originally developed for handling nonresponse turn out to be useful even when nonresponse is not an issue.

To return to causal research: the issues of inference and design are important—and that is the subject of most of the present book—but the statistical modeling issues are *not* so strongly affected. Whether your data are observational or experimental, you'll want to construct a model conditional on variables that can affect treatment assignment and also variables that can have potentially important interactions—and, in practice, these two sets of variables often overlap a lot. This is a point implicitly made by Greenland (2005) (and by Imai, King, and Stuart, chapter 8 in this book, in the social science context): the most important sources of bias commonly arise from treatment interactions which are interesting in their own right.

The same sort of analysis that researchers use to adjust for potential confounders in an observational study is also useful for accounting for interactions in an experimental context. True, with experimental data, you *can* get clean estimates of average causal effects by using simple averages. But why do that? Field experiments are often expensive and have small sample sizes; why not get the most out of your data? Here I'm not talking just about estimating higher moments of a distribution but about estimating nonlinear relationships and interactions. From this statistician's perspective, it's a crime to spend a million dollars on data collection and then do a five-dollar statistical analysis.

1. Starting from the Goal, or Starting from What We Know

Policy analysis (and, more generally, social science) proceeds in two ways. From one direction, there are questions whose answers we seek—how can we reduce poverty, fight crime, help people live happier and healthier lives, increase the efficiency of government, better translate public preferences into policy, and so forth? From another direction, we can gather discrete bits of understanding about pieces of the puzzle: estimates of the effects of particular programs as implemented in particular places. A large part of social science involves performing individual studies to learn useful bits of information, and another important aspect of social science is the synthesis of these "stylized facts" into inferences about larger questions of understanding and policy. Much of my own social science work has gone into trying to discover and quantify some stylized facts about American politics, with various indirect policy implications that we generally leave to others to explore.

Much of the discussion in the present book is centered on the first of the approaches described in the paragraph above, with the question framed as follows: What is the best design for estimating a particular causal effect or causal structure of interest? Typical quantitative research, though, goes in the other direction, giving us estimates of the effects of incumbency on elections, or the effects of some distribution plan on attitudes, or the effect of a particular intervention on political behavior, and so forth. Randomized experiments are the gold standard for this second kind of study, but additional model-based quantitative analysis (as well as historical understanding, theory, and qualitative analysis) is needed to get to the larger questions.

It would be tempting to split the difference in the present debate and say something like the following: randomized experiments give you accurate estimates of things you don't care about; observational studies give biased estimates of things that actually matter. The difficulty with this formulation is that inferences from observational studies also have to be extrapolated to correspond to the ultimate policy goals. Observational studies can be applied in many more settings than experiments, but they address the same sort of specific microquestions. For all the reasons given by Gerber, Green, and Kaplan (chapter 1 in this book), I think experiments really are a better choice when we can do them, and I applaud the expansion in recent years of field experiments in a wide variety of areas in political science, economics, sociology, and psychology.

I recommend we learn some lessons from the experience of educational researchers, who have been running large experiments for decades and realize that, first, experiments give you a degree of confidence that you can rarely get from an observational analysis; and, second, that the mapping from any research finding—experimental or observational—is in effect an ongoing conversation among models, data, and analysis.

Here, my immediate practical message is that before considering larger implications, it can be useful to think of the direct, specific implications of any study. This is clear for simple studies—any estimated treatment effect can also be considered as a descriptive finding, the difference between averages in treatment and control groups, among items that are otherwise similar (as defined by the protocols of the study).

Direct summaries are also possible for more complicated designs. Consider, for example, the Levitt (1997) study of policing and crime rates, which can be viewed as an estimate of the causal effect of police on crime, using political cycles as an instrument, or, more directly, as an estimate of the different outcomes that flow from the political cycle. Levitt found that in years when cities have mayoral elections the number of police on the street goes up (compared to comparable city-years without election) and the crime rate goes down. To me, this descriptive summary gives me a sense of how the findings might generalize to other potential interventions. In particular, there is always some political pressure to keep crime rates down, so the question might arise as to how one might translate that pressure into putting police on the street even in nonelection years.

For another example, historical evidence reveals that when the death penalty has been implemented in the United States, crime rates have typically gone down. Studies have found this at the national and the state levels. However, it is difficult to confidently attribute such declines to the death penalty itself, as capital punishment is typically implemented in conjunction with other crime-fighting measures such as increased police presence and longer prison sentences (Donohue and Wolfers 2006).

In many ways I find it helpful to focus on descriptive data summaries, which can reveal the limits of unstated model assumptions. Much of the discussion of the death penalty in the popular press as well as in the scholarly literature (not in the Donohue and Wolfers paper but elsewhere) seems to go to the incentives of potential murderers. But the death penalty also affects the incentives of judges, juries, prosecutors, and so forth. One of the arguments in favor of the death penalty is that it sends a message that the justice system is serious about prosecuting murders. This message is sent to the population at large, I think, not just to deter potential murderers but to make clear that the system works. Conversely, one argument against the death penalty is that it motivates prosecutors to go after innocent people and to hide or deny exculpatory evidence. Lots of incentives out there. One of the advantages of thinking like a statistician—looking at what the data say—is that it gives you more flexibility later to think like a social scientist and consider the big picture. With a narrow focus on causal inference, you can lose this.

2. Research Designs

I welcome the present exchange on the pluses and minuses of social science experimentation, but I worry that the discussion is focused on a limited perspective on the possibilities of statistical design and analysis.

In particular, I am concerned that *experiment* is taken to be synonymous with *randomized experiment*. Here are some well-known designs which have some aspect of randomization or experimentation without being full randomized experiments:

Natural experiments. From the Vietnam draft lottery to countless regression discontinuity studies, we have many examples where a treatment was assigned not by a researcher—and thus is not an experiment under the usual statistical definition of the term—but by some rule-based process that can be mathematically modeled.

Nonrandomized experiments. From the other direction, if a researcher assigns treatments deterministically, it is still an experiment even if not randomized. What is relevant in the subsequent statistical analyses are the factors influencing the selection (for a Bayesian treatment of this issue, see Gelman et al. 2003, chapter 7).

Sampling. Textbook presentations often imply that the goal of causal inference is to learn about the units who happen to be in the study. Invariably, though, these are a sample from a larger population of interest. Even when the study appears to include the entire population—for example, an analysis of all fifty states—the ultimate questions apply to a superpopulation such as these same states in future years.

Mixed experimental-observational designs. In practice, many designs include observational variation within an experiment. For example, Barnard et al. (2003) analyze a so-called broken experiment on school vouchers. Mixing of methods also arises when generalizing experimental results to new decision problems, as I discuss in the meta-analysis example later in this chapter.

Informal experimentation. One point often made by proponents of causal inference from observational data is that people (and, for that matter, political actors) do informal experimentation all the time. Our brains can do causal inference, so why can't social scientists? Humans do (model-based) everyday causal inference all the time (every day, as it were), and we rarely use experimental data, certainly not the double-blind stuff that is considered the gold standard. I have some sympathy for but also some skepticism about this argument (see Gelman 2011), in that the sorts of inferences used as examples by the proponents of everyday causal reasoning look much less precise than the sorts of inferences we demand in science, or even in social science.

In any case, our everyday causal reasoning is not purely observational. As Sloman (2005) points out, one of the purposes of informal experimentation in our ordinary lives is to resolve some of the causal questions left open by models and observational inference. In our lives we experiment all the time, on matters as small as trying out new recipes or new routes to work, to trying out new teaching methods in our classes, to the big personal decisions such as cohabitation as a potential prelude to marriage.

Formal experimentation. What are the mimimal conditions a study must have to be counted as an experiment in the statistical sense. Informal experimentation, as described above, is not enough. In my view, any experiment has two defining features:

1. *Deliberately assigned treatments.* Simply trying a new idea is not an experiment unless you make a clear decision of when and where you will try it and its alternatives. Without this clarity, you risk having an observational study in which conditions are assigned endogenously and then only labeled as experimental treatments after the fact.

2. *Systematic data collection*, which includes a measurement of the experimental treatments (what, exactly, was done in each case) and of the outcome, and also, ideally, of pretreatment variables. Without a measurement protocol there is no way to estimate treatment effects with any validity.

These are, under my definition, the only *necessary* features of a formal experiment. But one would like to have many more. Techniques such as randomization, blindness, large sample size, and measurement of background variables (to better allow extrapolation to the general population) allow us to have much more confidence in our inferences. As usual in statistics, the less care that goes into the data collection, the more that inferences are sensitive to model assumptions.

Self-experimentation. One way to focus on experimentation—in isolation of related but distinct ideas such as randomization—is to consider the most basic form, where the sample size is 1 and the experimenter and the subject are the same. Self-experimentation has a long history in medical research (Altman 1986), and more recently it has been advocated as a research method to be used more widely.

Seth Roberts is a professor of psychology with a background in rat learning experiments who has used self-experimentation to generate and study hypotheses about sleep, mood, and nutrition. Here are some of his findings (Roberts 2004): "Seeing faces in the morning on television decreased mood in the evening and improved mood the next day. . . . Standing 8 hours per day reduced early awakening and made sleep more restorative. . . . Drinking unflavored fructose water caused a large weight loss that has lasted more than 1 year. . . ." Self-experimentation generates new hypotheses and is also an inexpensive way to test and modify them, with the sort of flexibility that might be difficult to attain in a study of experimental volunteers funded by the National Institutes of Health.

These conditions are similar to those found in social science research and policy analysis, especially at the national level, where it is difficult to go beyond n=1. Practical policymaking is, in many ways, a form of self-experimentation on the local, state, or national level. Looked at from this perspective, an important research step is to go beyond informal trying out of ideas toward formal self-experimentation with its clearly defined treatments and measurement protocols. Successful small experiments, randomized or not, can lay the foundation for larger, more conclusive studies, although there are challenges involved in taking this last step (see Gelman and Roberts 2007).

Our love for the full field-experimentation package, including randomization, blindness, and large sample sizes, should not blind us to the advantages of experimentation in its simplest form. Good self-experimentation includes manipulations, that is, experimentation, but also careful and dense measurements: self-surveillance. Similarly, designers of observational studies and field experiments alike should be aware of the benefits to be gained by extensive measurement and also by exploratory data analysis—those statistical tools that allow us to check our assumptions and generate new ideas as well as to estimate and test fixed, prechosen hypotheses.

3. Example: Interactions in a Meta-Analysis

I now return to the second question posed at the beginning of this chapter: Given the manifest virtues of experiments, why do I almost always analyze observational data? The short answer is that almost all the data out there are observational. Rather than give a list of dozens of research projects, I will discuss a particular example, not one of my most important projects but one in which, even though we were working with data from clean randomized experiments, our ultimate analysis was observational.

Several years ago some colleagues and I were involved in a survey with a disappointingly low response rate. We did some research into how we could do better and discovered a paper by Singer et al. (1999) with a meta-analysis on the use of incentives to increase participation in surveys. Each experiment included in the meta-analysis had been conducted by randomly assigning different incentive conditions to participants in a survey. (Survey participants are already randomly selected, and so it is nearly effortless to embed an experiment within.) There were between two and five different conditions in each survey-experiment, with a total of 101 conditions in 39 surveys. Each condition had several descriptors (the dollar value of the incentive, whether the incentive was offered before or after the interview, whether the survey was conducted face to face or by telephone, whether the incentive was in cash or a gift, and the burden of the survey, that is, whether it was long or short) and an outcome, namely, the response rate of the people interviewed under that survey condition.

Singer et al. ran a regression of the increases in response rate (compared to the no-incentive condition) for these surveys and estimated an effect of 1.4 percentage points, plus 0.34 percentage points for each additional dollar of incentive. There was also some evidence that incentives were more effective when given before the interview, using an earlier mail contact. These estimates all made sense, but we did not fully believe some of the other results of the model. For example, the estimated effect for gift versus cash incentive was very large in the context of the other effects: the expected effect of a postpaid cash incentive of \$10 in a low-burden survey was $1.4 + 10*0.34 - 6.9 = -2.1$ percent, thus actually lowering the response rate. We find it implausible that giving a gift would lower the response rate.

But the estimate is based on a randomized experiment, so what grounds do we have to distrust it? The answer is that, although each individual study in the meta-analysis is experimental, the comparison of conditions *among* studies is observational.

Because of the nonrandomized design, which is unavoidable because the 39 different studies were conducted at different times with different goals, coefficient estimates cannot automatically be given direct causal interpretations, even if they are statistically significant. The estimated effect of -6.9 percent in response rate for a gift, compared with the equivalent incentive in cash, is presumably an artifact of interactions in the data between the form of the incentive and other variables that affect response rates. To put it most simply, the surveys in which gifts were considered as an experimental condition may be surveys in which, for some other reasons, incentives happened to be less effective.

The only consistently randomized factor in the experiments is the incentive indicator itself; the other factors are either observational (burden, mode) or experimental but generally not assigned randomly (value, timing, form). This is a common problem when a meta-analysis is used to estimate a "response surface" rather than simply an average effect (see Rubin 1989).

In this particular analysis, the implausible estimate arises because of treatment interactions that had not been included in the model. We addressed the problem in the usual fashion for observational data, that is, by fitting a regression model including interactions of the effect of incentive with survey, along with some interactions of the predictive factors with each other (Gelman, Stevens, and Chan 2003). Finally, having fit a model that we found plausible (albeit with some of the coefficients being less than two or even one standard error away from zero), we applied it to the conditions of the survey on which we were working. For this application, high levels of interactions are a modeling necessity, not merely a theoretical possibility, as we were considering various options for our survey.

4. Conclusions

In social science as in science in general, formal experiments (treatment assignment plus measurement) teach us things that we could never observe from passive observation or informal experimentation. I applaud the increasing spread of field experiments and recommend that modern statistical methods be used in their design and analysis. Using the simplest statistical methods just because we can is an inefficiency we cannot afford and shows insufficient respect for the participants in our surveys and experiments. Even in the unlikely setting that treatments have been assigned randomly according to plan and that there are no measurement problems, there is no need to limit ourselves to simple comparisons and estimates of average treatment effects.

In areas of design, measurement, and analysis, field experimenters can learn much from researchers in sample surveys (for the problem of extending from sample to population, which is often brought up as a concern with experiments) and from research in observational studies (for the problem of modeling complex interactions and response surfaces). And observational researchers—that would be most empirical social scientists, including me—should try our best to model biases and to connect our work to solid experimental research wherever possible.

Acknowledgments

I thank Dawn Teele for soliciting this chapter and the Institute for Education Sciences for partial support of this work.

NOTES

1. Box, Hunter, and Hunter refer to "changing" something—that is, experimentation—without reference to randomization, a point to which I return later in the chapter.

2. I restrict my discussion to social science examples. Social scientists are often tempted to illustrate their ideas with examples from medical research. When it comes to medicine, though, we are, with rare exceptions, at best ignorant laypersons (in my case, not even reaching that level), and it is my impression that by reaching for medical analogies we are implicitly trying to borrow some of the scientific and cultural authority of that field for our own purposes. Evidence-based medicine is the subject of a large literature of its own (see, for example, Lau, Ioannidis, and Schmid 1998).

8

MISUNDERSTANDINGS BETWEEN EXPERIMENTALISTS AND OBSERVATIONALISTS ABOUT CAUSAL INFERENCE

Kosuke Imai, Gary King, and Elizabeth A. Stuart

1. Introduction

Random treatment assignment, blocking before assignment, matching after data collection, and random selection of observations are among the most important components of research designs for estimating causal effects. Yet the benefits of these design features seem to be regularly misunderstood by those specializing in different inferential approaches. Observationalists often have inflated expectations of what experiments can accomplish; experimentalists ignore some of the tools observationalists have made available; and both regularly make related mistakes in understanding and evaluating covariate balance in their data. We attempt to clarify some of these issues by introducing a general framework for understanding causal inference.

As an example of some of the confusion in the literature, in numerous articles across a diverse variety of academic fields, researchers evaluate the similarity of their treated and control groups achieved through blocking or matching by conducting hypothesis tests, most commonly the t-test for the mean difference of each of the covariates in the two groups. We demonstrate that when these tests are used as stopping rules in evaluating matching adjustments, as is frequently done in practice, they will often yield misleading inferences. Relatedly, in experiments, many researchers conduct such balance tests after randomization to see whether additional adjustments need to be made, perhaps via regression methods or other parametric techniques. We show that this procedure is also fallacious, although for different reasons.

These and other common fallacies appear to stem from a basic misunderstanding some researchers have about the precise statistical advantages of their research designs and about other paradigmatic designs to which they compare their work. We attempt to ameliorate this situation here.

To illustrate our points, we use two studies comparing the five-year survival of women with breast cancer who receive breast conservation (roughly, lumpectomy plus radiation) versus mastectomy. By the 1990s multiple randomized studies indicated similar survival rates for the two treatments. One of these was Lichter et al. (1992), a study done by the National Institutes of Health (NIH) which randomized 237 women to mastectomy or breast conservation, within blocking strata defined by age, clinical node status, and the presence or absence of cardiac disease. To study whether this result generalized to women more broadly, the U.S. Government Accounting Office (GAO) used observational data from women being treated in general medical practices across the United States (U.S. General Accounting Office 1994; Rubin 1997). The data came from the National Cancer Institute's Surveillance, Epidemiology, and End Results (SEER) database, with information on 5,000 cancer patients, which includes nearly all women diagnosed with breast cancer in five states and four metropolitan areas. We illustrate our results by examining the design of these studies rather than their findings but note that the GAO study did find that the results from the randomized trials also held in the broader population. However, our results apply to all key designs for making causal inferences and not only to these studies.

2. Quantities of Interest

Consider an observed sample of n units taken from a finite population of N units, where typically N is much greater than n. Stochastic processes that may not be fully observed or known generate variables representing the sample selection I_i and treatment assignment T_i mechanisms. As a result of these mechanisms, unit i is in our sample if $I_i = 1$ and not if $I_i = 0$; unit i received the treatment if $T_i = 1$ and not if $T_i = 1$. Without loss of generality, assume that the treated and control groups in the sample are each of size $n/2$ so that n is an even number. For each unit, two potential outcome variables exist, $Y_i(1)$ and $Y_i(0)$, which represent the fixed values of the outcome variable when T_i is 1 or 0, respectively. In the sample, the potential outcome variable that corresponds to the actual value of the treatment variable is observed, whereas the other is not observed, and so we write the observed outcome as $Y_i = T_i Y_i(1) + (1 - T_i)Y_i(0)$ for units with $I_i = 1$. In our framework, therefore, (I_i, T_i, Y_i) are random variables.

We define the (unobserved) *treatment effect* for unit i as,

$$\text{TE}_i \equiv Y_i(1) - Y_i(0). \tag{1}$$

The quantity TE_i may vary across units as a function of the observed X_i and unobserved U_i pretreatment characteristics of unit i. We observe the covariates X_i but not U_i in the sample, and possibly neither in the remainder of the population. In practice, researchers often do not attempt to estimate TE_i for each i, and instead estimate only its average over either the sample, producing the *sample average treatment effect*, or SATE,

$$\text{SATE} \equiv \frac{1}{n} \sum_{i \in \{I_i = 1\}} \text{TE}_i.$$

or over the population, producing the *population average treatment effect*, or PATE,

$$\text{PATE} \equiv \frac{1}{N} \sum_{i=1}^{N} \text{TE}_i.$$

In the breast cancer studies, the SATE is the effect of mastectomy versus breast cancer for the women in a particular study. PATE, the quantity of real interest for women subsequently diagnosed with breast cancer, is the effect of breast conservation versus mastectomy among a larger population, for example, all women diagnosed with breast cancer for whom either treatment would be an appropriate therapy.

3. A Decomposition of Causal Effect Estimation Error

A simple baseline estimator of either SATE or PATE is the difference in the sample means of the observed outcome variable between the treated and control groups,

$$D \equiv \frac{1}{n/2} \sum_{i \in \{I_i=1, T_i=1\}} \Upsilon_i - \frac{1}{n/2} \sum_{i \in \{I_i=1, T_i=0\}} \Upsilon_i.$$

Then, the difference between PATE and this estimator, which we call *estimation error*, is

$$\Delta \equiv \text{PATE} - D \tag{2}$$

By studying estimation error, we focus on the most basic goal of statistical inference—the deviation of an estimate from the truth—rather than on all of the various commonly used approximations to this goal, such as unbiasedness, consistency, efficiency, asymptotic distribution, admissibility, mean square error, etc. These statistical criteria can each be computed from our results (by taking expectations, limits, variances, etc.), but all are secondary to understanding and ultimately trying to reduce estimation error in a particular study.

We simplify the decomposition of estimation error by considering an additive model that rules out interactions between the observed X and unobserved U covariates,

$$\Upsilon_i(t) = g_t(X_i) + h_t(U_i). \tag{3}$$

with unknown functions g_t and h_t, for $t = 0,1$. Then, the key result is that estimation error Δ can be decomposed into additive terms

$$\Delta = \Delta_S + \Delta_T = \Delta_{S_x} + \Delta_{S_U} + \Delta_{T_x} + \Delta_{T_U}. \tag{4}$$

where $\Delta_S = \text{PATE} - \text{SATE}$ and $\Delta_T = \text{SATE} - D$ represent *sample selection* and *treatment imbalance*, respectively (see Heckman et al. 1998; King and Zeng 2006). In the second line of equation (4), we further decompose sample selection error Δ_S into two components, Δ_{S_x} and Δ_{S_U}, due to selection on observed (X) and unobserved (U) covariates, respectively. Treatment imbalance Δ_T similarly decomposes into components Δ_{T_x} and Δ_{T_U} due to imbalance with respect to these observed and unobserved covariates.

We now derive and interpret each of the components under the additive model of equation (3). To focus on the key issues in this chapter, our decomposition assumes away other forms of estimation error that need to be attended to in any actual empirical analysis, such as posttreatment bias, measurement error, simultaneity, lack of compliance with the treatment assignment, and missing data, among others.

3.1. Sample Selection

The first component, sample selection error, is given by,

$$\Delta_S \equiv \text{PATE} - \text{SATE} = \frac{N-n}{N}(\text{NATE} - \text{SATE}),$$

where NATE is the *nonsample average treatment effect* and is defined by applying the SATE formula to the observations in the population but not in the sample, i.e.,

$$\text{NATE} = \sum_{i \in \{I_i = 0\}} \frac{\text{TE}_i}{(N-n)}.$$

Thus, the sample selection error component of causal estimation error vanishes if one of three conditions holds:

a. The sample is a census of the entire population, so that $I_i = 1$ for all observations and thus $n = N$;

b. The treatment effect in the sample is the same as in the rest of the population, SATE = NATE;

c. We redefine the problem so that the population of interest is coincident with the sample, in which case SATE and PATE are equivalent.

A special case of no sample selection error occurs when TE_i is constant over i, in which case SATE = NATE. In the presence of heterogeneous treatment effects, random sampling guarantees no sample selection bias rather than no sample selection error, i.e., $E(\Delta_S) = 0$.

From the definition of TE_i in equation (1), under the additive model of equation (3) and after a little algebra, the sample selection error Δ_S as defined above can be decomposed into the two additive components relating to observed and unobserved covariates:

$$\Delta_{S_x} = \frac{N-n}{N}\left[\frac{1}{N-n} \sum_{i \in \{I_i = 0\}} \{g_1(X_i) - g_0(X_i)\} - \frac{1}{n} \sum_{i \in \{I_i = 1\}} \{g_1(X_i) - g_0(X_i)\} \right],$$

$$\Delta_{S_u} = \frac{N-n}{N}\left[\frac{1}{N-n} \sum_{i \in \{I_i = 0\}} \{h_1(X_i) - h_0(X_i)\} - \frac{1}{n} \sum_{i \in \{I_i = 1\}} \{h_1(X_i) - h_0(X_i)\} \right].$$

Alternatively, these components can be expressed in the following form,

$$\Delta_{S_x} = \frac{N-n}{N} \int \{g_1(X) - g_0(X)\} \, d\{\tilde{F}(X|I=0) - \tilde{F}(X|I=1)\}, \qquad (5)$$

$$\Delta_{S_v} = \frac{N-n}{N} \int \{h_1(U) - h_0(U)\} \, d\{\tilde{F}(U|I=0) - \tilde{F}(U|I=1)\}, \qquad (6)$$

where $\tilde{F}$ represents the empirical (possibly multivariate) cumulative distribution function. Since by equation (3), the potential outcomes are deterministic functions of X and U, the treatment effect in the sample is the same as in the population when the distribution of X and U are identical in each. Specifically, when the empirical distribution of the observed pretreatment covariates X is identical in the population and sample—$\tilde{F}(X|I=0) = \tilde{F}(X|I=1)$ —then Δ_{S_x} vanishes. Similarly, when the empirical distribution of all unobserved pretreatment covariates is identical in the population and sample—$\tilde{F}(U|I=0) = \tilde{F}(U|I=1)$—then Δ_{S_v} vanishes. Since X is observed only in sample (and U is not observed at all) these conditions cannot be verified from the observed sample alone. However, if the population distribution of X is known, weighting or imputing can be used to adjust for the bias due to Δ_{S_x}. Alternatively, if one assumes that the treatment effect is constant over X_i, then $g_1(X_i) - g_0(X_i)$ is constant, implying $\Delta_{S_x} = 0$. Similarly, if the treatment effect is assumed to be constant over U_i, then $\Delta_{S_v} = 0$.

In the breast cancer studies, sample selection error refers to differences between the women in each study and those in the general population who are candidates for either treatment. We might expect sample selection error to be smaller in the observational study with 5,000 patients broadly representative of at least five states and four metropolitan areas than in the small random assignment study with just 237 women, all of whom agreed to participate and were willing and able to travel to NIH for follow-up visits. In fact, the published studies on this experiment do not even contain information on exactly how the patients were selected. For the randomized study, observable sample selection error might include differences in income, information, education, and disease severity, while selection error that would be difficult for us to observe and adjust for might include psychological conditions related to a woman's decision to participate in a randomized trial.

3.2. Treatment Imbalance

From previous definitions under the additive model of equation (3) and after a little algebra, the treatment imbalance error term $\Delta_T = \text{SATE} - D$ as defined above can be decomposed into the two additive components,

$$\Delta_{T_x} = \frac{1}{n/2}\left\{\sum_{i\in\{I_i=1,T_i=0\}} \frac{g_1(X_i)-g_0(X_i)}{2} - \sum_{i\in\{I_i=1,T_i=1\}} \frac{g_1(X_i)-g_0(X_i)}{2}\right\}$$

for observed covariates and a corresponding expression for Δ_{T_v} for unobserved covariates, with $h_j(\cdot)$ and U_i replacing $g_j(\cdot)$ and X_i, respectively. These terms can also be expressed as,

$$\Delta_{T_x} = \int \frac{g_1(X)-g_0(X)}{2} \mathrm{d}\{\tilde{F}(X|T=0,I=1)-\tilde{F}(X|T=1,I=1)\}, \quad (7)$$

$$\Delta_{T_v} = \int \frac{h_1(U)-h_0(U)}{2} \mathrm{d}\{\tilde{F}(U|T=0,I=1)-\tilde{F}(U|T=1,I=1)\}. \quad (8)$$

These components vanish if the treatment and control groups are balanced (i.e., have identical empirical distributions) for the observed X_i and unobserved U_i covariates. For example, $\Delta_{T_x} = 0$ if the following equality holds,

$$\tilde{F}(X|T=1,I=1) = \tilde{F}(X|T=0,I=1), \quad (9)$$

which is entirely in sample and observable. If this condition is not met, one needs to adjust the data to meet this condition so that valid inference can be made. In contrast, verifying the exact value of Δ_{T_v} is impossible since U is by definition unobserved.

In the breast cancer example, treatment imbalance error arises from observable and unobservable differences between women who receive breast conservation versus mastectomy. The randomization in Lichter et al. (1992) ensures that, if the study is large enough, no systematic differences exist between the women who receive the two therapies. Their table 1 compares the characteristics of women in the two treatment groups and shows few differences. In contrast, because it was not randomized, the GAO breast cancer study is likely to suffer from some treatment imbalance since doctors do not base treatment decisions on random number generators. Matching methods described in 1994 and Rubin (1997) attempt to deal as well as possible with observed differences but, without randomization, the samples may still differ in unobserved (and thus unadjusted) ways.

4. Generalizations

Blocking in experimental research involves the random assignment of units to treatment and control groups within strata (blocks) defined by a set of observed pretreatment covariates. Blocking guarantees that the treated and control groups are identical with respect to these covariates so that they cannot affect our inferences. In contrast, *matching* is a procedure that involves dropping, repeating, or grouping observations from an observed data set in order to reduce covariate imbalances between the treated and control groups that were not avoided during data collection. Blocking takes place before randomization of treatments, whereas matching is implemented only after treatments are assigned. Although their goals are so close that the terms are often used interchangeably, we keep the distinction here.

In this section we show how the essential logic of our decomposition remains unchanged when blocking on all observed covariates, and when the quantity of interest is the causal effect on the average of the treated units rather than all units. (Changing to an infinite population perspective requires imagining a superpopulation from which the N population units are randomly drawn, and then averaging over this extra variation. Our resulting estimand changes from PATE to the *superpopulation average treatment effect* SPATE, i.e. SPATE $\equiv E\{Y(1) - Y(0)\} = E(\text{PATE})$. We denote the estimation error for SPATE as Δ^* and define it as $\Delta^* \equiv \text{SPATE} - D = \Delta_S + \Delta_T + \text{SPATE} - \text{PATE}$, which directly extends our decomposition in section 3. No other results or analyses need change.)

4.1. Decomposition with Complete Blocking

Suppose we select our n observations, completely block on X, and then randomly assign T to half of the units within each block. Letting

χ denote the set of unique observed values of the rows of X, our decomposition in equation (4) then becomes,

$$\Delta = \Delta_S + \text{SATE} - D = \Delta_{S_X} + \Delta_{S_U} + \sum_{x \in \chi} w_x \Delta_{T_{U|x}},$$

where W_x is the proportion of units in each strata x of χ, and

$$\Delta_{T_{U|x}} = \int \frac{h_1(U) - h_0(U)}{2} d\{\tilde{F}(U \mid T = 0, X = x, I = 1) - \tilde{F}(U \mid T = 1, X = x, I = 1)\}.$$

This result demonstrates that some basic intuition of our decomposition in equation (4) remains the same, where blocking eliminates Δ_{T_X} and does not affect Δ_S. It also shows that Δ_{T_U} changes to the weighted average of $\Delta_{T_{U|x}}$, defined within strata of unique values of X. Since U and X are not necessarily independent, Δ_{T_X} and Δ_{T_U} may be related. Thus, blocking on the observed confounders may have an effect on the unobserved confounders.

4.2. Average Treatment Effect on the Treated

For some purposes we might consider the quantity of interest to be the treatment effect averaged over only the treated units. For example, a medical researcher may wish to learn the effect of a drug on those who receive or would receive the treatment and no others. In our motivating example, we may be interested in the effect of receiving breast conservation, for the women who choose that therapy. For this purpose, common practice is to define the sample or population *average treatment effect on the treated*, which are, respectively,

$$\text{SATT} \equiv \frac{1}{n/2} \sum_{i \in \{I_i = 1, T_i = 1\}} \text{TE}_i$$

and

$$\text{PATT} \equiv \frac{1}{N^*} \sum_{i \in \{T_i = 1\}} \text{TE}_i,$$

where $N^* = \sum_{i=1}^{N} T_i$ is the number of treated units in the population. (The definition of the SATT assumes, as we do throughout, that half of the units receive the treatment and half do not.)

An analogous version of our PATE estimation error decomposition in Equation (4)also holds for the estimation error for PATT, $\Delta' \equiv \text{PATT} - D$, which is equal to,

$$\Delta' = \Delta'_{S_x} + \Delta'_{S_U} + \Delta'_{T_x} + \Delta'_{T_U}, \tag{10}$$

where

$$\Delta'_{S_x} = \frac{N^* - n/2}{N^*} \int \{g_1(X) - g_0(X)\} d\{\tilde{F}(X|T=1, I=0) - \tilde{F}(X|T=1, I=1)\}$$

$$\Delta'_{S_U} = \frac{N^* - n/2}{N^*} \int \{h_1(U) - h_0(U)\} d\{\tilde{F}(U|T=1, I=0) - \tilde{F}(U|T=1, I=1)\}$$

$$\Delta'_{T_x} = \int g_0(X) d\{\tilde{F}(X|T=0, I=1) - \tilde{F}(X|T=1, I=1)\}$$

$$\Delta'_{T_U} = \int h_0(U) d\{\tilde{F}(U|T=0, I=1) - \tilde{F}(U|T=1, I=1)\}.$$

Notice that only the terms involved in $\Upsilon_i(0)$ enter in treatment imbalance Δ'_{T_x} and Δ'_{T_U}. This is because SATT restricts itself to the treated units in sample for which $T_i = 1$ and thus the terms involving $\Upsilon_i(1)$ in SATT and D are identical. This means that terms involving $g_i(X_i)$ and $h_i(U_i)$ cancel on taking $\Delta_T = \text{SATT} - D$ and decomposing into Δ'_{T_x} and Δ'_{T_U}.

The sample selection error is given by

$$\Delta'_S \equiv \text{PATT} - \text{SATT} = \frac{N^* - n/2}{N^*}(\text{NATT} - \text{SATT}) = \Delta'_{S_x} + \Delta'_{S_U},$$

where

$$\text{NATT} \equiv \sum_{i \in (I_i=0, T_i=1)} \frac{\text{TE}_i}{N^* - n/2}$$

is the nonsample average treatment effect. As a result, all the intuition we develop for PATE and SATE apply also to PATT and SATT and to this decomposition as well.

Since almost any implementation of matching would affect Δ_S in estimating PATE and SATE, applications of matching typically change the goal to PATT or SATT. For example, if matching is implemented by selectively dropping only control units and the quantity of interest is changed to SATT, then researchers avoid the sample selection error completely, i.e., $\Delta'_s = 0$. PATT or SATT could be used for randomized experiments, but if the treated group is randomly selected these quantities will not differ systematically from PATE and SATE, respectively.

5. Reducing Estimation Error

We now attempt to clarify how the specific features of common research designs used in a variety of disciplines can help reduce estimation error. The decomposition we offer in section 3 provides the guide for demonstrating how each contributes to reducing different components of the error. We begin with the specific features of these designs and common statistical assumptions and then discuss the research designs themselves.

5.1. Design Features

We summarize the effects of different design features in table 1, which shows the effect of each design in reducing specific components of estimation error. For example, randomly sampling units from a population, normally considered the sine qua non of survey research, works to reduce sample selection error on average across experiments, i.e., $E(\Delta_{S_x}) = E(\Delta_{S_U}) = 0$, but not necessarily in any one sample. Only by changing the quantity of interest from PATE to SATE, or equivalently taking a census of the population, is the sample selection component exactly eliminated in sample ($\Delta_{S_x} = \Delta_{S_U} = 0$). Weighting can eliminate the observed component of estimation error but cannot affect the unobserved component except inasmuch as it is related to the (observed) variables from which the weights are built.

Randomly assigning the values of the treatment variable (as in the randomized breast cancer study), normally considered the sine qua non of experimental research, reduces the components of estimation error arising from observed and unobserved variables on average but not exactly in sample, i.e., $E(\Delta_{T_x}) = E(\Delta_{T_U})$. For example, if the randomized breast cancer experiment could have been conducted many times we would expect no differences between the women in the two treatment groups on average. However, in any one study, including the one actually conducted, differences may remain between the women who receive breast conservation and mastectomy that form a component of estimation error.

Table 8-1. Effects on the components of estimation error of various choices of design and statistical assumptions[†]

	Sample selection estimation error		Treatment imbalance estimation error	
	Observed Δ_{S_X}	Unobserved Δ_{S_U}	Observed Δ_{T_X}	Unobserved Δ_{T_U}
Design choice				
Random sampling	$\overset{avg}{=} 0$	$\overset{avg}{=} 0$		
Focus on SATE rather than PATE	$= 0$	$= 0$		
Weighting for non-random sampling	$= 0$	$= ?$		
Large sample size	$\to ?$	$\to ?$	$\to ?$	$\to ?$
Random treatment assignment			$\overset{avg}{=} 0$	$\overset{avg}{=} 0$
Complete blocking			$= 0$	$= ?$
Exact matching			$= 0$	$= ?$
Assumption				
No selection bias	$\overset{avg}{=} 0$	$\overset{avg}{=} 0$		
Ignorability				$\overset{avg}{=} 0$
No omitted variables				$= 0$

[†]For column Q, ' → A' (where A in the table is either a fixed but unknown point, denoted '?', or 0) denotes $E(Q) = A$ and $\lim_{n\to\infty} \{var(Q)\} = 0$, whereas '$\overset{avg}{=}$ A' indicates only $E(Q) = A$. No entry means no systematic effect, and '=?' indicates an effect of indeterminate size and direction. Matching is normally designed to estimate PATT or SATT and so this row in the table should be read as affecting components in equation (10) rather than equation (4).

Complete blocking followed by randomization eliminates imbalance on observed variables in sample, i.e., $\Delta_{T_X} = 0$, but its only effect on unobserved confounders is on the portion correlated with X, which is eliminated or reduced as well. When estimating the superpopulation average treatment effect, adding blocking to random treatment will always reduce estimation variance of the causal effect compared to randomization alone. If PATE is the estimand, then the same relationship also holds unless n is small. This is true no matter how badly the blocking variables are chosen. (This result, which to our knowledge has not appeared before in the literature, is given in the appendix below; related results are discussed in Cochran and Cox 1957; Greevy et al. 2004; and Imai 2007.) However, despite this efficiency gain, a blocked experiment has fewer degrees of

freedom and so can have lower power in small samples; simulations indicate that this is not an issue except in very small data sets (Imai et al.
2007), and so blocking is almost always preferable when feasible. The appendix also formalizes the common recommendation in the experimental
design literature that researchers increase the variation of the outcome
variables across blocks relative to that within blocks.

Lichter et al. (1992) blocked on three variables. If it had been feasible to block on other relevant variables, such as psychological status or
other clinical indicators of disease, efficiency could have been improved.
Of course, because patients cannot wait for another patient who matches
them on background characteristics to arrive at the hospital before they are
randomized to treatment, additional blocking may not have been feasible.

Exact matching in observational research has the same logical effect as
blocking in experimental research but also comes with four weaknesses
that blocking does not possess. First, to avoid selection bias even with
a random sample from the known population, the quantity of interest
must typically be changed from PATE to PATT or SATT. With PATE,
we would likely make $\Delta_{S_x} \neq 0$ while trying to make $\Delta_{T_x} = 0$; in contrast,
by switching to PATT or SATT, matching researchers can make $\Delta'_{T_x} = 0$
while not affecting Δ'_S. Second, by definition, random treatment assignment following matching is impossible. Third, exact matching is dependent on the already-collected data happening to contain sufficiently good
matches. With blocking, no such dependency arises, since the treatment
assignment is defined on the basis of the blocks.

Finally, matching (or parametric adjustment) in the worst-case scenario,
such as on only a subset of highly correlated covariates uncorrelated with
T but related to posttreatment variables, can increase bias compared to
an unadjusted difference in means. Although observationalists typically
argue that this exception for matching does not affect their research because they have sufficient prior theoretical knowledge to choose covariates appropriately, the possibility always exists. Adding matching to an
existing parametric adjustment procedure almost always reduces model
dependence, bias, variance, and mean square error, but a parametric adjustment and matching taken together (like parametric analysis on its
own) can, in this worst-case scenario, increase bias and variance compared
to an unadjusted difference in means.

This worst-case scenario with matching and parametric analysis cannot occur with blocking followed by random treatment assignment, even when blocking on irrelevant covariates or on only a subset of relevant covariates. This benefit of blocking may seem especially surprising to observationalists. However, the inefficiency and bias in procedures for observational data can be seen, by analogy, as a result of needing to estimate the coefficients from an incorrectly specified parametric model. In contrast, blocking is equivalent to parametric adjustment where the model specification *and* the exact numerical values of the coefficients on the potential confounders are known and so can be adjusted for exactly, even if all covariates are not available. Thus, except in very small samples, blocking on pretreatment variables followed by random treatment assignment cannot be worse than randomization alone. Blocking on variables related to the outcome is more effective in increasing statistical efficiency than blocking on irrelevant variables, and so it pays to choose the variables to block carefully. But choosing not to block on a relevant pretreatment variable prior to randomization, that is feasible to use, is not justified.

When the sample size is large, the variance of each of the four components of estimation error gets small. If n becomes large when the expected value of one of these components is zero, then the value of that component will become smaller and at the limit approach zero even in sample.

5.2. Assumptions

Experimentalists and observationalists often make assumptions about unobserved processes on the basis of prior evidence or theory. At worst, when the question is judged sufficiently important but no better evidence exists, these assumptions are sometimes based on no more than wishful thinking for lack of anything better to do. Either way, we need to understand these assumptions precisely, and what their consequences are for the components of estimation error.

The second portion of table 8-1 lists three assumptions that are commonly used in the same way and for some of the same purposes as design features in the rest of the table 8-1. For example, the assumption of no selection bias made in numerous studies is that $E(\Delta_S) = 0$, not necessarily that $\Delta_S = 0$ in the observed sample. We could strengthen this assumption (to $\Delta_S = 0$), but this level of optimism is rarely justified or made in the literature.

The assumption of ignorability, most often made in statistics, implies that the component of estimation error due to unobserved variables is zero in expectation ($E(\Delta_{T_U}) = 0$). In contrast, the assumption of no omitted variables (or no omitted variable bias), typically made in classical econometrics and many of the social sciences, is that U is either uncorrelated with X or has no causal effect on Y, conditional on X; the result is that $\Delta_{T_U} = 0$ exactly in sample. Assumptions need not be made about imbalance in observables since they can be checked directly, but the various types of parametric models and nonparametric adjustment procedures are routinely used to try to further reduce Δ_{T_x} (or Δ'_{T_x}).

5.3. Major Research Designs

The major research designs are each combinations of the features and assumptions described above. Table 8-2 summarizes how a particular design affects each of the four components of the estimation error.

We begin with what we call the *ideal experiment*, which involves selecting a large number of units randomly from a well-defined population of interest, measuring and blocking on all known confounders X and then randomly assigning values of the treatment variable T. In this situation, researchers can claim that

    a. $\Delta_{S_x} \approx 0$ and $\Delta_{S_U} \approx 0$ because random sampling ensures $E(\Delta_{S_x}) = E(\Delta_{S_U}) = 0$ and a large n makes the variances of Δ_{S_x} and Δ_{S_U} small while yielding $\dfrac{N-n}{N} \approx 0$ and, SATE $\approx$ NATE

    b. $\Delta_{T_x} \approx 0$ because of blocking, and

    c. $\Delta_{T_U} \approx 0$ because random assignment implies that $E(\Delta_{T_U}) = 0$ and the large n makes the variance of Δ_{T_U} across repeated treatment assignments small too.

If the confounders in X include all confounders rather than merely all confounders we happen to know, then $\Delta_{T_U} = 0$.

For numerous logistical reasons, ideal experiments are rarely run in practice, and many other research designs are used, depending on the constraints imposed by the research situation. For example, in the most common form of *randomized clinical trials* in medicine, n is small, the

Table 8-2. Components of bias when estimating PATE†

Design choice	Sample selection estimation error		Treatment imbalance estimation error	
	Observed Δ_{S_X}	Unobserved Δ_{S_U}	Observed Δ_{T_X}	Unobserved Δ_{T_U}
Ideal experiment	$\to 0$	$\to 0$	$= 0$	$\to 0$
Randomized clinical trials (limited or no blocking)	$\neq 0$	$\neq 0$	$\overset{\text{avg}}{=} 0$	$\overset{\text{avg}}{=} 0$
Randomized clinical trials (complete blocking)	$\neq 0$	$\neq 0$	$= 0$	$\overset{\text{avg}}{=} 0$
Social science field experiment (limited or no blocking)	$\neq 0$	$\neq 0$	$\to 0$	$\to 0$
Survey experiment (limited or no blocking)	$\to 0$	$\to 0$	$\to 0$	$\to 0$
Observational study (representative data set, well matched)	≈ 0	≈ 0	≈ 0	$\neq 0$
Observational study (unrepresentative but partially correctable data, well matched)	≈ 0	$\neq 0$	≈ 0	$\neq 0$
Observational study (unrepresentative data set, well matched)	$\neq 0$	$\neq 0$	≈ 0	$\neq 0$

†For column Q, ' $\to 0$' denotes $E(Q) = 0$ and $\lim_{n\to\infty} \{\text{var}(Q)\} = 0$, whereas ' $\overset{\text{avg}}{=} 0$' indicates $E(Q) = 0$ for a design with a small n and so asymptotic limits are not relevant. Quantities in the columns marked Δ_{S_X} and Δ_{S_U} can be set to 0 if the quantity of interest is changed from PATE to SATE. Matching is normally designed to estimate PATT or SATT and so designs using it should be read as affecting components in equation (10) rather than equation (4).

sample is drawn neither randomly nor from a known population of interest, treatment is randomly assigned, and blocking is only sometimes used. The randomized breast cancer study is one such example, as it was carried out using 237 nonrandomly selected women who agreed to be in the trial and who were randomly assigned to treatment with some blocking.

In these trials, researchers must admit that $\Delta_S \neq 0$, although they sometimes sidestep the problem by switching their quantity of interest from PATE to SATE and inferring to PATE only after their results are replicated in a different setting, perhaps by different research teams. Researchers then are left basing a claim that $\Delta_S \approx 0$ on the hope or argument that their subjects are similar enough to subjects everywhere ("a kidney is a kidney is a kidney is a kidney . . .") and so NATE $\approx$ SATE; this claim is somewhat more plausible if estimates from replications in diverse settings are relatively constant, but, as seems to be recognized, the generalizations wind up depending on qualitative arguments rather than on statistical science. As with partially correctable observational studies, randomized clinical trials sometimes select patients according to some known characteristics X and some unknown; in this situation, Δ_{S_x} can equal zero if a weighted difference in means is used instead of D, but even in this situation Δ_{S_U} is not 0 exactly, in the limit, or on average.

Randomized clinical trials that block on all the information in X benefit directly because $\Delta_{T_x} = 0$. However, medical researchers often block on only a few variables, and so $\Delta_{T_x} \neq 0$ and of course $\Delta_{T_U} \neq 0$. However, random assignment means that on average these error components vanish, i.e., $E(\Delta_{T_x}) = E(\Delta_{T_U}) = 0$. Since n is small in most of these (including most academic works as well as most phase I and II clinical trials), these expectations alone are not so comforting, but since the practice in this field is for many researchers to replicate roughly the same experiments, the concept of Δ_{T_x} and Δ_{T_U} vanishing on average across many repeated experiments is plausible.

In *social science field experiments*, researchers typically have large non-random convenience samples, such as from one city, nongovernmental organization, or company to which they were able to gain access and permission to run the experiment. They may or may not use blocking, but they are able to randomly assign the values of the treatment variable. For example, Green (2000) conducted a voter mobilization experiment containing many one- and two-voter households in New Haven. In these settings, since $\Delta_S \neq 0$ and replication of the experiment is not common, often the best researchers can do with regard to sample selection error is to settle for estimating SATE rather than PATE. If they use complete blocking prior to random assignment, $\Delta_{T_x} = 0$ and not otherwise. However, random assignment with a large n means that $E(\Delta_{T_x}) = E(\Delta_{T_U}) = 0$ and the variances of both Δ_{T_x} and Δ_{T_U} drop as n increases.

A related research design involves *survey experiments*, in which a large number of randomly selected respondents from a known population of interest are randomly assigned to treatment and control groups (the treatment in such studies often being different questionnaire wordings). This design is also sometimes used in public policy experiments when the population of interest is known. One example is the Job Corps evaluation, in which all applicants to the program were randomly assigned either to the treatment group, and were therefore allowed to enroll in Job Corps, or to the control group, in which case they were not allowed to enroll at that time (Schochet et al. 2003). If the sample was properly drawn, $E(\Delta_{S_x}) = E(\Delta_{S_v}) = 0$ with a small variance tending toward zero. Unfortunately, random sampling of survey respondents is becoming increasingly difficult with the rise in cell phones and unit nonresponse. Blocking is rarely used in these experiments unless respondents' characteristics are collected prior to the experiment, and so $\Delta_{T_x} \neq 0$, but Δ_{T_x} and Δ_{T_v} are both zero in expectation and have small variances.

Finally, purely *observational studies* typically have large samples that are often randomly selected, but blocking and random assignment are infeasible. The last three rows of table 2 include a summary of results for three general categories of observational studies. The first includes data that are representative of a fixed population, such as from a random sample. The second is not a random sample but includes enough information to correct for unrepresentativeness, such as via weighting. The third is based on a convenience sample with no known relationship to the population of interest. All three data types in the table are assumed to contain data that make high-quality matching possible.

As an example of the three types of observational studies, the GAO breast cancer researchers were interested in comparing breast cancer treatments among women who would not necessarily choose to have their treatment selected randomly. To study that question, nearly all women with breast cancer in five states and four metropolitan areas were included, but the women chose which treatment to receive (U.S. General Accounting Office 1994). In these studies, Δ_S is zero or reasonably close to it exactly or in expectation. When the population differs from the sample, the SATE is a sufficiently interesting quantity on its own that its difference from PATE becomes a definitional matter of minor importance. Studies that select on the basis of variables that are known in part and corrected via weighting, imputation, or some other procedure can eliminate or reduce Δ_{S_x} but cannot affect Δ_{S_v}, except inasmuch as X and U are related. Much of the work in observational studies goes into collecting the best pretreatment covariates and adjusting for them after the data are collected. If adjustment is done well, $\Delta_{T_x} \approx 0$, but unfortunately in general $\Delta_{T_U} \neq 0$, and the absence of random assignment means these studies cannot avoid error due to U even on average or as n grows. The hope of these researchers is that enough is known from theory, prior observational studies, or qualitative evidence (clinical information) that an assumption of ignorability or no omitted variable bias is close enough for reasonably accurate inferences.

5.4. What's the Best Design?

If an ideal experimental design is infeasible, which of the remaining research designs is best? This question is not directly material, since medical researchers cannot randomly select subjects to administer medical procedures, and those conducting observational studies of, say, the U.S. congressional elections, cannot randomly assign incumbency status to candidates for public office. However, none of these procedures reduces all four components of estimation error to zero with certainty.

From this perspective, the Achilles heel of observational studies is error due to imbalance in unobserved variables, whereas in experimental studies it is a small n and the lack of random selection. The estimation error in either can overwhelm all the good these research designs otherwise achieve, but both approaches have ways of attacking their biggest weaknesses. Neither is best; both are adapted as well as possible to the constraints of their subjects and research situation. Experimentalists may envy the large, randomly selected samples in observational studies, and observationalists may envy the ability of experimentalists to randomly assign treatments, but the good of each approach comes also with a different set of constraints that cause other difficulties.

6. Fallacies in Experimental Research

Numerous experimental researchers across many fields make two mistakes that are easy to understand and correct with reference to our decomposition of estimation error.

First, experimentalists often fail to block at all, whereas any observed covariates should be fully blocked if feasible. The common practice of re-randomizing, when the first set of random draws for treatment assignments is unsatisfactory, can be thought of as an inefficient form of blocking. To see this, note that re-randomizing is equivalent to rejection sampling, where sampling from a known unrestricted distribution and discarding any samples that do not meet desired restrictions is equivalent to sampling directly from the restricted population.

Blocking is not always feasible, such as when patients in a medical experiment trickle in over time, and treatment decisions need to be made for each quickly (as may have been the case in Lichter et al. 1992), or when important pretreatment covariates cannot be measured until after treatment. However, when feasible, blocking on potentially confounding covariates should always be used. As Box et al. (1978: 103), write, "Block what you can and randomize what you cannot." Randomization is remarkable because it can eliminate imbalance on all covariates in expectation, even if those covariates are unobserved. But randomization without blocking is incapable of achieving what blocking can, which is to eliminate one component of estimation error entirely, setting $\Delta_{T_x} = 0$, rather than merely ensuring that $E(\Delta_{T_x}) = 0$. Since individual researchers care about getting the right answer in their experiment, rather than on average over their career or on average across different researchers in the scientific community, failing to block on an observed covariate can be a huge missed opportunity. Greevy et al. (2004) point out that algorithms have been developed to make blocking on many covariates considerably easier than it once was, and that blocking even on irrelevant variables introduces no inferential problems, although it may reduce statistical power or efficiency relative to better-chosen blocking covariates.

Second, experimenters who block on some or all available covariates and then randomize sometimes evaluate the balance of the treated and control groups by conducting various hypothesis tests, such as the difference in means. Senn (1994: 1716) explained that this "common procedure" is "philosophically unsound, of no practical value, and potentially misleading." He writes, "1. over all randomizations the groups are balanced; 2. for a particular randomization they are unbalanced. No 'significant imbalance' can cause 1 to be untrue and no lack of significant balance can make 2 untrue. The only reason to employ such a test must be to examine the process of randomization itself. Thus, a significant result should lead to the decision that the treatment groups have not been randomized, and hence either that the trialist has dishonestly manipulated the allocation or that some incompetence . . . has occurred."

Any other purpose for conducting such a test is fallacious. Inappropriate randomization may be an issue in social science field experiments more often than in medical research, as the social scientist often conducts and implements random assignment only through a third party, such as a government, firm, or other organization.

These points are easy to understand using our decomposition, since under random assignment $E(\Delta_{T_x}) = E(\Delta_{T_u}) = 0$, but for unblocked randomization $\Delta_{T_x} \neq 0$ (and of course $\Delta_{T_u} \neq 0$ under random assignment with or without blocking). Hypothesis tests are used to evaluate expectations, which we know are zero due to randomization, but are not needed to evaluate the components of estimation error, which can be calculated directly, in sample, and without any need for averaging over random sampling from a superpopulation or repeated experiments. Moreover, even if the population from which X comes is sampled from a superpopulation, Δ_{T_x} and not its expectation is the relevant component of estimation error, and the difference in the empirical cumulative distribution function between the treated and control groups is a directly observable feature of the sample. So hypothesis tests in this circumstance have no relevant role. This point is also central for a related fallacy that arises in matching, to which we now turn, and for which the results we give are also relevant for experimenters.

7. The Balance Test Fallacy in Matching Studies

7.1. Matching

From the perspective of our decomposition, the only purpose of matching and blocking is to reduce imbalance in the observables Δ'_{T_x} and in any portion of imbalance in the unobservables $\Delta'_{T_{u|x}}$ for which U and X are related. Although blocking is easy to apply whenever the variables to block on are observed and treatment assignment is under the control of the investigator, matching requires sometimes difficult searching to find the best matches in the available data (Rosenbaum 2002; Rubin 2006).

Matching also operates by deleting (or duplicating) observations, and so to keep the quantity of interest fixed during this process, researchers typically focus on PATT or SATT and try to keep the treated group fixed.

Matching is not a method of estimation, so any application of it must be followed by a simple difference in means or some other method. In the best case, the data exactly match and thus satisfy equation (9) so that $\Delta'_{T_x} = 0$, without losing too many observations in the process. In this best case of exact matching, T and X are unrelated in the matched sample, and no further adjustments for X are necessary, so the PATT or SATT can be estimated by the simple difference in means, D. When imbalance Δ'_{T_x} is not eliminated, further adjustment for X after matching may be necessary, such as via the same parametric methods as are commonly applied when matching is not applied. Since methodological work on matching is growing fast, the list of available matching algorithms from which to choose is also growing (Ho et al. 2007).

Choosing the most appropriate algorithm for a given problem involves assessing how well equation (9) holds in the matched samples. Ideally that would involve comparing the (joint) empirical distributions of all covariates X between the matched treated and control groups. However, when X is high dimensional, this is generally infeasible and thus lower-dimensional measures of balance are used instead. Standard practice in observational studies is for researchers to evaluate an implication of equation (9) for the chosen matching algorithm by conducting t-tests for the difference in means for each variable in X between the matched treated and control groups, thus seemingly addressing imbalance in at least one important aspect of a high-dimensional relationship. Other hypothesis tests, such as χ^2–, F–, and Kolmogorov-Smirnov tests, are also sometimes used for each covariate, but the same problems we describe below still apply, and so for expository purposes we focus on the most commonly used t-test.

7.2. The Balance Test Fallacy

The practice of using hypothesis tests to evaluate balance is widespread and includes a large volume of otherwise high-quality work in economics (Smith and Todd 2005), political science (Imai 2005), sociology

(Lundquist and Smith 2005), psychology (Haviland and Nagin 2005), education (Crosnoe 2005), management science (Villalonga 2004), medicine (Mangano et al. 2006), public health (Novak et al. 2006), and statistics (Lu et al. 2001). Tables of t and other test statistics and/or their p-values are used as a justification in these and other published articles for the adequacy of the chosen matching method, and statistically insignificant t-tests are used as a stopping rule for maximizing balance in the search for the appropriate matched sample from which to draw inferences. Although we do not trace the exact consequences of this practice in the aforementioned studies, this approach is problematic for at least four reasons.

First, as an illustration, consider a data set on the School Dropout Demonstration Assistance Program, which sought to reduce dropout rates by a series of school "restructuring" initiatives, including curriculum reform and expansion of teacher training (Stuart and Rubin 2007). The design is observational: a school with the restructuring effort is compared with a control school. We use a subset of these data that includes 428 students from a treated school and 434 from a control school. The outcome variable Y is a test score (on a scale from 0 to 100), and X includes a variety of variables, but we focus here only on the baseline math test score. Matching analysis begins with the full data set and then selectively deletes students until equation (9) is best satisfied without losing too many observations. Suppose instead that we choose a matching algorithm that chooses observations from the control group to discard *randomly*, rather than (as usual) to maximize balance. That is, we literally draw observations from the control group with equal probability and discard them from the data. Clearly, this algorithm would not affect expected balance between the treated and control group, or the bias in the ultimate analysis that satisfying equation (9) is meant to improve. In other words, on average across different randomly generated deletions, Δ'_{T_x} would not drop. Yet, we can show that randomly deleting observations seems to do wonders according to the t-test. To do this, we create a sequence of matching solutions that randomly drop different numbers of control observations (with results averaged over 5,000 draws), and plot the average results in figure 8-1(a) (we discuss figure 8-1(b) later). The horizontal axis in figure 8-1(a) reports the number of control units randomly dropped, while the vertical axis gives the size of the t-test. We have shaded in the area

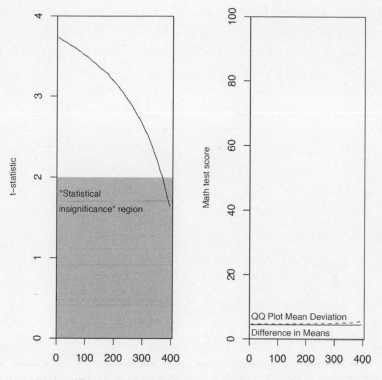

Fig. 8-1. Dangers in relying on *t*-statistics as a measure of balance (average value of a measure of balance when a given number of control units are randomly dropped from the data set (out of a total of 434): with larger numbers of control units dropped (i.e., smaller numbers of control units in the resulting sample), the value of the t-statistic becomes closer to 0, falsely indicating improvements in the balance, even though true balance does not vary systematically across the data sets (and efficiency declines); the difference in means and quantile-quantile plot mean deviation, which are given in (b), correctly indicate no change in bias as observations are randomly dropped.

below a *t*-test of 2, which is the region in which results are conventionally referred to as statistically insignificant. The line on the plot clearly shows that, according to the *t*-test, randomly dropping more control units does an "excellent" job at achieving balance, reducing the statistic from 3.7 to 1.6 in figure 8-1(a). This makes no sense at all.

Second, the problem in figure 1 can be seen by recognizing that dropping observations can influence not only balance but also statistical power, and unfortunately the *t*-test, like most statistical tests, is a function of both. The more observations dropped, the less power the tests have to detect imbalance in observed covariates. Formally, let n_{mt} and n_{mc} be the sample sizes for the matched treated and matched control groups, and define $r_m = n_{mt}/n_m$ where $n_m = n_{mt} + n_{mc}$. Then, write the two sample t-test statistic with unknown and unequal variances as,

$$\frac{\sqrt{n_m}\,(\overline{X}_{mt} - \overline{X}_{mc})}{\sqrt{\left\{ \dfrac{s_{mt}^2}{r_m} + \dfrac{s_{mc}^2}{1-r_m} \right\}}}$$

where

$$\overline{X}_{mt} = \sum_{i=1}^{n_m} \frac{T_i X_i}{n_{mt}}$$

and

$$\overline{X}_{mc} = \sum_{i=1}^{n_m} \frac{(1-T_i)X_i}{n_{mc}}$$

are the sample means, and

$$s_{mt}^2 = \frac{\sum_{i=1}^{n_m} T_i (X_i - \overline{X}_{mt})^2}{n_{mt}-1}$$

and

$$s_{mc}^2 = \frac{\sum_{i=1}^{n_m} (1-T_i)(X_i - \overline{X}_{mt})^2}{n_{mc}-1}$$

represent the sample variances of the matched treated and control groups, respectively. Hence, the difference in sample means as a measure of balance is distorted in the t-test by three factors:

a.   The total number of remaining observations n_m,
b.   The ratio of remaining treated units to the total number of remaining observations r_m, and
c.   The sample variance of X for the remaining treated and control units, s_{mt}^2 and s_{mc}^2.

Since the value of this (and other) hypothesis tests is affected by factors other than balance, they cannot even be counted on to be monotone functions of balance: The t-test can indicate balance is getting better while the actual balance is getting worse, staying the same, or improving. Although we choose the most commonly used t-test for illustration, the same problem applies to many other test statistics used in applied research. For example, the same simulation applied to the Kolmogorov-Smirnov test shows that its p-value monotonically increases as we randomly drop more control units. This is because a smaller sample size typically produces less statistical power and hence a larger p-value.

Third, from a theoretical perspective, balance is a characteristic of the sample, not of some hypothetical population, so, strictly speaking, hypothesis tests are irrelevant in this context (Ho et al. 2007). Whether the quantity of interest is SATT, PATT, or SPATT, balance affected by matching only affects Δ'_{T_x}. Virtually all methods of adjustment condition on the observed values of X, and so X can be dropped in these analyses only when equation (9) is satisfied in sample, not in some population from which the data are hypothetically or actually drawn. For the same reason that randomized blocks or paired matching are preferable to classical randomization in experimental design—that is, the imbalance in the variables that defines the blocks can be set to zero in-sample, without having to hope that the sample size is large enough for the advantages of randomization to kick in (see also Greevy et al. 2004: 264)—matching on all observed differences in X is preferable whenever feasible and other goals such as variance reduction are not harmed. The goal of reducing estimation error is reducing Δ'_{T_x} and not merely $E(\Delta'_{T_x})$, and so imbalance with respect to observed pretreatment covariates—the difference between $\tilde{F}(X|T = 1, I = 1)$ and $\tilde{F}(X|T = 0, I = 1)$—should be minimized without limit where possible, so long as we are not unduly compromising other goals in the process (such as efficiency).

Fourth and finally, we offer a simple model that conveys why matching contains no threshold below which the level of imbalance is always acceptable. To see this, consider data generated by the classical regression model $E(\Upsilon|T, X) = \theta + T\beta + X\gamma$ (Goldberger 1991), a special case of the model in Equation(3). Then the regression of Υ on a constant and T (without X) gives a difference in means, the (conditional) bias of which as an estimate of β is $E(\hat{\beta} - \beta|T,X) = G\gamma$, where G contains vectors of coefficients from regressions of each of the variables in X on a constant and T. Using matching to eliminate bias under this simplified data generation process involves dropping or repeating observations so that G is as close to a matrix of zeros as possible. But what happens to bias if G is smaller than it was before matching but still not zero? The answer is that the bias is reduced, but without knowledge of γ—which researchers eschew estimating to avoid inadvertently introducing selection error by choosing matching solutions that stack the deck for their favored hypotheses—it could be that a nonzero portion of G, when multiplied by its corresponding elements of γ, will generate arbitrarily large bias. This also shows that no measure of balance which is a function of X alone can be guaranteed to be a monotone function of bias without special assumptions (Rubin and Stuart 2006), so proper measures of imbalance should always be minimized without limit, subject to efficiency constraints. Thus, whether or not some hypothesis tests indicate that G is not significantly different from zero is immaterial: The smaller G is, the better, either above or below the t-test threshold of statistical significance, since G (i.e., balance) is a characteristic of the observed data.

An argument related to our last point has been made in the context of randomized experiments, where researchers have shown that even small (and statistically insignificant) differences in important (or what they call in this literature prognostic) covariates can result in large differences in the results of the experiment (Senn 1994; Pocock et al. 2002). However, the problem we describe in this section with statistical power and stopping rules being a function of the remaining sample size does not arise in randomized experiments.

Researchers analyzing data from randomized experiments that did not block on all observed covariates can check balance, but they do not need hypothesis tests to do so. The issue of balance is entirely in sample and involves no inference to populations or superpopulations. Thus, everything needed to check balance and determine it directly is available (Cochran 1965). Issues of sample selection and sampling bias arise only in Δ_S; in contrast, Δ_T always involves just the sample at hand, whether your perspective is sample-based, population-based, or superpopulation-based. If the samples are not balanced, then researchers may wish to settle for Δ_T being close to zero in expectation or they can adjust. Adjustment will improve balance and thus reduce Δ_{T_X}, but if not done properly can be at the expense of estimation variance or bias. Normally, however, even matching on irrelevant covariates will only slightly increase the variance (Rubin and Thomas 1996; Ho et al. 2007).

7.3. Better Alternatives

In any study where all observed covariates were not fully blocked ahead of time, balance should be checked routinely by comparing observed covariate differences between the treated and control groups. Any statistic used to evaluate balance should have two key features:

a. It should be a characteristic of the sample and not of some hypothetical population, and
b. The sample size should not affect the value of the statistic.

If matching is used, the difference between the groups should be minimized without limit. A difference in means is a fine way to start. Cochran (1968) suggests a rule of thumb that a mean difference should not differ more than a quarter of a standard deviation, though we emphasize that imbalance should be minimized without limit. Other options include higher order moments than the mean, nonparametric density plots, and propensity score summary statistics (e.g., Austin and Mamdani 2006; Rubin 2001).

A more general approach is quantile-quantile, or QQ, plots that directly compare the empirical distribution of two variables, although statistics based on QQ-plots can be sensitive to small features of the data. The graph on the right side of figure 8-1(b) plots for comparison the difference in means and a QQ-plot summary statistic, the average distance between the empirical quantile distributions of the treated and control groups calculated over the same samples as for figure 1(a). (Formally, this measure can be defined as $(1/n)\sum_{i=1}^{n} |\tilde{q}_{X_{mt}}(i\,/\,n) - \tilde{q}_{X_{mc}}(i\,/\,n)|$ where $\tilde{q}_{X_{mt}}$ and $\tilde{q}_{X_{mc}}$ are the empirical quantile functions of a covariate X for the matched treated and matched control groups, respectively, and $n = \min(n_{mt}, n_{mc})$.) Unlike the t-test, the level of balance does not change for either statistic as more units are randomly dropped. These statistics are by no means perfect, but they and the many other possibilities do not have the flaw we show hypothesis tests possess when used as a stopping rule for assessing balance. As is widely recognized, we also ultimately need better ways of comparing two multidimensional empirical distributions, but these should be sample quantities, not hypothesis tests.

Although these results indicate that future researchers should not use hypothesis tests as a balance stopping rule, a reasonable question is how to interpret the considerable volume of published literature that does so without reporting better balance statistics. One interpretation would be that published tables which report small p-values or large t-tests should cause readers to worry about balance, whereas the reverse would not suggest any level of comfort. In studies with small numbers of observations and thus larger p-values, low levels of imbalance relative to the unobserved importance of the covariates might be acceptable if the bias induced is swamped by the uncertainty of the ultimate quantity of interest at the analysis stage; however, because importance is unobserved, the threshold "low level" is not defined, and so p-value cut-offs (e.g., significance at the 0.05 level) are not of use for this purpose. Best practice should be to minimize imbalance for all covariates, using measures like those described above, and then to adjust for any remaining differences (Ho et al. 2007).

8. Concluding Remarks

Random selection and random assignment (which enable researchers to avoid some statistical assumptions) along with matching and blocking (which adjust nonparametrically for heterogeneity and potential confounders) are among the most practically useful ideas in the history of statistical science. At times, they are also among the most misunderstood. We have tried to lay out some of the key issues in this chapter so that they will be more transparent to all and so that future researchers from both experimental and observational research traditions will be able to avoid the fallacies of causal inference to which many have previously fallen prey.

Our decomposition and analysis describe the basic contributions of each approach and do not attempt to control for the many sophisticated data problems that inevitably arise in a wide range of statistical research in the real world. For example, even in the best experimental work, some information goes missing, randomly selected subjects sometimes refuse to participate, some subjects do not comply with treatment assignments, random numbers do not always get assigned as planned or must be assigned at a more aggregated level than desired, and outcomes are not always measured correctly or recorded appropriately. To account for these problems, when they cannot be fixed through better data collection, more sophisticated methods become necessary. But throughout that more advanced work, the more basic issues discussed here should remain at the forefront.

Appendix: Efficiency of Adding Blocking to Random Treatment

We first show that if the estimand is the SPATE, then blocking always improves classical randomization in terms of statistical efficiency. Suppose that blocking is done on the variable X whose support is χ. Then, the variances of D under classical randomization and blocking are given by

$$\text{var}^c(D) = \frac{2}{n}\left[\text{var}\{Y(1)\} + \text{var}\{Y(0)\}\right],$$

$$\text{var}^B(D) = \frac{2}{n}\sum_{x\in\chi} w_x\left[\text{var}_x\{Y(1)\} + \text{var}_x\{Y(0)\}\right],$$

where $\text{var}(\cdot)$ represents the (super) population variance, $\text{var}_x(\cdot)$ represents the conditional (super) population variance with covariate value $X_i = x$, and w_x is the known (super) population weight for the units with $X_i = x$. Then, if we define the within-block mean as $\overline{Y(t)}_x \equiv E\{Y(t)\mid X = x\}$ for $t = 0,1$, we have

$$\text{var}\{Y(t)\} = E\left[\text{var}_x\{Y(t)\}\right] + \text{var}\{\overline{Y(t)}_x\}$$

$$\geq E\left[\text{var}_x\{Y(t)\}\right] = \sum_{x\in\chi} w_x\,\text{var}_x\{Y(t)\}.$$

Thus, it follows that the variance under blocking is smaller than or equal to the variance under classical randomization, i.e., $\text{var}^C(D) \geq \text{var}^B(D)$.

Next, we consider the case where the estimand is PATE. In this case, the variances of D under complete randomization and blocking are given by

$$\text{var}^c(D) = \frac{1}{n}\Big[2\,\text{var}\{\Upsilon(1)\} + 2\,\text{var}\{\Upsilon(0)\} - \text{var}(\text{TE})\Big], \tag{11}$$

$$\text{var}^B(D) = \frac{1}{n}\sum_{x\in\chi} w_x\Big[2\,\text{var}\{\Upsilon(1)\} + 2\,\text{var}\{\Upsilon(0)\} - \text{var}(\text{TE})\}_,\Big] \tag{12}$$

where $\text{var}(\cdot)$ ($\text{var}_x(\cdot)$) now represents the finite (conditional) population variance, and $w_x = n_x/n$ with n_x being the number of observations with $X_i = x$. Note that the third term in each of the variance expressions cannot be estimated from the data. (However, if the treatment effect is constant across units, i.e., $\Upsilon_i(1) - \Upsilon_i(0)$ for all i, this term will be 0.)

Now, for any variable δ and finite sample size n, the standard analysis-of-variance formula implies that

$$(n-1)\,\text{var}(\delta) = \sum_{x\in\chi}\Big\{(n_x-1)\,\text{var}_x(\delta) + n_x\big(\bar{\delta}_x - \bar{\delta}\big)^2\Big\},$$

where $\bar{\delta}_x = \sum_{i\in\{X_i=x\}}\delta_i / n_x$, and $\bar{\delta} = \sum_{i=1}^{n}\delta_i/n$. Then,

$$\text{var}(\delta) = \sum_{x\in\chi}\left(w_x - \frac{1-w_x}{n-1}\right)\text{var}_x(\delta) + \left(w_x + \frac{w_x}{n-1}\right)(\bar{\delta}_x - \bar{\delta})^2$$

where $w_x = n_x/n$. Applying this result and after some algebra, the difference between equations (11) and (12) can be written as,

$$\text{var}^c(D) - \text{var}^B(D) = \Theta_B - \Theta_W, \tag{13}$$

where the two components Θ_B and Θ_W are closely related to the between-block variation and the within-block variation of the potential outcomes, respectively. They are defined as

$$\Theta_B = \frac{m-1}{m(n-1)}\,\text{var}_w\{\overline{\Upsilon(1)}_x + \overline{\Upsilon(0)}_x\},$$

$$\Theta_W = \frac{1}{n(n-1)}\sum_{x\in\chi}(1-w_x)\,\text{var}_x\{\Upsilon(1) + \Upsilon(0)\},$$

where m is the number of blocks, and

$$\text{var}_w(\delta) = \frac{m\sum_{x\in\chi}w_x(\delta_x - \bar{\delta}_x)^2}{(m-1)\sum_{x\in\chi}w_x}$$

is the weighted variance between blocks. Equation (13) gives the exact expression for the efficiency gain due to blocking. If we assume m stays constant while n grows, the first term, which is positive and $o(1)$, dominates the second term, which is negative but $o(n^{-1})$. Hence, unless the sample size is small, blocking improves efficiency. Moreover, applying the central limit theorem, the asymptotic variances under classical randomization and blocking are given by $n\mathrm{var}^{C}(D)$ and $n\mathrm{var}^{B}(D)$, respectively. Then, the difference between these two asymptotic variances equals

$$n\Theta_{\mathrm{B}} = \frac{m-1}{m}\ \mathrm{var}_{w}\left\{\overline{\Upsilon(1)}_{x} + \overline{\Upsilon(0)}_{x}\right\},$$

which is always positive. Thus, blocking is asymptotically more efficient than classical randomization when PATE is the estimand. Results similar to the ones given in this appendix can also be derived for the matched-pair design (see Imai 2007).

Acknowledgments

Our thanks to Alberto Abadie, Neal Beck, Jack Buckley, Alexis Diamond, Felix Elwert, Andrew Gelman, Ben Hansen, Guido Imbens, Paul Rosenbaum, Don Rubin, Jas Sekhon, Chris Winship, and the participants of the Northeast Political Methodology Program conference for many helpful comments; and the National Institutes of Aging (P01 AG17625–01), the National Institute of Mental Health and the National Institute of Drug Abuse (MH066247), the National Science Foundation (SES-0318275, IIS-9874747, SES-0550873), and the Princeton University Committee on Research in the Humanities and Social Sciences for research support. We also thank Antony Fielding (editor of the journal) for detailed comments that significantly improved the presentation of the results given in this paper. This article was reproduced with the permission of the *Journal of the Royal Statistical Society* A, where it first appeared in 2008,171, part 2, pp. 481–502.

9

METHODS ARE LIKE PEOPLE: IF YOU FOCUS ONLY ON WHAT THEY CAN'T DO, YOU WILL ALWAYS BE DISAPPOINTED

Ian Shapiro

Debates about methods in political science call to mind the job candidate who was asked in an interview to describe an introductory graduate seminar he could teach in his field.[1] His answer that he would begin with the well-established empirical findings provoked the further question: "That's fine for week one, but what would you do for the rest of the semester?" The story is only partly facetious; it reflects the disconnect between the ceaseless quest to refine methods—not to mention the no less endless debates about those refinements—and the manifest dearth of empirical findings about politics that have accumulated in the discipline. If political scientists were developing a growing body of knowledge about the major questions of politics, we would not be mired in debates about methods. People would just get on with it. The debates reflect the reality that if political science is a discipline at all, it is what Kuhn (1962) described as a pre-paradigmatic one. Not only is it devoid of a generally accepted or reigning theory. There is (also) widespread disagreement on what the research agenda should be, on which techniques are best, and even on the kinds of data that should be gathered. Copying practices from clinical research in medicine or from other sciences in which there are well-established theories and cumulating bodies of knowledge should be done cautiously, if at all, with a keen eye to the implications of this different setting.[2]

Another thing not to lose sight of is that all the available methods of studying politics are pretty bad. Even when there is agreement on the question, there is seldom agreement on how to tackle it or, indeed, on what counts as having tackled it. Part of this is due to the sheer complexity of politics and part of it is due to the scarcity of good data. Practitioners of large-n studies have to cope with the dearth of comparable data from different times and places, with the result that scholars typically work with proxies of what they are actually trying to study.[3] Case studies avoid this difficulty, but at the price of raising questions about whether and to what extent the findings travel. In theory people would do both: a large-n comparison combined, perhaps, with intensive case studies that fall on the regression line to help identify causal mechanisms as well as outliers to see why the theory breaks down when it does (see Gerring 2007). In reality, people seldom have the resources or the inclination. The price of entry for reliable case studies is often huge. It can require learning new languages, mastering new literatures, and acquiring other kinds of necessary street-level knowledge. Typically, political scientists who undertake intensive case studies are drawn to them because they already have many of the relevant skills for autobiographical reasons or because of their idiosyncratic interests; not because of where the cases fall in relation to a regression line. Interesting as the results might be, they will not rise to the level of testing a theory that was generated independently of the case in any sense that someone with a rudimentary knowledge of statistics would sanctify.[4]

I start with these observations because I think they go some way toward illuminating the appeal of the turn to field experiments in political science. Field experiments seem to hold out great promise to escape from the quagmire of indeterminacy that plagues so much of what passes for sound empirical work in political science. Here is an approach that takes advantage of randomization, that lends itself to the rigors of experimental controls, and that circumvents the tribulations of external validity that have long been known to plague lab experiments—the great bulk of which are conducted on wildly, if not weirdly, unrepresentative undergraduates in elite U.S. universities (see Heinrich et al. 2010). Finally, it seems to proponents, we have the Holy Grail—or at least a path that can be relied on to lead us there.

Perhaps, but before evaluating that claim we must take account of the reality that Weber (2004 [1917]) pointed out long ago: the scientific method directs us to study questions in particular ways, but it does not tell us which questions to study. A firm believer in the fact/value dichotomy, Weber insisted that the choice of research agenda rests on individual ethical commitments about which science has nothing to say. Even if one does not share Weber's hard-boiled positivism, the endemic disagreement in political science just mentioned suggests that, while people might agree that we should study important questions, there is unlikely to be much convergence any time soon among political scientists on what counts as an important question. One scholar's brilliant insight is the next one's banal truism. Perhaps the turn to field experiments sheds no light on how to deal with the resulting impasse, but no other widely accepted understanding of the political science enterprise does either—so debate about it is irrelevant to assessing the relative merits of field experiments.

Stated at that altitude of abstraction this proposition might seem unassailable, but it looks rather different from the trenches of actual research. Consider the following phenomena that political scientists have sought to study and that those drawn to political science often want to understand but that are not likely to lend themselves to field experiments:

- the effects of regime type on the economy, and vice versa;
- the determinants of peace, war, and revolution;
- the causes and consequences of the trend toward creating independent central banks;
- the causes and consequences of the growth in transnational political and economic institutions;
- the importance of constitutional courts in protecting civil liberties and property rights and in limiting the power of legislatures;
- the effects of other institutional arrangements, such as parliamentarianism v. presidentialism, unicameralism v. bicameralism, federalism v. centralism on such things as the distribution of income and wealth, the effectiveness of macroeconomic policies, and the types of social policies that are enacted;
- the dynamics of political negotiations to institute democracy.

These examples suggest that field experiments lend themselves to the study of behavioral variation in settings where the institutional context is comparatively fixed and where the stakes are relatively low so that the kinds of interventions required are both feasible and do not violate accepted ethical criteria for experimentation on human subjects. It is not surprising, therefore, that field experiments have been widely deployed by governments to evaluate public health interventions[5] and programs to limit corruption,[6] and by those interested in the study of voting behavior.[7] Field experiments do not lend themselves to the study of life-or-death and other high-stakes politics, war and civil war, questions about the macropolitical economy, or the determinants of regime stability and change. That still leaves a great deal to study that is worth studying. Indeed, creative use of the field experimental method might render it deployable in a wider array of areas than I have noted here.[8]

It is not my intention to denigrate field experiments. One of the worst features of methodological disagreement in political science is the propensity of protagonists to compare the inadequacies of one method with the adequacies of a second and then declare the first to be wanting.[9] This is little more than a shell game because all methods have limitations and none should be expected to be serviceable for all purposes. The better inference to draw is that if a method can do some things that are worth doing well, that is a sufficient justification for investing some research resources in it. Hence the title of this chapter.

If that were all there was to say, we could move on in a pluralistic multimethods vein. But Gerber, Green, and Kaplan (hereafter GGK) throw down a more challenging gauntlet in chapter 1 of this book, "The Illusion of Learning from Observational Research." GGK suggest that there are deeper worries. Because observational learning runs the risk of being illusory in ways that field experimental learning, they think, does not, ceteris paribus, resources should be invested in field experimental research. What should we make of this claim? The ceteris paribus clause turns out on inspection to be quite capacious, though this might not readily be grasped because there is a disjunction between the arresting title and setup of their chapter and the conclusion that their argument actually sustains.

Illusion stands in need of disambiguation. GGK's Illusion of Observational Learning Theorem shows that unobserved bias is less likely to infect a field experimental study of a question than an observational study of it. But their theorem does not establish that observational research is illusory in the sense that it is no better than, say, alchemy or astrology or even that it is no better than casual observation or journalism. A researcher might miss sources of bias in the research design of an observational study, leading to unwarranted confidence in its results, but well-designed observational studies should still be expected to be superior to studies that take no account of potential sources of bias or studies that have no research design at all. There is always some chance that apparent observational learning is illusory, but the likelihood varies, inter alia, with how well conventional research design criteria have been deployed.

More important, on GGK's account the results of observational studies can only be declared more likely illusory than the results of experimental studies when both are used to study an identical research question. Perhaps we should have more confidence in the results of an experimental study of the effects of phone calls versus face-to-face contact on voter turnout than in the observational study of that question, but GGK's Illusion of Observational Learning Theorem does not supply grounds for having greater confidence in the results of an experimental study of the effects of phone calls versus face-to-face contact on voter turnout than in the results of an observational study of the effects of deficit spending versus tax cuts on the duration of recessions. These are apples and oranges from the standpoint of their analysis.

This implies corresponding caveats about the commitment of resources dealt with in GGK's Research Allocation Theorem. Ceteris paribus, it makes more sense to spend the next marginal research dollar on a field experiment of phone calls versus face-to-face contact on voter turnout if the alternative is an observational study of that question. But the Research Allocation Theorem provides no basis to say that the next marginal dollar is better spent on the field experiment on voter turnout than on the observational study of deficit spending versus tax cuts on the duration of recessions.

This might provoke the retort that investing in research questions that do lend themselves to field experiments is nonetheless to be preferred on the grounds that it gives us a better prospect of reducing the likelihood of illusory findings than if we do not. With observational studies we could chase our tails in the dense fog of illusion for centuries—the social science equivalent of pre-experimental studies of bloodletting. Surely it makes more sense to study something where we have better prospects of making progress? To the extent that this supposition operates as an unstated presumption behind the enthusiasm for the field experimental research program, it stands in need of being stated explicitly and scrutinized.

Before getting to the larger issue of choosing research questions, I want to register a note of caution about this line of thinking even within research agendas that do lend themselves to field experimentation. As a field experimental research agenda advances, there might be good reasons to worry about diminishing returns to the research resources invested in a given stream of research; that scholars will be learning more and more about less and less.

Consider the study of voter turnout. We certainly know much more about it due to Green and Gerber's field experimental research agenda on voter mobilization, and in particular the effects of face-to-face efforts such as traditional door-to-door canvassing as compared with mass mailings and the use of other kinds of media. They estimate that between a hundred and two hundred field experiments have been run in the past fifteen years in which researchers study the connection between mailings and/or phone calls and voter turnout.[10] Their 2008 book has chapters exploring the effects of different types of leaflets, direct mail, phone banks, e-mail, public events, and mass media. They conclude by calling for additional studies of the effects of mass media, voter registration, voting by mail, and the timing of get-out-the-vote efforts. These refinements might well be of interest to people running political campaigns, but that tells us nothing about whether it can be expected to generate knowledge that is worth having for any other purpose. To judge whether the increased knowledge promises anything other than the political science equivalent of economists giving marketing advice to businesses, we need to know more about the scholarly agendas to which it might plausibly be expected to contribute.

One possible answer has to do with upending conventional wisdom. Dispelling influential falsehoods is surely a useful part of almost any plausible account of the political science discipline and is one time-honored way in which it has proceeded for decades. The belief that a single power elite controls all major political decisions, that divided party control affects legislative output in Congress, that Thomas Hobbes was the universally despised "monster of Malmesbury," that candidate debates influence election outcomes, or that parties converge on the median voter are all instances where careful empirical scholarship has overturned conventional wisdom, or at least called it seriously into question.[11] Part of the value of Green and Gerber's work on turnout is that it fits into this tradition. It has often been conjectured that face-to-face canvassing to get out the vote is being rendered obsolete by new communications technologies. Prima facie this is not an unreasonable suspicion. Green and Gerber's early field experiments upended that view; surely that was a notable contribution. But the refinements they have since been exploring and calling for at what they describe as the research frontiers of this area of inquiry give one pause. Is it really worth anyone's other than a political campaign's time to know exactly how much less cost-effective leafleting is than canvassing in getting out the vote? or just how much more expensive direct mail is? or how much more effective emails from personal friends are at getting out the vote than mass emails? or that mail and phone campaigns can get people to vote by mail rather than in person, but they do not increase turnout rates? (Green and Gerber 2008: 53, 72, 107, 143).[12]

The impulse to yell, "Enough, already!" springs, I think, from contemplating the potentially endless research stream of turnout experiments without paying any attention to how we should think about, let alone compute, the value of the expected payoffs from proceeding down that path. If we follow GGK's lead in estimating the value of resources spent on a stream of research by reference to opportunity costs of their possible deployment on something else, it is logical to think about the conditions under which the returns should be expected to diminish.

Some types of research clearly should not be thought about in that way. When scientists are looking for causes of cancers, having large fleets of researchers isolate and get exact answers to well-defined, if small, research questions that are close cousins of one another might make a great deal of sense. One of them could hit on a definitive breakthrough that moves the entire field forward, but no one knows in advance who that is going to be. In such circumstances there is a diversified attack on an agreed-upon problem, considerable established knowledge but a lot that is not known, and a stock of theory that motivates researchers about where to look next. One can imagine a day when the big questions about the causes of and treatments for cancers have been answered. Then serious questions will arise about the marginal benefits of additional studies. We are a long way away from there.[13]

But turnout and the other political science examples I mentioned earlier are not like that. There is no equivalent to finding a cure for cancer motivating the research. If the motivation is, as I supposed earlier, to scotch or call into question a widespread misconception, once that has been done then the value added of endless refinements might well be of diminishing interest. This brings us to the role of theory in motivating and refining empirical research agendas, to which I now turn.

As well as calling for more field experiments on turnout, in their discussion of research frontiers Green and Gerber take up the issue of theory, remarking that "the main challenge is to isolate the active ingredient that causes some GOTV [get-out-the-vote] strategies to work and others to fail." In fact it is the only theoretical challenge they mention, observing that "this research agenda remains in its infancy" (Green and Gerber 2008: 143). We get some insight as to why they zero in on this as the most important theoretical challenge from the account of the role of theory in GGK. Theory development, they say, "depends critically on the stock of basic, carefully assessed, empirical claims." They complain that social scientists "tend to look down on this type of science as narrow and uninspiring, grasping instead for weak tests of expansive and arresting propositions." They blame this surplus of reach over grasp for the fact that "social scientists have accumulated relatively few secure empirical premises from which to extrapolate," an unfortunate state of affairs "because developing secure empirical premises speeds the rate at which learning occurs as new experimental and observational results become available."

I have nothing against inductive theory building (see Green and Shapiro 1994: 185–88; 1995), but GGK's understanding of it is overly narrow. If theories are to be developed only on the basis of well-tested empirical claims, then theorizing will be geared exclusively toward accounting for either regularities or anomalies that are thrown up in particular streams of well-tested empirical research. Such theorizing might well be worthwhile for advancing a particular stream of research, but it will tell us nothing about whether the stream is worth advancing given the risks of diminishing returns and the opportunity costs of doing something else instead. This inevitably raises questions about why the research is being done in the first place.

Green and Gerber (2008: 2) address their research to people who want to increase voter turnout, in effect bracketing the questions about why. For political campaigns the answer might be obvious, but Green and Gerber also mention nonpartisan groups who seek to mobilize voters. Once we consider groups for whom the self-evident motive of winning is absent, then it becomes relevant why the group in question wants to ramp up turnout. If, for instance, their goal is to expand civic participation, then potential trade-offs arise over whether ever more fine-grained knowledge about how to get people to vote is worth spending resources on rather than on, say, figuring out ways to get people not to avoid jury service, to get them to participate in town meetings, or to engage in other civic activities. This is to say nothing of those who have adduced reasons to wonder about benign interpretations of increased turnout, as in Almond and Verba's (1963, 1980) and Hibbing and Theiss-Morse's (2002) contentions that not voting might reflect satisfaction with the status quo; Bateson's (2012) finding that turnout increases when people have been victimized by crime; Verba, Schlozman, and Brady's (1995) claim that not voting reflects people's recognition that participating won't do them much good; or the older concerns registered by Mill (1991[1861]) and Converse (1964) that ignorant voters can be manipulated to turn out for causes they do not understand.

Nor is this point restricted to nonpartisan groups. Partisan groups whose members work to increase turnout are often motivated by policy agendas. Consider the decades-long debate as to whether racial integration is more profitably pursued through the courts or through electoral politics (Rosenberg 1993). The costs of turning out voters are relevant to that debate, but so are many other things, ranging from the costs of litigation, to the likelihood of its success, to knowledge about the responsiveness of legislators, once elected, to voters' preferences. Activists must make judgments about the optimal allocation of their resources in the face of the available stock of knowledge and theory about all these things. The changing costs and value of marginal increments to knowledge about any one of them is relevant to their decision, but this is meaningful only when considered in relation to the others. It might be that there is a dearth of well-tested empirical knowledge about some of the possible courses of action they must consider, but to forgo theorizing about them for that reason in favor of theorizing instead about why some turnout strategies are more effective than others would be nuts. The joke about hunting for lost keys under the lamppost because that's where the light happens to be comes to mind.

In short, theorizing that loses sight of the purposes for which research is being conducted runs the risk of being seen as pointless. This is an important caution. I suspect that part of the disaffection with 1960s behaviorism in the study of American politics that spawned the model mania of the 1980s about which Green and I complained in *Pathologies of Rational Choice Theory* was that the behaviorists had become mindlessly preoccupied with demonstrating propositions of the order that Catholics in Detroit vote Democrat (see Taylor 1985: 90).[14] As a result, the mainstream of political science discipline that they came to define seemed to others to be both utterly devoid of theoretical ambition as well as detached from consequential questions of politics; frankly boring. To paraphrase Kant, theoretical ambition without empirical research may well be vacuous, but empirical research without theoretical ambition will be blind.[15]

In this regard it is worth contrasting the literature on voter turnout to date with one of the other research agendas I mentioned that was also launched when careful empirical research called a piece of conventional wisdom seriously into question. In *Who Governs?* Dahl (1962) deployed an intensive study of decision making in New Haven to upend the view, popularized by C. Wright Mills (1956) and others, that power is typically exercised by a small elite. But Dahl's work also spawned a decades-long literature on power that had both empirical and theoretical strands. On the empirical side there was a series of successor studies of power in urban politics from Polsby (1963), Domhoff (1987), Gaventa (1980), and others, culminating in Rae (2005). On the theoretical side, Dahl's (1957) programmatic argument provoked a comparably wide-ranging literature from Bachrach and Baratz (1962), Wolfinger (1971), Lukes (1974), Isaac (1987), Shapiro and Wendt (1992), Hayward (2000) and others, with a good deal of cross-fertilization between the two. The result is that we now have a considerably more nuanced and sophisticated understanding of how power actually operates in bureaucratic and quasi-bureaucratic settings, techniques have been developed to study the so-called second and third faces of power empirically (declared impossible by some of the early behavioral theorists),[16] and there has been a reframing of theoretical agendas—as in Gaventa's attempt to specify the conditions under which quiescence, rather than rebellion, is what stands in need of explanation.

The empirical results in much of this literature are surely less secure than those in the field experimental literature on turnout. Indeed, some of the more notable contributions, such as Gaventa (1980) and Rae (2005), are perhaps better characterized as exercises in explanatory description than as efforts to line up independent and dependent variables for either large-n or experimental studies geared to isolating unambiguously demonstrable causal propositions. Among the contributions of such works is a kind of historical scholarship that is more self-conscious about causation than that which historians typically engage in. But, particularly for researchers who are predisposed to an inductive approach to theory building as at least one of the paths forward for the discipline, such scholarship should not be discounted. Describing the world is essential to theory building, but it is also contentious. An important task for political scientists is to foster critical reflection about prevailing descriptions, point out the theoretical agendas they presuppose and support, and consider the advantages and limitations of alternatives. A view that biases theory building to what has already been well tested empirically excludes too much and risks marginalizing itself over time.[17]

In *Pathologies* Green and I made the case for problem-driven research, in which "the elaboration of theories is designed to explain phenomena that arise in the world." We contrasted this with method-driven research, which occurs "when a theory is elaborated without reference to what phenomena are to be explained, and the theorist subsequently searches for phenomena to which the theory in question can be applied" (194). Green and I were concerned primarily with theories in search of applications, but methods in search of applications are no less problematic. We argued that the best course is to start with a problem, identify what is known about it from the existing stock of theory and empirical knowledge, and then try to design a research strategy that can do better (180–84, 188).

To be sure, embracing problem-driven research does not tell researchers which problems to study, and people disagree over which problems merit scholarly attention. But researchers are kidding themselves if they think they can duck this question by choosing research streams that are most likely to produce accumulations of knowledge. Even if they are right—and I have suggested reasons for having misgivings about the extent to which they are—they answer the question implicitly by the choices they make and the examples they set for students and junior colleagues. They would do better to make the strongest case they can for the problems they choose to study without appealing to the fact, if it is one, that they lend themselves to field experimental research—or to any other method of political inquiry.

NOTES

1. This essay draws from and builds on Shapiro (2004).

2. Some would say that economics is not as different from political science in these respects as many economists like to believe, pointing, for example, to the dissensus on the causes and best responses to the financial crisis that began in 2008. I am sympathetic to this view but will not take it up here. See Cassidy (2010).

3. For instance, in the literature on whether democracies are downwardly redistributive scholars often focus on changes in inequality, which is influenced by many things other than government policies. A better dependent variable would be redistributive policies enacted by legislatures, but it would be incredibly difficult to get cross-nationally comparable data on such policies. But by using changes in inequality scholars are inevitably vulnerable to objections that they have not controlled, or not controlled in the right way, for the many possible things that influence that. See Shapiro (2003a: 104–45). Comparable considerations attend the debates about the use of per capita income as a proxy for state capacity in the literature on civil wars. See Fearon and Laitin (2003), Quinn et al. (2003), and Glynn (2009).

4. My own case study of the repeal of the estate tax in the United States in 2001 (Graetz and Shapiro 2005) involved a three-year commitment that included learning the history of U.S. tax policy, the budget and related committee process of the U.S. federal government, and some 150 intensive interviews—and we didn't have to learn new languages. We developed tentative suspicions about how representative our findings are of other kinds of distributive politics (see Shapiro 2011: 27–31), but we don't know whether they are correct.

5. For example, McCracken et al. (2007) established through a randomized experiment in Guatemala that chimney woodstoves reduce exposure to fine particles when compared with traditional open wood fires, with concomitant improvements in the subjects' diastolic blood pressure. Duflo et al. (2011) showed through randomized

studies of sub-Saharan teenagers that subsidizing education reduces dropout rates, teen pregnancy, and teen marriage, but that, in order to have an impact on HIV and other sexually transmitted diseases, subsidies must be combined with explicit instruction about the risks. Roberts et al. (2001) deployed a field experiment to establish the measurable health benefits of clean water in a Malawian refugee camp.

6. Useful field experiments of corruption include Olken (2007), who found that centralized monitoring is more effective than grassroots monitoring in reducing corruption in Indonesian villages, especially where village heads planned to run for re-election. Ferraz and Finan (2008) found that empowering citizens with information about their local elected officials reduces reelection prospects of corrupt Brazilian mayors, and Lagunes (2012) found that monitoring construction permit applications in Mexico is effective only when the monitoring officials face the risk of sanction from above.

7. See Green and Gerber (2008), discussed further below, for a compilation of the field experimental work on voter turnout.

8. Some examples of ingenious field experiments: Sherman et al. (1995) capitalized on the random assignment of court-ordered raids on crack houses to run a field experiment on their deterrent effects—which turn out not to be great. Howell et al. (2002) deployed evidence from programs that randomly awarded school vouchers to treatment and control groups in three U.S. cities to find that African American students who switched from public to private schools did significantly better those who did not. Paluck and Green (2009) studied the effects of the media on prejudice and conflict in Rwanda via an experiment in which the treatment group that listened to radio soaps with messages about reducing prejudice, violence, and trauma became more trusting, empathic, and cooperative than did the control group, whose placebo soaps excluded such messages.

9. For discussion of an analogous phenomenon that plagues normative debates in political theory, see Shapiro (2005: 152–77).

10. In correspondence.

11. On the debate about power elites, see Dahl (1962) and the related literature on power discussed below. On divided party control, see Mayhew (1991), Howell et al. (2000), Rogers (2005), and Binder (2011). On the demolition of the "Monster of Malmesbury" thesis, see Skinner (1966) and Parkin (2007). On the effects of debates, see Katz and Feldman (1962), Sears and Chaffee (1979), and Holdbrook (1996). For the convergence thesis in electoral competition, see Downs (1957). On the subsequent empirical literature, see Green and Shapiro (1994: 147–78).

12. A notable exception here is the field experimental literature establishing that substantial increases in turnout can be achieved by telling voters their own voting records and those of their neighbors, or by sending them leaflets telling them that their voting records will be publicized in their communities (see Green and Gerber 2008: 68–71; Gerber, Green, and Larimer 2008). These findings are consequential not only for evaluating rational self-interest theories of turnout, as Green, Gerber, and Larimer note, but also for social psychology literatures on shaming as well as debates about interdependent utilities among economists.

13. This is not to deny that even now there are important questions about the opportunity costs of cancer research versus other kinds of medical research. See Shapiro (2003b: 101–3).

14. For discussion of perhaps analogous reactive oscillation of legal scholarship between overambitious theory and atheoretical bean counting, see Gilmore (1979).

15. Kant's (1929 [1781]: 93) formulation was, "Thoughts without content are empty, intuitions without concepts are blind."

16. The second face of power concerns "non-decisions" which Bachrach and Baratz (1962) identified as resulting from the mobilization of bias. Lukes (1974) defined power's third face as involving the manipulation of preferences.

17. I take up these issues further in Shapiro (2004).

REFERENCES

Abadie A. 2002. Bootstrap tests for distributional treatment effects in instrumental variables models. *Journal of the American Statistical Association* 97(457): 284–92.

Abbring, J. H., and J. J. Heckman. 2008. Econometrics evaluation of social programs, part III: distributional treatment effects, dynamic treatment effects, dynamic discrete choice and general equilibrium policy evaluation. In *Handbook of Econometrics*, ed. J. J. Heckman and E. Leamers. Vol. 6B. Amsterdam: Elsevier Sci. Ltd. North Holl, 2008.

Abdul Latif Jameel Poverty Action Lab (ALJ-PAL). 2005. Fighting poverty: what works? Fall, no. 1. Cambridge: MIT.

Acemoglu, D., and J. Angrist. 2001a. How large are human-capital externalities? Evidence from compulsory schooling laws. In *NBER Macroeconomics Annual 2000*, ed. B. S. Bernanke and K. Rogoff, 15: 9–74. Cambridge, Mass.: NBER.

———. 2009. Theory, general equilibrium, political economy and empirics in development economics. *Journal of Economic Perspectives* 24(3): 17–32.

———, S. Johnson, and J. A. Robinson. 2001b. The colonial origins of comparative development: An empirical investigation. *American Economic Review* 91(5): 1369–1401.

Achen, C. H. 1986. *The Statistical Analysis of Quasi-Experiments*. Berkeley: University of California Press.

Alderman, H. 2002. Do local officials know something we don't? Decentralization of targeted transfers in Albania. *Journal of Public Economics* 83(3): 375–404.

Almond, G., and S. Verba. 1963. *The Civic Culture: Political Attitudes and Democracy in Five Nations*. Princeton: Princeton University Press.

———, and S. Verba, eds. 1980. *The Civic Culture Revisited*. London: Sage.

Altman, D. G. 1998. Within trial variation—a false trail. *Journal of Clinical Epidemiology* 51(4): 301–3.

Altman, L. K. 1986. *Who Goes First?: The Story of Self-Experimentation in Medicine.* Berkeley: University of California Press.

Angrist, J., E. Bettinger, E. Bloom, M. Kremer, and E. King. 2002. Vouchers for private schooling in Colombia: Evidence from randomized natural experiments. *American Economic Review* 92(5): 1535–58.

———, D. Lang, and P. Oreopoulos. 2009. Incentives and services for college achievement: Evidence from a randomized trial. *American Economic Journal: Journal of Applied Economics* 1: 136–63.

———, and V. Lavy. 2009. The effect of high school matriculation awards: Evidence from group-level randomized trials. *American Economic Review* 99(4): 1384–1414.

———, E. Bettinger, and M. Kremer. 2006. Long-term educational consequences of secondary school vouchers: Evidence from administrative records in Colombia. *American Economic Review* 96(3): 847–62.

———, G. W. Imbens, and D. B. Rubin. 1996. Identification of causal effects using instrumental variables. *Journal of the American Statistical Association* 91(434): 444–55.

———. 1990. Lifetime earnings and the Vietnam-era draft lottery: Evidence from Social Security Administrative records. *American Economic Review* 80(3): 313–36.

———, and G. W. Imbens. 1994. Identification and estimation of local average treatment effects. *Econometrica* 62(2): 467–75.

———, and J. S. Pischke. 2010. The credibility revolution in empirical economics: How better research design is taking the con out of econometrics. *Journal of Economic Perspectives* 24(2): 3–30.

———, and V. Lavy. 1999. Using Maimonides' rule to estimate the effect of class size on scholastic achievement. *Quarterly Journal of Economics* 114(2): 533–75.

Ansolabehere, S., and S. Iyengar. 1995. *Going Negative: How Attack Ads Shrink and Polarize the Electorate.* New York: Free Press.

Arceneaux, K., A. S. Gerber, and D. P. Green. 2006. Comparing experimental and matching methods using a large-scale voter mobilization experiment. *Political Analysis* 14: 1–36.

Ashraf, N., J. Berry, and J. M. Shapiro. 2010. Can higher prices stimulate product use? Evidence from a field experiment in Zambia. *American Economic Review* 100(5): 2383–2413.

———, D. Karlan, and W. Yin. 2006. Tying Odysseus to the mast: Evidence from a commitment savings product in the Philippines. *Quarterly Journal of Economics* 121(2): 635–72.

Attanasio, O., A. Barr, J. Camillo, G. Genicot, and C. Meghir. 2008a. Group formation and risk pooling in a field experiment. Mimeograph, Georgetown University.

———, A. Kugler, and C. Meghir. 2008b. Training disadvantaged youth in Latin America: Evidence from a randomized trial. Working Paper, Institute for Fiscal Studies.

————, C. Meghir, and A. Santiago. 2012. Education choices in Mexico: Using a structural model and a randomized experiment to evaluate Progresa. *Review of Economic Studies* 79(1): 37–99.

Austin, P. C., and M. M. Mamdani. 2006. A comparison of propensity score methods: A case study estimating the effectiveness of post-ami statin use. *Statistical Medicine* 25: 2084–2106.

Bachrach, P., and M. S. Baratz. 1962. The two faces of power. *American Political Science Review* 56: 947–52.

Banaji, M. 2001. Implicit attitudes can be measured. In *The Nature of Remembering: Essays in Honor of Robert G. Crowder*, ed. H. L. Roediger III, J. S. Nairne, I. Neath, A. Surprenant, 117–50. Washington: American Psychological Association.

Banerjee, A. R., E. Duflo, R. Glennerster, and S. Khemani. 2010a. Pitfalls of participatory programs: Evidence from a randomized evaluation in education in India. *American Economic Journal: Economic Policy* 2(1): 1–30.

————, S. Cole, E. Duflo, and L. Linden. 2007. Remedying education: Evidence from two randomized experiments in India. *Quarterly Journal of Economics* 122(3): 1235–64.

————, E. Duflo, R. Glennerster, and D. Kothari. 2010b. Improving immunization coverage in rural India: A clustered randomized controlled evaluation of immunization campaigns with and without incentives. *British Journal of Medicine* 340: 1–9.

————, and E. Duflo. 2005. Growth theory through the lens of development economics. In *Handbook of Economic Growth*, ed. S. Durlauf, P. Aghion, 1A:473–552. Amsterdam: Elsevier Sci. Ltd. North Holl.

————, S. Jacob, M. Kremer, J. Lanjouw, and P. Lanjouw. 2005. Moving to universal education! Costs and trade-offs. Mimeograph, Department of Economics, MIT.

————. 2002. The uses of economic theory: Against a purely positive interpretation of theoretical results. Working Paper 007, Department of Economics, MIT.

————. 2005. New development economics and the challenge to theory. *Economic and Political Weekly* 40(40): 4340–44.

————. 2007. *Making Aid Work*. Cambridge: MIT Press.

————. 2009. Big answers for big questions: The presumption of growth policy. In *What Works in Development: Thinking Big and Thinking Small*, ed. Jessica Cohen and William Easterly, 207–32. Washington: Brookings Institution Press.

————. 2005. New development economics and the challenge to theory. *Economic and Political Weekly*, October 1, 4340–44.

————. 2007. Inside the machine: Toward a new development economics. *Boston Review*, September 4.

————, and R. He. 2008. Making aid work. In *Reinventing Foreign Aid*, ed. William R. Easterly, 47–92. Cambridge: MIT Press.

Barnard, J., C. E. Frangakis, J. L. Hill, and D. B. Rubin. 2003. Principal stratification approach to broken randomized experiments: A case study of school choice vouchers in New York City. *Journal of the American Statistical Association* 98: 299–323.

Barnes, J. 1977. *The Ethics of Inquiry in Social Science: Three Lectures.* Oxford: Oxford University Press.

Barrett, C. B., and M. R. Carter. 2010. The power and pitfalls of experiments in development economics: Some non-random reflections. *Applied Economic Perspectives and Policy* 32(4): 515–48.

Barro, Robert J., 1998. *Determinants of Economic Growth: A Cross-Country Empirical Study.* Cambridge: MIT Press.

———, and X. Sala-i-Martin. 1995. *Economic Growth.* New York: McGraw-Hill.

Basu, K. 2005. The new empirical development economics: Remarks on its philosophical foundations. *Economic and Political Weekly* 40(40): 4336–39.

Bateson, G. 2012. Crime victimization and political participation. *American Political Science Review* 106(3): 570–87.

Bauer, T. Peter. 1971. *Dissent on Development: Studies and Debates in Development Economics.* London: Weidenfeld and Nicolson.

———. 1981. *Equality, the Third World, and Economic Delusion.* Cambridge: Harvard University Press.

Baumrind, D. 1985. Research using intentional deception: Ethical issues revisited. *American Psychologist* 40(2): 165.

Beaman, L., R. Chattopadhyay, E. Duflo, R. Pande, and P. Topalova. 2009. Powerful women: Does exposure reduce bias? *Quarterly Journal of Economics* 124(4): 1497–1540.

Behrman, J. R., P. Sengupta, and P. E. Todd. 2005. Progressing through Progresa: An impact assessment of Mexico's school subsidy experiment. *Economic Development and Cultural Change* 54(1): 237–75.

Berry, J. 2008. Child control in education decisions: An evaluation of targeted incentives to learn in India. Mimeograph, Department of Economics, MIT.

Bertrand, M., D. Chugh, and S. Mullainathan. 2005. Implicit discrimination. *American Economic Review* 95(2): 94–98.

———, S. Djankov, R. Hanna, and S. Mullainathan. 2007. Corruption in driving licensing process in Delhi. *Quarterly Journal of Economics* 122(4): 1639–76.

———, D. Karlan, S. Mulainathan, E. Shafir, and J. Zinman. 2010. What's advertising content worth? Evidence from a consumer credit marketing. *Quarterly Journal of Economics* 125(1): 263–306.

———, S. Djankov, R. Hanna, and S. Mullainathan. 2007. Obtaining a driver's license in India: An experimental approach to studying corruption. *Quarterly Journal of Economics* 122(4): 1639–76.

Bhargava, A. 2008. Randomized controlled experiments in health and social sciences: Some conceptual issues. *Economics and Human Biology* 6: 293–98.

Binder, S. 2011. Legislative productivity and gridlock. In *The Oxford Handbook of the American Congress,* ed. Eric Schickler and Frances E. Lee, 641–60. Oxford: Oxford University Press.

Bjorkman, M., and J. Svensson. 2009. Power to the people: Evidence from a randomized field experiment of a community-based monitoring project in Uganda. *Quarterly Journal of Economics* 124(2): 735–69.

Bleakley, H. 2007. Disease and development: evidence from hookworm eradication in the American south. *Quarterly Journal of Economics* 122(1): 73–117.

Bloom, H. S., C. Michalopoulos, C. J. Hill, and Y. Lei. 2002. Can nonexperimental comparison group methods match the findings from a random assignment evaluation of mandatory welfare-to-work programs? Working Paper, Manpower Demonstration Research Corporation.

Blundell, R., and M. Costa Dias. 2009. Alternative approaches to evaluation in empirical microeconomics. *Journal of Human Resources* 44(3): 565–640.

Bobonis, G., E. Miguel, C. P. Sharma. 2006. Anemia and school participation. *J. Hum. Resour.* 41(4): 692–721.

Bonetti, S. 1998. Experimental economics and deception. *Journal of Economic Psychology* 19(3): 377–95.

Boone, P. 1996. Politics and the effectiveness of foreign aid. *European Economic Review* 40: 289–329.

Bosk, C. L., and R. G. Vries. 2004. Bureaucracies of mass deception: Institutional Review Boards and the ethics of ethnographic research. *Annals of the American Academy of Political and Social Science* 595: 249–63.

Box, G. E. P., W. G. Hunter, and J. S. Hunter. 1978. *Statistics for Experimenters*. New York: Wiley-Interscience.

———, and G. C. Tiao. 1973. *Bayesian Inference in Statistical Analysis*. Reading, Mass.: Addison-Wesley.

Brady, H. E. 2003. Models of causal inference: Going beyond the Neyman-Rubin-Holland theory. Paper prepared for the Annual Meeting of the Midwest Political Science Association, Chicago, Illinois.

———. 2009. Causation and explanation in social science. In *The Oxford Handbook of Political Science*, ed, Robert E. Goodin, 1054–1107. Oxford: Oxford University Press.

———, D. Collier, and J. M. Box-Steffensmeier. 2009. Overview of political methodology: Post-behavioral movements and trends. In *The Oxford Handbook of Political Science*, ed. Robert E. Goodin, 1005–53. Oxford: Oxford University Press.

Bruhn, M., and D. McKenzie. 2009. In pursuit of balance: Randomization in practice in development field experiments. *American Economic Journal: Applied Economics* 1(4): 200–232.

Burnside, C., and D. Dollar. 2000. Aid, policies, and growth. *American Economic Review* 90(4): 847–67.

Camerer, C., G. Loewenstein, and M. Rabin. 2004. *Advances in Behavioral Economics*. London: Sage Foundation and Princeton: Princeton University Press.

Card, D. 1999. The causal effect of education on earnings. In *Handbook of Labor Economics 3*, ed. O. Ashenfelter and D. Card, 1801–63. Amsterdam: Elsevier.

Cartwright, N. 2007a. Are RCTs the gold standard? *Biosocieties* 2: 11–20.

———. 2007b. *Hunting Causes and Using Them: Approaches in Philosophy and Economics*. Cambridge: Cambridge University Press.

———. 2010. What are randomized trials good for? *Philosophical Studies* 147: 59–70.

Cassidy, J. 2010. *How Markets Fail: The Logic of Economic Calamities*. New York: Farrar Straus Giroux.

Chattopadhyay, R., and E. Duflo. 2004. Women as policy makers: Evidence from a randomized controlled experiment in India. *Econometrica* 72(5): 1409–43.

Clemens, M., S. Radelet, and R. Bhavnani. 2004. Counting chickens when they hatch: The short-term effect of aid on growth. Center for Global Development, Working Paper 44, November.

Cochran, W. G. 1965. The planning of observational studies of human populations (with discussion). *Journal of the Royal Statistical Society A*, 128: 234–65.

———. 1968. The effectiveness of adjustment by subclassification in removing bias in observational studies. *Biometrics* 24: 295–313.

———, and Cox, G. 1957. *Experimental Designs*. New York: Wiley.

Cohen, J., and P. Dupas. 2007. Free distribution or cost-sharing? Evidence from a randomized malaria prevention experiment. *Global Economy and Development Working Paper* 11, Brookings Institution, December.

———, and P. Dupas. 2010. Free distribution or cost-sharing? Evidence from a randomized malaria prevention experiment. *Quarterly Journal of Economics* 125(1): 1–45.

Concato, J., N. Shah, and R. I. Horwitz. 2000. Randomized, controlled trials, observational studies, and the hierarchy of research designs. *New England Journal of Medicine* 342(25): 1887–92.

Conning, J., and M. Kevane. 2002. Community-based targeting mechanisms for social safety nets: A critical review. *World Development* 30(3): 375–94.

Converse, P. E. 1964. The nature of belief systems in mass publics. In *Ideology and Discontent*, ed. David E. Apter, 206–61. Glencoe: Free Press of Glencoe.

Cook, T. D., and D. T. Campbell. 1979. *Quasi-Experimentation: Design and Analysis Issues for Field Settings*. Boston: Houghton Mifflin.

———, and M. R. Payne. 2002. Objecting to the objections to using random assignment in educational research. In *Evidence Matters: Randomized Trials in Education Research*, ed. F. Mosteller and R. Boruch, 150–78. Washington: Brookings Institution Press.

Cox, D. R. 1958. *Planning of Experiments*. New York: Wiley.

Crosnoe, R. 2005. Double disadvantage or signs of resilience?: The elementary school contexts of children from Mexican immigrant families. *American Educational Research Journal* 42: 269–303.

Crump, R., J. Hotz, G. W. Imbens, and O. Mitni. 2008. Nonparametric tests for treatment effect heterogeneity. *Review of Economic Statistics* 90(3): 389–405.

Dahl, R. 1957. The concept of power. *Behavioral Science* 2(3): 201–15.

———. 1962. *Who Governs? Democracy and Power in an American City*. New Haven: Yale University Press.

Dalgaard, C. J., and H. Hansen. 2001. On aid, growth, and good policies. *Journal of Development Studies* 37(6): 17–41.

———, H. Hansen, and F. Tarp. 2004. On the empirics of foreign aid and growth. *Economic Journal* 114(F): 191–216.

Davey Smith, G., and M. Egger. 1998. Incommunicable knowledge? Interpreting and applying the results of clinical trials and meta-analysis. *Journal of Clinical Epidemiology* 51(4): 289–95.

———, and S. Ibrahim. 2002. Data dredging, bias, or confounding: They can all get you into the *BMJ* and the Friday papers. Editorial, *British Medical Journal* 325: 1437–38.

Dawes, R. M., J. M. Orbell, R. T. Simmons, and A. J. C. van de Kragt. 1986. Organizing groups for collective action. *American Political Science Review* 80: 1171–85.

de Mel, S., D. McKenzie, and C. Woodruff. 2008. Returns to capital in microenterprises: Evidence from a field experiment. *Quarterly Journal of Economics* 123(4): 1329–72.

———, D. McKenzie, and C. Woodruff. 2009. Are women more credit constrained? Experimental evidence on gender and microenterprise returns. *Am. Econ. J. Appl. Econ.* 1(3): 1–32.

de Rooij, E. A., D. P. Green, and A. S. Gerber. 2009. Field experiments on political behavior and collective action. *Annual Review of Political Science* 12(1): 389–95.

Deaton, A. 2009. Instruments of development: Randomization in the tropics, and the search for the elusive keys to economic development. *Proceedings of the British Academy* 162: 123–60. Oxford: Oxford University Press.

———. 2010a. Understanding the mechanisms of economic development. *Journal of Economic Perspectives* 24(4): 3–16.

———. 2010b. Instruments, randomization, and learning about development. *Journal of Economic Literature* 48(2): 424–55.

Dehejia, R. 2005a. Practical propensity score matching: A reply to Smith and Todd. *Journal of Econometrics* 125(1–2): 355–64.

———. 2005b. Program evaluation as a decision problem. *Journal of Econometrics* 125: 141–73.

———, and S. Wahba. 1999. Causal effects in non-experimental studies: Re-evaluating the evaluation of training programs. *Journal of the American Statistical Association* 94: 1053–62.

Dixit, A., and J. Londregan. 1996. The determinants of success of special interests in redistributive politics. *Journal of Politics* 58(4): 1132–55.

Domhoff, W. G. 1987. *Who Really Rules? New Haven and Community Power*. New Brunswick: Transaction.

Donohue, J. J., and J. Wolfers. 2006. Uses and abuses of empirical evidence in the death penalty debate. *Stanford Law Review* 58: 791–845.

Downs, A. 1957. *An Economic Theory of Democracy*. New York: Harper and Row.

Doyle, M. W. 1986. Liberalism and world politics. *American Political Science Review* 80(4): 1151–69.

Druckman, J. N., D. W. Green, J. Kuklinski, and A. Lupia. 2006. The growth and development of experimental research in political science. *American Political Science Review* 100(4): 627–35.

Duflo, E. 2004c. Scaling up and evaluation. *Annual World Bank Conference on Development Economics 2004.* Washington: World Bank.

———. 2004a. The medium-run consequences of educational expansion: Evidence from a large school construction program in Indonesia. *J. Dev. Econ.* 74(1): 163–97.

———. 2004b. Scaling up and evaluation. In *Accelerating Development*, ed. F. Bourguignon, B. Pleskovic, 342–67. Washington: World Bank.

———. 2007. Field experiments in development economics. In *Advances in Economic Theory and Econometrics*, ed. R Blundell, W. Newey, T. Persson. Econ. Soc. Monogr. 42, chap. 13. Cambridge: Cambridge University Press.

———, and M. Kremer. 2003. Use of randomization in the evaluation of development effectiveness. Paper prepared for the World Bank Operations Evaluation Development Conference on Evaluation and Development Effectiveness.

———, and M. Kremer. 2004. Use of randomization in the evaluation of development effectiveness. In *Evaluating Development Effectiveness*, World Bank Ser. Eval. Dev., ed. O. Feinstein, G. K. Ingram, G. K. Pitman, 7:205–32. New Brunswick: Transaction.

———, M. Kremer, and J. Robinson. 2008c. How high are rates of return to fertilizer? Evidence from field experiments in Kenya. *Am. Econ. Rev. Pap. Proc.* 98(2): 482–88.

———, M. Kremer, and J. Robinson. 2008d. Why are farmers not using fertilizer? Procrastination and learning in technology adoption. Mimeograph, Department of Economics, MIT.

———, M. Kremer, and J. Robinson. 2009. Nudging farmers to use fertilizer: Evidence from Kenya. MIT, processed.

———, M. Kremer, and R. Glennerster. 2008b. Using randomization in development economics research: A toolkit. In *Handbook of Development Economics*, ed. T. Schultz and J. Strauss, vol. 4, chap. 15. Amsterdam: Elsevier Sci. Ltd. North Holl.

———, P. Dupas, and M. Kremer. 2008a. Peer effects, pupil teacher ratios, and teacher incentives: Evidence from a randomized evaluation in Kenya. Mimeograph, Department of Economics, MIT.

———, P. Dupas, and M. Kremer. 2011. Education, HIV and early fertility: Experimental evidence from Kenya. Manuscript, UCLA.

———, P. Dupas P, M. Kremer, and S. Sinei. 2006. Education and HIV/AIDS prevention: Evidence from a randomized evaluation in western Kenya. Working Paper 402, World Bank Policy Research.

———, R. Hanna, and S. Ryan. 2007. Monitoring works: Getting teachers to come to school. BREAD Working Paper 103. Working Paper 11880, NBER.

———, and R. Pande. 2007. Dams. *Quarterly Journal of Economics* 122(2): 601–46.

Dunning, T. 2008. Improving causal inference: Strengths and limitations of natural experiments. *Political Research Quarterly* 61(2): 282–93.

Dupas, P. 2007. Relative risks and the market for sex: Teenage pregnancy, HIV, and partner selection in Kenya. Mimeograph, UCLA.

Easterly, W. R. 2006. *The White Man's Burden: Why the West's Efforts to Aid the Rest Have Done So Much Ill and So Little Good.* Oxford: Oxford University Press.

———. 2009. Can the West save Africa? *Journal of Economic Literature* 47(2): 373–447.

———, ed. 2008. *Reinventing Foreign Aid.* Cambridge: MIT Press.

———, R. Levine, and D. Roodman. 2003. Aid, policies, and growth: Comment. *American Economic Review* 94(3): 774–80.

Eldersveld, S. J. 1956. Experimental propaganda techniques and voting behavior. *American Political Science Review* 50 (March): 154–65.

Fearon, J., and D. Laitin. 2003. Ethnicity, insurgency, and civil war. *American Political Science Review* 97(1): 75–90.

Ferraz, C., and F. Finan. 2008. Exposing corrupt politicians: The effects of Brazil's publicly released audits on electoral outcomes. *Quarterly Journal of Economics* 123(2): 703–45.

Fisher, R. A. 1960 [1935]. *The Design of Experiments.* 8th ed. New York: Hafner.

Fiszbein, A., and N. Schady, eds. 2009. *Conditional Cash Transfers: Reducing Present and Future Poverty.* Washington: World Bank.

Flay, B. R., A. Biglan, R. F. Boruch, F. González Castro, D. Gottfredson, S. Kellam, E. K. Mościcki, S. Schinke, J. C. Valentine, and P. Ji. 2005. Standards of evidence: Criteria for efficacy, effectiveness and dissemination. *Prevention Science* 6(3): 1–25.

Frank, R. H. 2007. *The Economic Naturalist: In Search of Explanations for Everyday Enigmas.* New York: Basic Books.

Freedman, D. A. 2004. *Statistical Models: Theory and Practice,* New York. Cambridge University Press.

———. 2006. Statistical models of causation: What inferential leverage do they provide? *Evaluation Review* 30(6): 691–713.

———. 2008. On regression adjustments to experimental data. *Advances in Applied Mathematics* 40: 180–93.

Freund, J. E. 1971. *Mathematical Statistics.* 2d ed. New York: Prentice-Hall.

Fried, B., P. Lagunes, and A. Venkataramani. 2010. Corruption and inequality at the crossroad: A multimethod study of bribery and discrimination in Latin America. *Latin American Research Review* 45(1): 76–97.

Gaventa, J. 1980. *Power and Powerlessness: Quiescence and Rebellion in an Appalachian Valley.* Urbana: University of Illinois Press.

Geller, D. M. 1982. Alternatives to deception: Why, what, and how? In *The Ethics of Social Research: Surveys and Experiments,* ed. J. E. Sieber, 39–55. New York: Springer.

Gelman, A. 2011. Causality and statistical learning. *American Journal of Sociology* 117(3): 955–66.

———, and T. C. Little. 1997. Poststratification into many categories using hierarchical logistic regression. *Survey Methodology* 23: 127–35.

———, and S. Roberts. 2007. Weight loss, self-experimentation, and web trials: A conversation. *Chance* 20(4): 57–61.

———, J. B. Carlin, H. S. Stern, and D. B. Rubin. 2003. *Bayesian Data Analysis.* 2d ed. London: Chapman and Hall.

———, M. Stevens, and V. Chan. 2003. Regression modeling and meta-analysis for decision making: A cost–benefit analysis of incentives in telephone surveys. *Journal of Business and Economic Statistics* 21(2): 213–25.

Gerber, A. S. 2011. Field experiments in political science. In *Cambridge Handbook of Experimental Political Science*, ed. J. N. Druckman, D. P. Green, J. H. Kuklinski, and A. Lupia, 115–38. Cambridge: Cambridge University Press.

———, and D. P. Green. 2000. The effects of canvassing, telephone calls, and direct mail on voter turnout: A field experiment. *American Political Science Review* 94: 653–63.

———, D. P. Green, E. Kaplan, and H. Kern. 2009. Treatment, control, and placebo: Efficient estimation for three-group experiments. Working Paper.

———, D. P. Green, and C. W. Larimer. 2008. Social pressure and voter turnout: Evidence from a large-scale field experiment. *American Political Science Review* 102(1): 33–48.

———, D. P. Green, and E. H. Kaplan. 2003. The illusion of learning from observational research. Manuscript, Institution for Social and Policy Studies, Yale University.

Gerring, J. 2007. *Case Study Research: Principles and Practices.* Cambridge: Cambridge University Press.

Gilmore, G. 1979. *The Ages of American Law.* New Haven: Yale University Press.

Giné, X., D. Karlan, and J. Zinman. 2010. Put your money where your butt is: A commitment savings account for smoking cessation. *American Economics Journal: Applied Economics* 2(4): 213–35.

Glazerman, S., D. M. Levy, and D. Myers. 2002. Nonexperimental replications of social experiments: A systematic review. Mathematica Policy Research, Inc.

Glewwe, P., M. Kremer, and S. Moulin. 2009. Many children left behind? Textbooks and test scores in Kenya. *Am. Econ. J. Appl. Econ.* 1: 112–35.

———, N. Ilias, and M. Kreme. 2003. Teacher incentives. Working Paper, Department of Economics, Harvard University.

———, M. Kremer, S. Moulin, and E. Zitzewitz. 2004. Retrospective vs. prospective analyses of school inputs: The case of flip charts in Kenya. *Journal of Development Economics* 74: 251–68.

Glynn, A. 2009. Does oil cause civil war because it causes state weakness? Mimeo, Harvard University.

Goduka, I. N. 1990. Ethics and politics of field research in South Africa. *Social Problems* 37(3): 329–40.

Goldberger, A. 1991. *A Course in Econometrics.* Cambridge: Harvard University Press.

Gosnell, H. F. 1927. *Getting-Out-the-Vote: An Experiment in the Stimulation of Voting.* Chicago: University of Chicago Press.

Graetz, M., and I. Shapiro. 2005. *Death by a Thousand Cuts: The Fight over Taxing Inherited Wealth.* Princeton: Princeton University Press.

Gray, B. H. 1978. Complexities of informed consent. *Annals of the American Academy of Political and Social Science* 437: 37–48.

Green, D. P., and A. S. Gerber. 2003a. Reclaiming the experimental tradition in political science. In *The State of the Discipline III*, ed. Helen Milner and Ira Katznelson, 805–32. Washington: American Political Science Association.

———, and A. S. Gerber. 2003b. The underprovision of experiments in political science. *Annals of the American Academy of Political and Social Science* 589 (September).

———, and A. S. Gerber. 2008. *Get Out the Vote: How to Increase Voter Turnout.* 2d ed. Washington: Brookings Institution Press.

———, and D. Winik. 2010. Using random judge assignments to estimate the effects of incarceration and probation on recidivism among drug offenders. *Criminology* 48(2): 357–87.

———, and I. Shapiro. 1994. *Pathologies of Rational Choice Theory: A Critique of Applications in Political Science.* New Haven: Yale University Press.

———, and I. Shapiro. 1995. Pathologies revisited: Reflections on our critics. *Critical Review* 91–92: 235–76.

———. 2009. Regression adjustments to experimental data: Do David Freedman's concerns apply to political science? Manuscript from 26th Annual Meeting of the Society for Political Methodology, Yale University, July 23–25, 2009.

———, S. E. Ha, and J. G. Bullock. 2010. Enough already about "black box" experiments: Studying mediation is more difficult than most scholars suppose. *Annals of the American Academy of Social and Political Science* (March): 200–208.

Greenland, S. 2005. Multiple-bias modeling for analysis of observational data (with discussion). *Journal of the Royal Statistical Society A*, 168: 267–306.

Greevy, R., B. Lu, J. H. Silver, and P. Rosenbaum. 2004. Optimal multivariate matching before randomization. *Biostatistics* 5: 263–75.

Groopman, J. E. 2009. Diagnosis: what doctors are missing. *New York Review of Books* 56(17): November 5.

Gugerty, M. K., and M. Kremer. 2008. Outside funding and the dynamics of participation in community associations. *American Journal of Political Science* 52(3): 585–602.

Guillaumont, P., and L. Chauvet. 2001. Aid and performance: A reassessment. *Journal of Development Studies* 37(6): 66–92.

Habyarimana, J., D. Posner, M. Humphreys, and J. Weinstein. 2009. *Coethnicity: Diversity and the Dilemmas of Collective Action.* London: Russell Sage.

Hansen, H., and F. Tarp. 2000. Aid effectiveness disputed. *Journal of International Development* 12: 375–98.

———, and F. Tarp. 2001. Aid and growth regressions. *Journal of Development Economics* 64: 547–70.

Harmon, A. 2010. New drugs stir debate on rules of clinical trials. *New York Times*, September 19, 2010.

Haviland, A. M., and D. S. Nagin. 2005. Causal inferences with group-based trajectory models. *Psychometrika* 70: 557–78.

Hayward, C. 2000. *Defacing Power*. Cambridge: Cambridge University Press.

Heckman J. J., and E. Leamers, eds. 2008. *Handbook of Econometrics*. Vol. 6B. Amsterdam: Elsevier Sci. Ltd. North Holl.

————, H. Ichimura, J. Smith, and P. Todd. 1998. Characterizing selection bias using experimental data. *Econometrica* 66: 1017–98.

————, H. Ichimura, and P. Todd. 1997a. Matching as an econometric evaluation estimator: Evidence from evaluating a job training program. *Review of Economic Studies* 64: 605–54.

————, L. Lochner, and C. Taber. 1999. Human capital formation and general equilibrium treatment effects: A study of tax and tuition policy. *Fiscal Studies* 20(1): 25–40.

————, D. Schmierer, and S. Urzua. 2010. Testing the correlated random coefficient model. *Journal of Econometrics* 158(2): 177–203.

————, J. Smith, and N. Clements. 1997b. Making the most out of programme evaluations and social experiments: Accounting for heterogeneity in programme impacts. *Review of Economic Studies* 64: 487–535.

————, S. Urzua, and E. J. Vytlacil. 2006. Understanding instrumental variables in models with essential heterogeneity. *Review of Economic Statistics* 88(3): 389–432.

————, and E. J. Vytlacil. 2008a. Econometric evaluation of social programs, part 1: Using the marginal treatment effect to organize alternative economic estimators to evaluate social programs and to forecast their effect in new environment. In *Handbook of Econometrics*, ed. J. J. Heckman and E. Leamers, Vol. 6B:4779–4874. Amsterdam: Elsevier Sci. Ltd. North Holl, 2008.

————, and E. J. Vytlacil. 2008b. Econometrics evaluation of social program part II: Using the marginal treatment effect to organize alternative economic estimators to evaluate social programs and to forecast their effect in new environment. In *Handbook of Econometrics*. ed. J. J. Heckman and E. Leamers, Vol. 6B:4875–5144. Amsterdam: Elsevier Sci. Ltd. North Holl, 2008.

————, and J. Smith. 1995. Assessing the case for social experiments. *Journal of Economic Perspectives* 9(2): 85–110.

————. 1992. Randomization and social policy evaluation. In *Evaluating Welfare and Training Programs*, ed. C. F. Manski and I. Garfinkel, 201–30. Cambridge: Harvard University Press.

————. 2010. Building bridges between structural and program evaluation approaches to evaluating policy. *Journal of Economic Literature* 48(2): 356–98.

————. 1997. Instrumental variables: a study of implicit behavioral assumptions used in making program evaluations. *Journal of Human Resources* 32(3): 441–62.

————. 2000. Causal parameters and policy analysis in economics: A twentieth-century retrospective. *Quarterly Journal of Economics* 115: 45–97.

————, and E. J. Vytlacil. 1999. Local instrumental variables and latent variable models for identifying and bounding treatment effects. *Proceedings of the National Academy of Sciences* 96(8): 4730–34.

————, and E. J. Vytlacil. 2007. Econometric evaluation of social programs, part II: Using the marginal treatment effect to organize alternative econometric estimators to evaluate social programs, and to forecast their effects in new environments. In *Handbook of Econometrics*, ed. J. J. Heckman and E. Leamers. Vol. 6B:4875–5143. Amsterdam: Elsevier Sci. Ltd. North Holl, 2008.

————, and S. Urzua. 2010. Comparing IV with structural models: What simple IV can and cannot identify. *Journal of Econometrics* 156(1): 27–37.

————, R. J. Lalonde, and J. A. Smith. 1999. The economics and econometrics of active labor market programs. *Handbook of Labor Economics*, ed. Orley C. Ashenfelter and David Card, 1865–2097. New York: Elsevier.

Heinsman, D. T., and W. R. Shadish. 1996. Assignment methods in experimentation: When do nonrandomized experiments approximate answers from randomized experiments? *Psychological Methods* 1(2): 154–69.

Henrich, J., R. Boyd, S. Bowles, C. Camerer, E. Fehr, H. Gintis, and R. McElreath. 2001. In search of homo economicus: Behavioral experiments in 15 small-scale societies. *American Economic Review* 91(2): 73–78.

Henrich, J., S. J. Heine, and A. Norenzayan. 2010. The weirdest people in the world. *Behavioral and Brain Sciences* 32(2/3): 61–83.

Hibbing, J., and E. Theiss-Morse. 2002. *Stealth Democracy: American's Beliefs about How Government Should Work*. Cambridge: Cambridge University Press.

Hirano, K., and J. Porter. 2005. Asymptotics for statistical decision rules. *Econometrica* 71(5): 1307–38.

Ho, D., K. Imai, G. King, and E. Stuart. 2007. Matching as nonparametric preprocessing for reducing model dependence in parametric causal inference. *Political Analysis* 15: 199–236.

Hoddinott, J., J. A. Maluccio, J. R. Behrman, R. Flores, and R. Martorell. 2008. Effect of a nutrition intervention during early childhood on economic productivity in Guatemalan adults. *Lancet* 371(9610): 411–16.

Holbrook, T. M. 1996. *Do Campaigns Matter?* Thousand Oaks, Calif.: Sage Publications.

Holland, P. 1986. Statistics and causal inference. *Journal of the American Statistical Association* 81(396): 945–60.

Horwitz, R. I., B. M. Singer, R. W. Makuch, and C. M. Viscoli. 1996. Can treatment that is helpful on average be harmful to some patients? A study of the conflicting information needs of clinical inquiry and drug regulators. *Journal of Clinical Epidemiology* 49: 395–400.

————, B. M. Singer, R. W. Makuch, and C. M. Viscoli. 1997. On reaching the tunnel at the end of the light. *Journal of Clinical Epidemiology* 50(7): 753–55.

Howell, W. G., and P. E. Peterson. 2002. *The Education Gap: Vouchers and Urban Schools*. Washington: Brookings Institution Press.

———, et al. 2000. Divided government and the legislative productivity of Congress, 1945–94. *Legislative Studies Quarterly* 25(2): 285–312.

———, P. J. Wolf, D. E. Campbell, and P. E. Peterson. 2002. School vouchers and academic performance: Results from three randomized field trials. *Journal of Policy Analysis and Management* 21(2): 191–217.

Howson, C., and P. Urbach. 1993. *Scientific Reasoning: The Bayesian Approach.* 2d ed. Chicago: Open Court.

Hoxby, C. M. 2000. Does competition among public schools benefit students and taxpayers? *American Economic Review* 90(5): 1209–38.

Hsieh, C. T., and M. Urquiola. 2006. The effects of generalized school choice on achievement and stratification: Evidence from Chile's voucher program. *Journal of Public Economics* 90: 1477–503.

Humphreys, M., and J. M. Weinstein. 2009. Field experiments and the political economy of development. *Annual Review of Political Science* 12(1): 367–78.

Hutton, J. L. 2001. Are distinctive ethical principles required for cluster randomized controlled trials? *Statistics in Medicine* 20(3): 473–88.

Imai, K. 2005. Do get-out-the-vote calls reduce turnout? The importance of statistical methods for field experiments. *American Political Science Review* 99: 283–300.

———. 2007a. Variance identification and efficiency analysis in experiments under the matched-pair design. *Technical Report.* Department of Politics, Princeton University, Princeton.

———, G. King, and C. Nall. 2007b. The essential role of pair-matching in cluster-randomized experiments, with application to the Mexican universal health insurance evaluation. *Technical Report.* Department of Politics, Princeton University, Princeton.

Imbens, G. W., and J. Angrist. 1994. Identification and estimation of local average treatment effects. *Econometrica* 61(2): 467–76.

———, and J. M. Wooldridge. 2009. Recent developments in the econometrics of program evaluation. *Journal of Economic Literature* 47(1): 5–86.

———. 2004. Nonparametric estimation of average treatment effects under exogeneity: A review. *Review of Economics and Statistics* 86: 4–29.

———. 2010. Better LATE than nothing: Some comments on Deaton (2009) and Heckman and Urzua (2009). *Journal of Economic Literature* 48(2): 399–423.

———, D. B. Rubin, and B. I. Sacerdote. 2001. Estimating the effect of unearned income on labor earnings, savings and consumption: Evidence from a survey of lottery winners. *American Economic Review* 91(4): 778–94.

International Initiative for Impact Evaluation (3IE), 2008, http://www.3ieimpact.org/

Isaac, J. 1987. *Power and Marxist Theory.* Ithaca: Cornell University Press.

Ivy, A. C. 1948. The history and ethics of the use of human subjects in medical experiments. *Science* 108: 1–5.

Iyengar, S., and D. R. Kinder. 1987. *News That Matters: Television and American Opinion.* Chicago: University of Chicago Press.

Jensen, R. 2010. The (perceived) returns to education and the demand for schooling. *Quarterly Journal of Economics* 125(2): 515–48.

Jones, J. 1981. *Bad Blood: The Tuskegee Syphilis Experiment.* New York: Free Press.

Jurajda, Štěpán, and Daniel Münich. 2009. Admission to selective schools, alphabetically. Charles University, Prague. CERGE-EI, processed (March).

Kanbur, R. M. 2001. Economic policy, distribution, and poverty: The nature of the disagreements. *World Development* 29(6): 1083–94.

Kant, I. 1929 [1781]. *Critique of Pure Reason.* Translated by Norman Kemp Smith. London: Macmillan.

Karlan, D. 2005. Using experimental economics to measure social capital and predict real financial decisions. *American Economic Review* 95(5): 1688–99.

———, and J. Zinman. 2005. Observing unobservables: Identifying information asymmetries with a consumer credit field experiment. Working Paper 94, Department of Economics, Yale University.

———, and J. Zinman. 2008. Credit elasticities in less developed economies: Implications for micro-finance. *American Economic Review* 98(3): 1040–68.

———, and J. Zinman. 2010. Expanding credit access: Using randomized supply decisions to estimate the impacts. *Review of Financial Studies* 23(1): 433–64.

———, N. Ashraf, and W. Yin. 2006. Female empowerment: Impact of a commitment savings product in the Philippines. CGD Document of discussion 949.

Katz, E., and J. J. Feldman. 1962. The debates in the light of research: A survey of surveys. In *The Great Debates*, ed. S. Kraus, 173–223. Bloomington: Indiana University Press.

Katz, L. F., J. R. Kling, and J. B. Liebman. 2001. Moving to opportunity in Boston: Early results of a randomized mobility experiment. *Quarterly Journal of Economics* 116: 607–54.

King, G., and L. Zeng. 2006. The dangers of extreme counterfactuals. *Political Analysis* 14: 131–59.

———, R. O. Keohane, and S. Verba. 1994. *Designing Social Inquiry: Scientific Inference in Qualitative Research.* Princeton: Princeton University Press.

Kramer, G. H. 1970. The effects of precinct-level canvassing on voting behavior. *Public Opinion Quarterly* 34 (Winter): 560–72.

Kremer, M., and A. Holla. 2008. Pricing and access: Lessons from randomized evaluation in education and health. Mimeograph. Department of Economics, Harvard University.

———, E. Miguel, and R. Thornton. 2009. Incentives to learn. *Review of Economics and Statistics* 91(3): 437–56.

———, and E. Miguel. 2007. The illusion of sustainability. *Q. J. Econ.* 122(3): 1007–65.

Kuhn, T. 1962. *The Structure of Scientific Revolutions.* Chicago: University of Chicago Press.

Lagunes, P., B. Fried, and A. Venkataramani. 2010. Corruption and inequality at the crossroad: A multimethod study of bribery and discrimination in Latin America. *Latin American Research Review* 45(1): 76–97.

————. 2012. The watchful eye and the cracking whip: A field experiment on corruption monitoring in Mexico. Working Paper, Yale University, New Haven.

Lanoue, D. J. 1992. One that made a difference: Cognitive consistency, political knowledge, and the 1980 presidential debate. *Public Opinion Quarterly* 56: 168–84.

Lau, J., J. P. A. Ioannidis, and C. H. Schmid. 1998. Summing up evidence: One answer is not always enough. *Lancet* 351: 123–27.

Lax, J., and J. Phillips. 2009. How should we estimate public opinion in the states? *American Journal of Political Science* 53(1): 107–21.

Leamer, E. E. 1983. Let's take the con out of econometrics. *American Economic Review* 73(1): 31–43.

————. 2010. Tantalus on the road to asymptotia. *Journal of Economic Perspectives* 24(2): 31–46.

————. 1985. Vector autoregressions for causal inference? *Carnegie-Rochester Conference Series on Public Policy* 22: 255–304.

Lee, D. S., and T. Lemieux. 2010. Regression discontinuity designs in economics. *Journal of Economic Literature* 48(2): 281–355.

Lensink, R., and H. White. 2001. Are there negative returns to aid? *Journal of Development Studies* 37(6): 42–65.

Leonhardt, D. 2008. Making economics relevant again. *New York Times*, February 20.

Levitt, S., and J. A. List. 2009. Field experiments in economics: The past, the present, and the future. *European Economic Review* 53(1): 1–18.

————. 1997. Using electoral cycles in police hiring to estimate the effect of police on crime. *American Economic Review* 87(3): 270–90.

————. 2002. Using electoral ycles in police hiring to estimate the effect of police on crime: Reply. *American Economic Review* 92(3): 1244–50.

Levy, S. 2006. *Progress against Poverty: Sustaining Mexico's Progresa–Oportunidades Program*. Washington: Brookings Institution Press.

Lichter, A. S., M. E. Lippman Jr., D. N. Danforth Jr., T. d'Angelo, S. M. Steinberg, E. Demos, H. D. MacDonald, C. M. Reichert, M. Merino, S. M. Swain, K. Cowan, L. H. Gerber, J. L. Bader, P. A. Findlay, W. Schain, C. R. Gorrell, K. Straus, S. A. Rosenberg, and E. Glatstein. 1992. Mastectomy versus breast-conserving therapy in the treatment of stage I and II carcinoma of the breast: A randomized trial at the National Cancer Institute. *Journal of Clinical Oncology* 10: 976–83.

List, J. A. 2006. Field experiments: A bridge between lab and naturally occurring data. *Advances in Economic Analysis and Policy* B. E. Press 6(2): 1–45.

Loudon, I. 2000. *The Tragedy of Childbed Fever*. Oxford: Oxford University Press.

Lu, B., E. Zanuto, R. Hornik, and P. R. Rosenbaum. 2001. Matching with doses in an observational study of a media campaign against drug abuse. *Journal of the American Statistical Association* 96: 1245–53.

Lukes, S. 1974. *Power: A Radical View*. London: Macmillan.

Lundquist, J. H., and H. L. Smith. 2005. Family formation among women in the U.S. military: Evidence from the NLSY. *Journal of Marriage and Family* 67: 1–13.

Maluccio, J. A., J. Hoddinott, J. R. Behrman, R. Martorell, A. R. Quisumbing, and A. D. Stein. 2009. The impact of improving nutrition during early childhood on education among Guatemalan adults. *Economic Journal* 119(537): 734–63.

Mangano, D. T., J. C. Tudor, and C. Dietzel. 2006. The risk associated with aprotinin in cardiac surgery. *New England Journal of Medicine* 354(4): 353–65.

Mankiw, N. G., D. Romer, and D. N. Weil. 1992. A contribution to the empirics of economic growth. *Quarterly Journal of Economics* 107(2): 407–37.

Manski, C. F. 1996. Learning about treatment effects with random assignment of treatments. *Journal of Human Resources* 31(4): 709–33.

———. 2000. Identification problems and decisions under ambiguity: Empirical analysis of treatment response and normative analysis of treatment choice. *J. Econom.* 95: 415–42.

———. 2002. Treatment choice under ambiguity induced by inferential problems. *J. Stat. Plan. Inference* 105: 67–82.

———. 2004. Statistical treatment rules for heterogeneous populations. *Econometrica* 2(4): 1221–46.

———, and I. Garfinkel. 1992. Introduction. In *Evaluating Welfare and Training Programs*, ed. C. F. Manski, and I. Garfinkel, 1–22. Cambridge: Harvard University Press.

Martin, D. C., P. Diehr, E. B. Perrin, and T. D. Koepsell. 1993. The effect of matching on the power of randomized community intervention studies. *Statistical Medicine* 12: 329–38.

Mayhew, D. R. 1991. *Divided We Govern: Party Control, Lawmaking and Investigations, 1946–2002.* New Haven: Yale University Press.

McCleary, R. M., and R. J. Barro. 2006. Religion and economy. *Journal of Economic Perspectives* 20(2): 49–72.

McConahay, J. B. 1982. Self-interest versus racial attitudes as correlates of anti-busing attitudes in Louisville: Is it the buses or the blacks? *Journal of Politics* 44(3): 692–720.

McCracken, J. P., K. Smith, A. Diaz, M. A. Mittleman, and J. Schwartz. 2007. Chimney stove intervention to reduce long-term wood smoke exposure lowers blood pressure among Guatemalan women. *Environmental Health Perspectives* 115(7): 996–1001.

McCrary, J. 2008. Manipulation of the running variable in regression discontinuity design: A density test. *Journal of Econometrics* 142(2): 698–714.

McDermott, R. 2002. Experimental methods in political science. *Annual Review of Political Science* 5(1): 31–61.

McKenzie, D., and C. Woodruff. 2008. Experimental evidence on returns to capital and access to finance in Mexico. *World Bank Econ. Rev.* 22(3): 457–82.

Miguel, E., and M. Kremer. 2004. Worms: Identifying impacts on education and health in the presence of treatment externalities. *Econometrica* 72(1): 159–217.

———, S. Satyanath, and E. Sergenti. 2004. Economic shocks and civil conflict: An instrumental variables approach. *Journal of Political Economy* 112(4): 725–53.

Milgram, S. 1974. *Obedience to Authority: An Experimental View*. New York: Taylor and Francis.

Mill, J. S. 1843. *A System of Logic, Ratiocinative and Inductive: Being a Connected View of the Principles of Evidence and the Methods of Scientific Investigation*. John W. Parker.

————. 1991 [1861]. *Considerations on Representative Government*. New York: Prometheus Books.

Mills, C. W. 1956. *The Power Elite*. Oxford: Oxford University Press.

Mokyr, J. 2009. *The Enlightened Economy: An Economic History of Britain, 1700–1850*. New Haven: Yale University Press.

Morton, B. 2002. EITM: Experimental implications of theoretical models. *Political Methodologist* 10(2): 14–16.

Morton, R., and K. Williams. 2010. *Experimental Political Science and the Study of Causality: From Nature to the Lab*. Cambridge: Cambridge University Press.

————. 2008. Experimentation in political science. In *Oxford Handbook of Political Methodology*, ed. J. M. Box-Steffensmeier, H. E. Brady, and David Collier. Oxford: Oxford University Press.

Mullally, C., S. R. Boucher, and M. R. Carter. 2010. Perceptions and participation: Mistaken beliefs, encouragement designs, and demand for index insurance. Manuscript, University of California, Davis.

Murnane, R. J., and R. R. Nelson. 2007. Improving the performance of the education sector: The valuable, challenging, and limited role of random assignment evaluations. *Economics of Innovation and New Technology* 16(5): 307–22.

Nelson, T. E., K. Sanbonmatsu, and H. K. McClerking. 2007. Playing a different race card: Examining the limits of elite influence on perceptions of racism. *Journal of Politics* 69(2): 416–29.

Novak, S. P., S. F. Reardon, S. W. Raudenbush, and S. L. Buka. 2006. Retail tobacco outlet density and youth cigarette smoking: A propensity-modeling approach. *American Journal of Public Health* 96: 670–76.

Olken, B. 2007. Monitoring corruption: Evidence from a field experiment in Indonesia. *Journal of Political Economy* 115(2): 200–49.

Orcutt, G. H., and A. G. Orcutt. 1968. Incentive and disincentive experimentation for income maintenance purposes. *American Economic Review* 58(4): 754–72.

Palfrey, T. R. 2009. Laboratory experiments in political economy. *Annual Review of Political Science* 12(1): 379–88.

Paluck, E. L., and D. P. Green. 2009a. Deference, dissent, and dispute resolution: An experimental intervention using mass media to change norms and behavior in Rwanda. *American Political Science Review* 103(4): 622–44.

————. 2009b. Reducing intergroup prejudice and conflict using the media: A field experiment in Rwanda. *Journal of Personality and Social Psychology* 96: 574–87.

Parkin, J. 2007. *Taming the Leviathan: The Reception of the Political and Religious Ideas of Thomas Hobbes in England, 1640–1700*. Cambridge: Cambridge University Press.

Patten, S. C. 1977. The case that Milgram makes. *Philosophical Review* 86(3): 350–64.

Pawson, R., and N. Tilley. 1997. *Realistic Evaluation*. London: Sage.

Pearl, J. 2000. *Causality: Models, Reasoning, and Inference*. Cambridge: Cambridge University Press.

Peto, R., R. Collins, and R. Gray. 1995. Large-scale randomized evidence: Large, simple trials and overviews of trials. *Journal of Clinical Epidemiology* 48(1): 23–40.

Pocock, S. J., S. E. Assmann, L. E. Enos, and L. E. Kasen. 2002. Subgroup analysis covariate adjustment and baseline comparisons in clinical trial reporting: Current practice and problems. *Statistical Medicine* 21: 2917–30.

Pogge, T. 2005. World poverty and human rights. *Ethics and International Affairs* 19(1): 1–7.

Polsby, N. 1963. *Community Power and Political Theory*. New Haven: Yale University Press.

Porter, R. 2000. *The Creation of the Modern World: The Untold Story of the British Enlightenment*. New York: W. W. Norton.

Poverty Action Lab. 2007. Clinton honors global deworming effort. http://www .povertyactionlab.org/deworm/ (accessed December 15, 2008).

Posner, D. N. 2004. The political salience of cultural difference: Why Chewas and Tumbukas are allies in Zambia and adversaries in Malawi. *American Political Science Review* 98(4): 529–45.

Przeworski, A. 2007. Is the science of comparative politics possible? In *Handbook of Comparative Politics*, ed. C. Boix and S. Stokes, 147–71. Oxford: Oxford University Press.

Quinn, K., M. Hechter, and E. Wibbels. 2003. Ethnicity, insurgency, and civil war revisited. Mimeograph, Yale University.

Rae, D. 2005. *City: Urbanism and Its End*. New Haven: Yale University Press.

Rahman, A. 1999. Micro-credit initiatives for equitable and sustainable development: Who pays? *World Development* 27(1): 67–82.

Rajan, R., and A. Subramanian. 2008. Aid and growth: What does the data really show? *Review of Economics and Statistics BE Press* 90(4): 643–65.

Ravallion, M. 2009. Should the Randomistas Rule? *BE Press Economists' Voice*.

Reiss, P. C., and F. A. Wolak. 2007. Structural econometric modeling: Rationales and examples from industrial organization. In *Handbook of Econometrics*, ed. J. J. Heckman and E. Leamers, Vol. 6A:4277–4415. Amsterdam: Elsevier Sci. Ltd. North Holl, 2008.

Ridker, P., C. P. Cannon, D. Morrow, N. Rifai, L. M. Rose, C. H. McCabe, M. A. Pfeffer, and E. Braunwald. 2005. C-reactive protein levels and outcomes after statin therapy. *New England Journal of Medicine* 352(1): 20–28.

———, E. Danielson, F. A. Fonseca, J. Genest, A. M. Gotto Jr., J. J. Kastelein, W. Koenig, P. Libby, A. J. Lorenzatti, J. G. MacFadyen, and others. 2008. Rosuvastatin to prevent vascular events in men and women with elevated C-reactive protein. *New England Journal of Medicine* 359: 2195–2207.

Roberts, L., Y. Chartier, O. Chartier, G. Malenga, M. Toole, and H. Rodka. 2001. Keeping clean water clean in a Malawi refugee camp: A randomized intervention trial. *Bulletin of the World Health Organization* 79(4): 280–87.

Roberts, S. 2004. Self-experimentation as a source of new ideas: Ten examples about sleep, mood, health, and weight (with discussion). *Behavioral and Brain Sciences* 27: 227–88.

Rodrik, D. 2009. The new development economics: We shall experiment, but how shall we learn? In *What Works in Development: Thinking Big and Thinking Small*, ed. Jessica Cohen and William Easterly. Washington: Brookings Institution Press.

Rogers, J. R. 2005. The impact of divided government on legislative production. *Public Choice* 123.1: 217–33.

Roodman, D. 2008. The anarchy of numbers: Aid, development, and cross-country empirics. *World Bank Economic Review* 21(2): 255–77.

Rosenbaum, P. R. 2002. *Observational Studies*. 2d ed. New York: Springer.

———. 2010. *Design of Observational Studies*. New York: Springer-Verlag.

Rosenberg, G. 1993. *The Hollow Hope: Can Courts Bring About Social Change?* Chicago: University of Chicago Press.

Rosenstone, S. J. and J. M. Hansen. 1993. *Mobilization, Participation, and Democracy in America*. New York: Macmillan.

Rubin, D. B. 1973. Matching to remove bias in observational studies. *Biometrics* 29: 159–84.

———. 1989. A new perspective on meta-analysis. In *The Future of Meta-Analysis*, ed. K. W. Wachter and M. L. Straf. New York: Russell Sage Foundation.

———. 1997. Estimating causal effects from large data sets using propensity scores. *Annals of Internal Medicine* 127: 757–63.

———. 2001. Using propensity scores to help design observational studies: Application to the tobacco litigation. *Health Services and Outcomes Research Methodology* 2: 169–88.

———. 2006a. *Matched Sampling for Causal Effects*. Cambridge: Cambridge University Press.

———, and E. A. Stuart. 2006b. Affinely invariant matching methods with discriminant mixtures of proportional ellipsoidally symmetric distributions. *Annals of Statistics* 34: 1814–26.

———, and N. Thomas. 1996. Matching using estimated propensity scores, relating theory to practice. *Biometrics* 52: 249–64.

Sachs, J. 2005. *The End of Poverty: Economic Possibilities for Our Time*. New York: Penguin.

———. 2008. *Common Wealth: Economics for a Crowded Planet*. New York: Penguin.

Sackett, D. L., et al. 2000. *Evidence-Based Medicine: How to Practice and Teach EBM*. 2d ed. Amsterdam: Churchill Livingtone.

Sampson, R. J. 2008. Moving to inequality: Neighborhood effects and experiments meet social structure. *American Journal of Sociology* 114(1): 189–231.

Sanbonmatsu, L., J. R. Kling, G. J. Duncan, and J. Brooks-Gunn. 2006. Neighborhoods and academic achievement: Results from the moving to opportunity experiment. *Journal of Human Resources* 41(4): 649–91.

Schochet, P., S. McConnell, and J. Burghardt. 2003. National Job Corps study: Findings using administrative earnings records data: final report. *Technical Report.* Mathematica Policy Research, Princeton.

Schuler, S., S. Hashemi, and S. Badal. 1998. Men's violence against women in rural Bangladesh: Undermined or exacerbated by microcredit programmes? *Development in Practice* 8(2): 148–57.

Schultz, T. P. 2004. School subsidies for the poor: Evaluating the Mexican Progresa poverty program. *Journal of Development Economics* 74(1): 199–250.

Sears, D. O., and S. H. Chaffee. 1979. Uses and effects of the 1976 debates: An overview of empirical studies. In *The Great Debates*, ed. S. Kraus, 223–61. Bloomington: Indiana University Press.

Senn, S. 1994. Testing for baseline balance in clinical trials. *Statistics in Medicine* 13: 1715–26.

———, and F. Harrell. 1997. On wisdom after the event. *Journal of Clinical Epidemiology* 50(7): 749–51.

Shadish, W. R., and K. Ragsdale. 1996. Random versus nonrandom assignment in controlled experiments: Do you get the same answer? *Journal of Consulting and Clinical Psychology* 64 (6): 1290–1305.

Shapiro, Ian. 2004. Problems, methods, and theories in the study of politics: What's wrong with political science and what to do about it. In *Problems, Methods, and Theories in the Study of Politics*, ed. I. Shapiro, R. M. Smith, and T. E. Masoud, 19–41. Cambridge: Cambridge University Press.

———. 2003a. *The State of Democratic Theory.* Princeton: Princeton University Press.

———. 2003b. *The Moral Foundations of Politics.* New Haven: Yale University Press.

———. 2005. *The Flight from Reality in the Human Sciences.* Princeton: Princeton University Press.

———. 2011. *The Real World of Democratic Theory.* Princeton: Princeton University Press.

———, and A. Wendt. 1992. The difference that realism makes: Social science and the politics of consent. *Politics and Society* 20(2): 197–224.

Sherman, L. W., D. Rogan, T. Edwards, R. Whipple, D. Shreve, D. Witcher, and W. Trimble. 1995. Deterrent effects of police raids on crack houses: A randomized, controlled experiment. *Justice Quarterly* 12(4): 755–81.

Sims, C. A. 2010. But economics is not an experimental science. *Journal of Economic Perspectives* 24(2): 59–68.

Singer, E., J. Van Hoewyk, N. Gebler, T. Raghunathan, and K. McGonagle. 1999. The effects of incentives on response rates in interviewer-mediated surveys. *Journal of Official Statistics* 15(2): 217–30.

Singer, P. 2004. *One World: The Ethics of Globalization.* New Haven: Yale University Press.

Skinner, Q. 1966. Thomas Hobbes and his disciples in France and England. *Comparative Studies in Society and History* 8(2): 153–67.

Skloot, R. 2010. *The Immortal Life of Henrietta Lacks.* New York: Crown.

Sloman, S. 2005. *Causal Models: How People Think About the World and Its Alternatives.* Oxford: Oxford University Press.

Smith, J., and P. E. Todd. 2001. Reconciling conflicting evidence on the performance of matching estimators. *American Economic Review, Papers and Proceedings* 91(2): 112–18.

———, and P. E. Todd. 2005. Does matching overcome LaLonde's critique of non-experimental estimators? (with discussion). *Journal of Econometrics* 125: 305–75.

Sobel, M. E. 2008. Identification of causal parameters in randomized studies with mediating variables. *Journal of Educational and Behavioral Statistics* 33: 230–51.

Stuart, E. A., and D. B. Rubin. 2008. Matching with multiple control groups with adjustment for group differences. *Journal of Education and Behavioral Statistics* 33(3): 279–306.

Taylor, C. 1985. Neutrality in political science. In *Philosophical Papers II: Philosophy and the Human Sciences.* Cambridge: Cambridge University Press.

The Lancet. 2004. The World Bank is finally embracing science. Editorial, 364, August 28, 731–32.

Thorne, B. 1980. You still takin' notes? Fieldwork and problems of informed consent. *Social Problems* 27(3): 284–97.

Thornton, R. 2007. The demand for and impact of HIV testing: Evidence from a field experiment. *American Economic Review* 98(5): 1829–63.

Todd, P. E., and K. I. Wolpin. 2006. Using experimental data to validate a dynamic behavioral model of child schooling: Assessing the impact of a school subsidy program in Mexico. *American Economic Review* 96(5): 1384–1417.

———, K. I. Wolpin. 2010. Structural estimation and policy evaluation in developing countries. *Annual Review of Economics* 2: 21–50.

Topalova, P., and E. Duflo. 2003. Unappreciated service: Performance, perceptions, and women leaders in India. Mimeograph, MIT.

Urbach, P. 1985. Randomization and the design of experiments. *Philosophy of Science* 52(2): 256–73.

Urquiola, M., and E. Verhoogen. 2009. Class-size caps, sorting, and the regression-discontinuity design. *American Economic Review* 99(1): 179–215.

U.S. General Accounting Office. 1994. Breast conservation versus mastectomy: Patient survival in day-to-day medical practice and randomized studies. Report to the chairman, subcommitee on human resources and intergovernmental relations, committee on government operations, House of Representatives. *Technical Report GAOPEMD-95-9.* U.S. General Accounting Office, Washington.

Valentino, N. A., V. L. Hutchings, and I. K. White. 2002. Cues that matter: How political ads prime racial attitudes during campaigns. *American Political Science Review* 96(1): 75–90.

van den Berg, G. 2008. An economic analysis of exclusion restrictions for instrumental variable estimation. Amsterdam: VU University, CEPR Discussion Paper No. DP6157.

Verba, S., K. Schlozman, and H. Brady. 1995. *Voice in America: Civic Voluntarism in American Politics.* Cambridge: Harvard University Press.

Villalonga, B. 2004. Does diversification cause the 'diversification discount'? *Financial Management* 33: 5–27.

Voss, D. S., A. Gelman, and G. King. 1995. Pre-election survey methodology: Details from nine polling organizations, 1988 and 1992. *Public Opinion Quarterly* 59: 98–132.

Wand, J. N., K. W. Shotts, J. S. Sekhon, W. R. Mebane Jr., M. C. Herron, and H. E. Brady. 2001. The butterfly did it: The aberrant vote for Buchanan in Palm Beach County, Florida. *American Political Science Review* 95 (4): 793–810.

Wantchekon, L. 2003. Clientelism and voting behavior: Evidence from a field experiment in Benin. *World Politics* 55(3): 399–422.

Weber, M. 2004 [1917]. Science as a vocation. In *The Vocation Lectures*, ed. D. Owen, and T. B. Strong, 1–31. Indianapolis: Hackett.

Weiss, C. H. 2002. What to do until the random assigner comes. In *Evidence Matters: Randomized Trials in Education Research*, ed. F. Mosteller and R. Boruch. Washington: Brookings Institution Press.

Wennberg, D. E., F. L. Lucas, J. D. Birkmeyer, C. E. Bredenberg, and E. S. Fisher. 1998. Variation in carotid endarterectomy mortality in the Medicare population. *Journal of the American Medical Association* 279(16): 1278–81.

Whyte, W. 1988. *Learning from the Field: A Guide from Experience*. New York: Sage Publications.

Wittgenstein, L. 1969. *On Certainty*. New York: Harper and Row.

Wolfinger, R. E. 1971. Nondecisions and the study of politics. *American Political Science Review* 65(4): 1063–80.

Wood, E. 2006. The ethical challenges of field research in conflict zones. *Qualitative Sociology* 29(3): 373–86.

———. 2007. Field research. In *Oxford Handbook of Comparative Politics*, ed. C. Boix and S. Stokes, 123–46. Oxford: Oxford University Press.

Wooldridge, J. M. 2002. *Econometric Analysis of Cross-Section and Panel Data*. Cambridge: MIT Press.

World Bank. 2008a. The Spanish Impact Evaluation Fund.

———. 2008b. De nouveaux modes de gestion pour accroitre les performances de l'enseignement primaire malgache. Working Paper, World Bank.

Worrall, J. 2007a. Evidence in medicine and evidence-based medicine. *Philosophy Compass* 2(6): 981–1022.

———. 2007b. Why there's no cause to randomize. *British Journal of Philosophy of Science* 58: 451–88.

CONTRIBUTORS

Abhijit V. Banerjee, Ford Foundation International Professor of Economics, Department of Economics, Massachusetts Institute of Technology.

Christopher B. Barrett, Stephen B. and Janice G. Ashley Professor in the Charles H. Dyson School of Applied Economics and Management, and Professor in the Department of Economics, Cornell University.

Michael R. Carter, Professor in the Department of Agricultural and Resource Economics, Director, BASIS Collaborative Research Support Program and I4 Index Insurance Innovation Initiative, University of California, Davis.

Angus Deaton, Dwight D. Eisenhower Professor of International Affairs, Professor of Economics and International Affairs, Princeton University.

Esther Duflo, Abdul Latif Jameel Professor of Poverty Alleviation and Development Economics; Director of the Jameel Poverty Action Lab, Massachusetts Institute of Technology, Department of Economics.

Andrew Gelman, Departments of Statistics and Political Science, Columbia University.

Alan S. Gerber, Professor of Political Science; Director of the Center for the Study of American Politics, Department of Political Science, Yale University.

Donald P. Green, Professor of Political Science, Columbia University.

Kosuke Imai, Associate Professor, Department of Politics, Princeton University.

Edward H. Kaplan, School of Management, School of Public Health, Department of Engineering, Yale University.

Gary King, Albert J. Weatherhead III University Professor and Director of the Institute for Quantitative Political Science, Harvard University.

Ian Shapiro, Sterling Professor of Political Science; Director of the MacMillan Center, Yale University, Department of Political Science.

Susan C. Stokes, John S. Saden Professor of Political Science; Director of the Yale Program on Democracy, Yale University.

Elizabeth A. Stuart, Associate Professor, Department of Mental Health and Department of Biostatistics, Johns Hopkins Bloomberg School of Public Health.

Dawn Langan Teele is a Research Fellow at the London School of Economics and Political Science.

INDEX